A Collection of Biographies of 4 Kriya Yoga Gurus by Swami Satyananda Giri:

Yogiraj Shyama Charan Lahiri Mahasay,

*Yogacharya Shastri Mahasaya
(Hansaswami Kebalanandaji Maharaj),*

Swami Sri Yukteshvar Giri Maharaj,

*Yogananda Sanga
[Paramhansa Yoganandaji
As I have Seen and Understood Him]*

English translations by Yoga Niketan

Yoga Niketan
www.yoganiketan.net
email: yoganiketan@yoganiketan.net
surface mail contact:

Yoga Niketan
PO Box 1133
Battle Creek, Michigan
49016–1133
USA

iUniverse, Inc.
New York Lincoln Shanghai

**A Collection of Biographies of 4 Kriya Yoga Gurus
by Swami Satyananda Giri**
Yogiraj Shyama Charan Lahiri Mahasay,

Yogacharya Shastri Mahasaya
(Hansaswami Kebalanandaji Maharaj),

Swami Sri Yukteshvar Giri Maharaj,

Yogananda Sanga
[Paramhansa Yoganandaji
As I have Seen and Understood Him]

iUniverse books may be ordered through booksellers or by contacting:

iUniverse
2021 Pine Lake Road, Suite 100
Lincoln, NE 68512
www.iuniverse.com
1-800-Authors (1-800-288-4677)

ISBN-13: 978-0-595-38675-8 (pbk)
ISBN-13: 978-0-595-67634-7 (cloth)
ISBN-13: 978-0-595-83058-9 (ebk)
ISBN-10: 0-595-38675-X (pbk)
ISBN-10: 0-595-67634-0 (cloth)
ISBN-10: 0-595-83058-7 (ebk)

Printed in the United States of America

CONTENTS

Yogiraj Shyama Charan Lahiri Mahasay

A Biography

by Swami Satyananda Giri

English Translation by Yoga Niketan

muukam karoti vaachaalam pangum langhayate girim
yat-kripaa tam aham vande paramaananda-maadhavam

Whose Grace makes the dumb eloquent and the lame climb mountains, Him, the supremely blissful Lord of Lakshmi, I worship.

This translated book maintains that an almost literal translation of the Bengali words of the original author best serves both seekers and Kriyavans. No attempt has been made for the translations to be poetic or interpretive for the above-mentioned reason. If the reader notices irregular English grammar (including non-traditional sentence structure, punctuation, etc.), please understand that it is intentional. The translator has tried as best as he could to keep the work as close to the Bengali phrasing in the original without it being unreadable or incomprehensible.

Pranam, The Translator: Yoga Niketan

Yogiraj Sri Sri Shyama Charan Lahiri Mahasaya

PREFACE

I could not have imagined that I would be writing about the pioneer who, at the end of this age, brought back into the open the simple and direct yogadharma (path of yoga)—the Divine Yogavatar Sri Sri Shyamacharan Lahiri Mahasaya. A few days ago, a friend (who is not very much in the public eye) from my village made a subtle suggestion that created an impression in my mind which, during last Falgun (February-March), suddenly became an impulsion, which I let be known with joy and wonderment. A dear young kriyaban student made me enthusiastic about my inspiration. Then, at the vernal equinox in Chaitra (March-April), I received a supernatural blessing at the holy Kararashram in Puri and what was previously an inspiration and impulsion began to become reality.

[translator's note: In Bengali culture the title "Thakur" is used to denote the status of a divine being. Manifestations of the Divine— Krishna, Kali, Vishnu, Durga etc. etc. are called "Thakur"; God in no particular form is also called "Thakur"; a great yogic incarnation such as Sri Sri Lahiri Mahasaya and Sri Sri Ramakrishna are respectfully and affectionately addressed as "Thakur" as well. The closest translation to that is "Lord", as in Lord Jesus Christ; it is considered a little bit above the term "Guru" or "Master". In this translation, unless otherwise noted, the term "Lord" as used in addressing Sri Sri Lahiri Mahasaya is a translation of the term "Thakur" in Bengali. One further note, the world famous poet Rabindranath Tagore's real last name was Thakur, but that does not have the same connotation as "Lord".]

The Lord's advanced disciples used to keep His life so guarded that any inquiry about Him would bring about a typical response like, "What would you understand about my Lord; what could you possibly write about that immense Divinity?" Some would become fearful of the idea that a biography might be written about Yogiraj Lahiri Mahasaya—perhaps there could be misinterpretations; maybe the work would represent Him as ordinary and small. They desired to maintain the untainted and clear vision of Sri Guru in the sadhana bestowed upon them by Him.

Acharya Sri Bhupendranath Sanyal Mahasaya began writing a biography of Yogiraj about 43 years ago, and although he received quiet support from some of his brother disciples, a significant fellow kriyaban and brother disciple convinced him to stop that work. But who will stop what is bound by Nature to happen? Although it's true that the true understanding and experience of the Presence of such Divine incarnations is within and beyond the senses, but still it leaves us unsatisfied, even though we understand that we should try to be with Them in that way. Regardless of the fact that the ultimate goal of the sannyasi is in the realization of the Oneness, the wonderful stories and Lila (divine and miraculous play) of such an ascended being are naturally very attractive to all of us. Somehow, the heart cannot enamour itself like it wants without knowing about the human game that the Adi-Guru played. Even if there are corruptions in the life-picture, the devotee will still take to heart the greatness and create the story accordingly. In time, such a story also serves its purpose.

It is very difficult to discuss anything about Sri Sri Lahiri Mahasaya. There is much about Him that we do not know. Besides that, trying to understand His spiritual life is also not at all easy. From associating with His children, grandchildren and relatives, getting some help from the contents of old letters and having access to some previously published written works have we been able to know a little something about Him. In those days, He was known to many as "Kashibaba" or "Lahiribaba". "Yogavatar", "Yogivara", "Munivara", "Thakur" were also some of the many respectful terms with which He was addressed by His devotees. Naturally, we also have spoken of Him withsuch titles. A few years ago, my dear friend and Yogiraj's grandson, Sriyukta Ananda Mohan Lahiri took upon himself this daunting task, and with great determination, a good deal of financial expense and hard work was able to find much material that was previously unknown about the Lord; we all are indebted to him. Although some things were known about Yogiraj previously, it was Ananda Babu who first published a biography about Him. Ananda Babu has even more material in his possession, which are priceless, and we wait anxiously to know more about them. In a small booklet by Sriyukta Abhayacharan Lahiri, we also find some indication of this. He too has given us the assurance that he will publish an extended biography of Yogiraj. Acharya Sanyal Mahasaya has given us a glimpse of Yogiraj's life in a few words about His life as part of Sanyal Mahasaya's Gita publication. The sloka addressed to Yogeshwar is taken from Sanyal Mahasaya's slokamala (garland of slokas). Of course, different devotees would paint the Lord's picture in many ways, owing to their innumerable experiences and creative expression. Having had the great fortune to be in the holy company of the Lord's devotees and followers, through them, along with my dear friend Ananda Babu's help, I have come to know about many incidents and stories of Yogiraj's life. I am humbly grateful to them for this.

Ananda Babu was correct in saying that in order to understand the Lord, one has to have a clear and comprehensive knowledge of the historical elements of India, including the state of society at the time, the overall prevailing mentality, etc. The venerable Srimat Swami Sri Yukteswar Giri Maharaj showed through his immaculate reason and research that Yogiraj's time was that of an age in transition. It was clear from the developments in literature, science and philosophy, along with revolutionary changes in societal structures and government that a new era was clearly taking place. Once dormant, spiritual awareness was revealing itself through the great beings of the time. Our Lord's analysis of the scriptures indicated this natural awakening and evolution. As a supplement, I have thought it my duty to say a couple of things from my ordinary understanding about Kriya Yoga. The perspectives and explorations of knowledgeable Kriyabans coming up at this time could create a huge body of literature.

We often see many occurrences of supernatural incidents in the life stories of Great Beings. Naturally, such incidents will also be found in the pages of this book. It seems that it is not possible to understand all of these things with our limited capacity of mind. Intellectual science has proved the possibility of many things that seemed impossible. The findings of these sciences can partly help us in our understanding of spiritual subjects. But in this area, sometimes it seems best to not speak of the impossible because we do not have the ability to discriminate between the true and the false, and even knowing the truth, we do not know the skills of implementing it in life and thus creating unnecessary problems. One of the Lord's sayings may shed some light on this subject. The gist of this statement is this: there is not much of a difference in experiencing the ordinary and the supernatural. Just as the ordinary or worldly experience is a result of effort, so is the experience of the supernatural. As one cannot have the sensation of touch without awareness of the skin and the body, in a similar way, an inexperienced sadhak cannot wait after attaining some progress in Kriya, and have sudden and spontaneous supernatural knowledge without awareness of his inner senses. Personally, I feel that, leaving aside those supernatural incidents, it seems that by making easily attainable the yoga-dhyana, samadhi etc. which are horrifically portrayed nowadays as severe, unattainable and impossible, the Lord showed the greatest proof of supernatural powers. Stripping spirituality of clever speech, archaic language and history of countless ages and instead embracing the work itself, choosing to conduct oneself rightly in life instead of merely analyzing scriptures, keeping vigilance upon oneself, being mindful of the experience of the visible after contemplating the unseen, kindling the inspiration within to move towards God while respecting the natural process of a human being's life etc. were some of the essential and important ways that the Lord showed the Path and thus truly brought the "new age" to life.

What I have written is not much. I have endeavored to present a taste of His lila in just a few words. Perhaps this work will not have the flow of the typical historical account and there will probably be some things that won't be covered. [However,] if the publishing of these few pages lead the reader to experience even a shred of the compassion of that Great Being, then I will believe that this minuscule offering has successfully served its purpose. The one who first told me about the Priceless Divine Being nearly 36 years ago, the one by whose kindness I was able to receive the blessings of the Lord's great saint-disciples, the one who was my friend in my boyhood and remained my lifelong friend—a companion on the chariot of life, the one from whom I eagerly await even more extensive literature about the Yogavatar filled with the mysteries of sadhana—to begin this book, I first gratefully acknowledge and bow down with the greatest humility and reverence to Guru Swami Srimat Yogananda Paramahansaji.

End preface—Mahvishub Sankranti 241 Dwapara, 1347
Bengali year.
Swami Satyananda Giri
Kararashram
Swargadwar
Puri

CHAPTER ONE

ABIRBHAV (Appearance or Arrival)
(Birth—childhood—youth, etc.)

Sri Sri Shyamacharan was born in the first part of the 13th century of the Bengali calendar in an orthodox Brahmin family in a village known as Ghurnigram, near the town of Krishnanagar, in the Nadia district of Bengal. There is a great deal of disagreement about His date of birth. Supposedly, the astrological charts of the deceased were to be burned with the body, as was the practice of that lineage. But there is some doubt as to whether the Lord or anyone in the family had any idea about His birth date because we had learned from Acharya Sanyal Mahasaya that he had seen a note in the Lord's handwriting saying, "Birth date not exactly known".

(translator's note: the quoted phrase appears in English in the Bengali original and then is translated into Bengali in parentheses for the reader. It may be assumed that aforementioned note of Yogiraj was written by Him in English.)

Yogiraj's grandson, the late Ananda Mohan Lahiri was able to prove after much research and work that He arrived on this Earth on the 16th of Ashwin, 1235 (Bengali calendar). The date was confirmed by Sriyukta Abhayacharan Lahiri later. The Lord's venerable senior disciples have pointed out some statements made by Yogiraj which they heard directly from Him and have said that even though the exact date may not be known, the time of birth could be another three or four years before the aforementioned date. Whatever the case may be, it doesn't seem like it makes that much of a difference.

Shyamacharan was born in an esteemed lineage as the first child of the second wife of the late Gourmohan Lahiri Sarkar Mahasaya. His first wife died while in pilgrimage; she had borne three children. The Jalangi river, which is connected to the river Padma, sometimes, like the Padma, takes on a horrific all-devouring form. The late Gourmohan Lahiri's paternal house was situated on the banks of the Jalangi but was consumed by the river when the Lord was but an infant. Having visited that place with Ananda Babu I could see that the Lahiri house that was on the Padma river banks was also swept away, and that house ended up on the opposite bank of the river. The destruction caused by the ruthless Padma of eminent estates through-out history is a reminder of the transitory nature of worldly existence.

A temple of Shiva built by the Lahiri family was also taken to the bottom of the river along with the house. Legend has it that a devotee was able to rescue the temple's Shivalingam from the river's bowels and then offered it to a new temple, and that temple is now known as the respected "Ghurni's Shivatala" (Whirlpool's Shiva center).

The Lahiri family was well known for holding gatherings of spiritual recitations and worship as well as other righteous work. It is said that the Lord's father, the late Gourmohan Lahiri, was a dedicated practi-tioner of the path of Yoga and that His mother was a devotee of the Lord Shiva. The babe Shyamacharan would sit as if immersed in a meditative state during the worship of Lord Shiva. Perhaps the child-Yogavatar was enjoying His Oneness with Mahadeva, the Lord of Yogis.

Gourmohan Lahiri Sarkar Mahasaya eventually left the Nadia district with the infant Shyamacharan and his family and settled in Kashi (Benares or Varanasi). Shyamacharan lost His mother at this early age. Even though Bengal to Benares was a two-day journey overland and water in those days, the Lahiri family, for many generations, had a his-tory of traveling to Benares for numerous reasons. So Gourmohan Lahiri Mahasaya was easily able to settle into life in Benares. He had constructed an edifice for Shiva worship here as well. We have not been able to find anything extensive about the Lord's infancy, child-hood or youth. Besides His personal sanctification, there is no question that the pure lineage and culture of ancient Aryan wisdom in which He was born, the gradual dominance of western educational systems, and the inevitable conflicts of change during this time of Yuga-transi-tion had significantly influenced His human existence. He must have also been touched spiritually by the Sadhus and Mahatmas (sages and saints) of Benares. Although His father followed the strict ordinances of his ancient Brahmin scholarly lineage, Gourmohan Lahiri did not ignore modern trends of thought.

The child Shyamacharan studied Hindi and Urdu in a primary school in Benares, as His father had wished Him to do. Gradually, He moved on to study Bengali, Sanskrit, Farsi and English at Raja Jaynarayan Ghosal's school and the Government Sanskrit College. It is said that He studied English up to the "Juniorship" level. Even after the advent of the University institution, we have heard that some small colleges were respected as mini-Universities in those days. Because of His spiritual insight, Shastra-based spiritual matters were of special interest to Him, however He also studied the Vedas and philosophical treatises regularly. He probably was not a big scholar in the grammar and lexicography elements of ordinary language. We have heard that even at old age He would recite the Vedas in the presence of Vedic scholars, and that with the pundits He too would drink a small amount of ghee.

The young Shyamacharan was straightforward and simple in nature. He was more interested in duty and work than fancy food and clothing. His beautiful radiance and grace, muscular physique, athletic swimming ability, adroitness at work, serious nature, courage and other such traits earned Him the respect and adoration of His peers. Recitation of the Vedas, bathing in the Ganges, and the Sandhya (dusk) worship were a regular part of daily life in His youth.

At the start of adulthood, Sri Shyamacharan married eight-year old Srimati Kashimoni Devi, the daughter of Sriyukta Devanarayan Sanyal Mahasaya. In time, Kashimoni Devi was initiated into the Path of Yoga by the Lord; she continued her life as an ideal and sacred life-partner with Him, and in this way maintained and managed all of the duties of the household. From serving and attending to the poorest of visitors who would come to their home and performing other such works of selfless service, she ran all of the domestic affairs with great care and order. This holy and pious woman left this plane in Benares in the year 1337 (Bengali calendar) at the age of 94. It was in Benares that her two sons, the late Tinkori Lahiri Mahasaya—the oldest—and the late Dukori Lahiri Mahasaya—the youngest—were born. By the Grace of the Lord, His sons eventually became highly advanced sadhaks and initiated many men and women into Kriya Yoga. In 1851, Sri Shyamacharan became an employee of the ruling British government as a clerk for the military. He received promotions and gradually moved up the ranks in His job. Sri Sri Lahiri Mahasaya also had to relocate to many different places, such as Gazipur, Mirzapur, Danapur, Nainital, Benares and others as the military needed. Two and a half years into His job, His father passed away and He had to bear the full responsibility of the entire household. In 1863, He began living in a rented house in Simanchouhatta. He bought a house free and clear in Garudeshwar Mahalla the very next year. His children were born after He received initiation. At that time, although immersed deeply in the spiritual, Sri Shyamacharan performed all of the worldly duties of the ideal householder. He earned His living through honest and hard work, was known for His loyalty and trustworthiness, discipline and thrift. With stability and ease, He carried out the life of His household. He showed equal respect for everyone, even though He was the highest of Acharyas. If disciples or devotees would bow to touch His feet, He would redirect the pranam to Narayan (God); He did not allow anyone to touch His feet. As He was one Who always carried out His duties, He would also give proper reprimand to those who would neglect theirs. He was aware of and involved in social and philanthropic work as well. In certain schools and other institutions of education, especially in the "Bangalitola" section of Benares, special sections of these institutions were dedicated in honor of Him at their inception. "Where is the time to do sadhana after all the work we have to do in our daily life?" was a familiar cry among householders having to struggle with responsibilities that call from every direction, and perhaps it was to demonstrate a resolution to this complaint of everyday people that the Lord, Saint of Acharyas, although immersed in Spirit, fully attended to all the work of a householder. Those who are caught up in the current of worldly obligations and who either cannot turn inwards to experience Spirit or are hesitant to try should give special consideration to this demonstration by the Lord, the Being of the Age.

CHAPTER TWO

INITIATION

The year is 1268 in the Bengali calendar, 1861 in the Christian calendar. Sri Shyamacharan has passed through most of His youth. He is now over thirty years of age. The work at the office, maintaining domestic life, bathing in the Ganges, japa, puja, recitation of scriptures, all are going on regularly, but the reason for His being here and what will be the real work of His life is about to present itself. The ash covered fire had been only smoldering and giving off smoke; now it was about to be inflamed. What can we ordinary people know about the beautiful plan of the Creator as He is playing it out beyond our sight? We only see after the fruit appears, and we praise Him after we taste the fruit.

In the fall of that year, Lahiri Mahasaya suddenly and unexpectedly received orders to relocate to a place near Nainital called Ranikhet where there were preparations being made for the construction of military barracks. There were no railway lines to in that area at that time, and it is assumed that Lahiri Mahasaya most likely took the aid of an "ekka" (carriage drawn by a single horse) type of transportation from Danapur and arrived at His new place of work. He lived in a tent with His attendants during His stay and whatever little work there was for Him to do, He would finish in a short time and then wander off—going here and there in the beautiful mountains of that region. The desire to find Truth had always been working in Him and because of this, He would feel attracted to seek out the company of sadhus and sannyasis. So, one day when He heard from one of His servants that some sadhus lived in a certain mountain, His curiosity naturally grew keen.

In any case, as He was wandering in the mountains one afternoon, He heard someone calling His name—"Lahiri! Lahiri!"—from somewhere up. He was taken aback, hearing His name being called in this unknown, uninhabited place. Somewhat anxious to satisfy His curiosity,

13

He sought to find the source of the voice. He grew tired after walking quite a while and saw that the sun was going down. Even though He was feeling some trepidation, He kept on walking, just to have audience with a sadhu and to resolve this mystery. Eventually He came upon a clean and well-kept cave at the top of the mountain. A tall, divinely radiant sadhu was standing there—a beatific, joyful smile on His face. It seemed that this holy man was standing there because He was waiting for Lahiri Mahasaya to come. Laughing warmly, Sadhuji said in Hindi, "Shyamacharan, come and rest here. I was calling you." Sri Shyamacharan was surprised to hear His name from this unknown sadhu. All kinds of ideas and thoughts about this situation were spinning in His head, but some sort of attraction pulled Him to follow Sadhuji into the cave. Entering, He found some asanas (material or seat for sitting on the floor for meditation), kamandalus (sacred water pots) and other such things that were used by ascetic monks. Sadhuji pointed to an asana at a particular part of the cave and asked, "Do you recognize this asana?" Lahiri Mahasaya was dumbstruck at this question and the more He looked at Sadhuji's gently laughing countenance, everything seemed to make less and less sense. Still, He was beginning to feel some kind of familiar attraction towards this unknown place. Sadhuji touched Him and gently caressed His head with affection. Suddenly, it seemed to Shyamacharan that He just woke up from a deep sleep. He saw that this was His own place of sadhana and His own asana! How familiar this cave was! And how familiar was this Extraordinary Mahatma who was standing with Him—His eternal and deathless Srigurudev! It all came back to Him: in His last life He had become a sannyasi and in the presence of Sriguru became absorbed in sadhana in this very place. Later, He left His body. Overwhelmed by remembering all this, Sri Shyamacharan collapsed at Sriguru's feet and immediately begged to receive complete shelter in Him. Gurudev's tranquil words of consolation and solace brought some relief to Lahiri Mahasaya's mind. He then came to know that it was Sriguru's Divine Power that had caused Him to be suddenly relocated to Ranikhet.

Though He didn't want to return to His present life after having surrendered all to His Guru's Feet, upon Sriguru's instructions Lahiri Mahasaya returned to the Ranikhet office. He began attending satsang on different mountains at the feet of His Guru. Administering medicine and proper nutrition and gradually bringing Shyamacharan to a physically pure and healthy state, Sadhuji sat Him down on His asana and initiated Him in the rare and priceless path of Kriya Yoga Sadhana. The dust and dullness of consciousness was removed; the radiance of Divine Knowledge appeared. His initiation was complete.

[translator's note: the terms "diksha prapta" is emphasized by Swami Satyananda; in western terms it is a similar meaning to being "born again". The translator has tried to remain as close to the literal as possible, but this is the inferred meaning.]

This was not only a sacred moment for Him, but for all humankind. It was the beginning of recovering the Lost Treasure—so many thirsty men and women would now find a place to quench their yearning with the rejuvenating water of life. It was as if Mother Ganges Herself began flowing to helpless devotees as Mandakini, Her heavenly form. That holy moment was a hidden event, unseen by people in an undiscovered and secret cave. For beings praying for shelter, for the distressed and desperate, for sincere seekers, the powerful seed of the Tree that would be their future sanctuary was now planted with the greatest love and care. Blessed and grateful was this Arya (noble) land—this India, Guru of the world.

Pure and sanctified, Sri Shyamacharan sat on the sacred asana and began to ascend the different levels of Pranayam Kriya Yoga, experiencing worlds of incredible wonder. The outward bound senses were withdrawn and rested within; He became immersed in beatific awareness. The Lord was Samadhistha (absorbed in samadhi). How time disappeared! Where was the office? Where was the job? Where was His domestic life? Coming out of samadhi, He fell at Sriguru's Lotus Feet and begged to remain with His Divine Presence forever; the taste of the Satchitananda-filled Brahman made Him want to leave everything behind. Guru Mahamuni Babaji Maharaj lovingly embraced Him and said that He would still have to fulfill His worldly duties for a few more years and that Kriya Yoga Sadhana would spread to the people of the world through His presence in the world. Realizing His new responsibility, Sri Shyamacharan submitted reverently to Sriguru's order. He then asked how and when He might see His Guru again. Sriguru reassured Him, "Whenever You think of me, I will be there."

At first, Babaji Maharaj had put severe restrictions on initiation and who was to be initiated; He instructed to initiate only those with certain high qualities into Kriya Yoga Sadhana. He even said that only those willing to give everything at the Feet of the Guru would be revealed the mysteries of sadhana. The compassionate heart of the Lord cried out to Sriguru, "If You have bestowed Your Grace upon Me, then I beg for Your Mercy to bestow even more Grace for all people, without distinction, that they may also receive this rarest Kriya Yoga Sadhana without such difficulty." Hearing this poignant prayer from the magnanimous heart of His disciple, the Great Being Srigurudev said, "So shall it be." He instructed that the aspirant should give at least 5 rupees at the initiation as a symbolic offering of physical penance, which Sri Shyamacharan should receive in Sriguru's name. Later, the Lord also instructed His disciples who were eligible to initiate others into Kriya to follow the same injunction. Probably because of Babaji Maharaj's orders, no initiator-guru is allowed to use this money on his own behalf. Through the lineage of Guru-parampara, we know that this money may be only used for the service of sadhus and good works.

Before leaving the place of initiation, Sri Shyamacharan was joyfully greeted with congratulations by the high holy men living in the caves of the mountain. We have heard of many supernatural events associated with the time and place of His initiation. It is not easy to comprehend the mysteries of these events in our minuscule intelligence. In any case, after having been absorbed in His True Self, beyond mind and the three gunas, the Lord descended from the state of Nirvikalpa and re-entered the world anew, an incarnation of Divine Yoga with a mission to establish the Path of Yoga and dispel the darkness in worldly life. Eventually, Yogiraj Munibar Sri Sri Shyamacharan Lahiri Mahasaya returned to Benares, the land of knowledge.

CHAPTER THREE

MAHAMUNI BABAJI MAHARAJ

The real name of Sri Sri Lahiri Mahasaya's Gurudev has never been disclosed. The Lord referred to Him as "Babaji". [translator's note: many holy men in India are called "babaji", an intimate term loosely associated with "father".] We know nothing about whether He was associated with any sect or lineage. We will only discuss whatever little we have been able to find about Him from Yogiraj's earliest disciples. Everyone's experience says that He is a Fully Realized, Immortal Being who has lived in a human body for almost 600 years; He is alive even today. His divinely beautiful, radiant form which seems to be forever in the years just before middle-age, has been witnessed. His Holiness Swami Sri Yukteswar Giri Maharaj used to say that His form has an amazing likeness to Lahiri Mahasaya's. The difference is that Babaji Maharaj has full, long hair and He was usually seen in the type of dhoti (cloth worn for the lower half of the body) that is the garb of Northwestern Indians. He would drape the excess of the cloth over one shoulder. He would speak in Hindi. Sri Shyamacharan returned to working at the office after His initiation. In conversations with friends or holy men, He would find Himself discussing about the best way to do sadhana in ordinary life, the powers of certain yogis and yogic powers in general. Sensing that the others doubted these things, He would proudly speak of the glorious yogic abilities of His Guru. One day while everyone was aroused with curiosity and suspicion, in order to dispel the doubts of the unbelievers, Lahiri Mahasaya asked them to wait outside a room. He entered that empty space, sat in asana and called upon His Guru. Mahamuni Babaji Maharaj, keeping His word, was drawn to His disciple and appeared in His subtle body at His asana. But He was angry at being called to only satisfy a curiosity. Saying, "You won't be able to get darshan for this kind of thing again!" He was about to disappear. Oh sadhu, understand that even such a great being and avatar can succumb to error; they are also not beyond reprimand! It is so whether you think that this behavior is for teaching a lesson to everyone or whether you think that is Lila. The supreme devotee Arjuna himself fell to so many mistakes in his path of sadhana and was reprimanded for it. And we, attaining any little thing say that we are beyond making mistakes, we know everything—beyond chastisement! In any case, Sri Shyamacharan fell desperately the Feet of Sriguru and begged for forgiveness of His error, and conveyed to Him what He was trying to do—change the minds of the unbelievers into believing. Sri Shyamacharan petitioned, "Since You have appeared by Your Grace, then show Yourself to the all the others!" The Ocean of Mercy, Babaji Maharaj agreed and the door to the room was opened. Everyone was astonished to see that another man had appeared in a locked room. This still did not end their suspicions. They thought that this could be a hallucination, or maybe a ghost. To dispel their doubts, "halua" (a dish made of semolina, ghee, milk and sugar) was made and Babaji ate. Everyone received "prasad" (sacrament). Eventually, the others went outside the room. Lahiri Mahasaya closed the door. "From now on, I will come when I see that You need Me," said Babaji Maharaj and disappeared. The door was opened again, and to everyone's amazement, Shyamacharan was alone in the empty room.

From Swami Sri Yukteswar Giri Maharaj, we have learned that Babaji was aware of modern movements—especially Western influence and ideology—and expressed that the Arya Shikhsha and Sadhana (the highest education and practice) is present in both the East and West. We know of three encounters with Swamiji Maharaj and Babaji Mahatma: once at the Prayag Kumbhamela in the year 1300 (Bengali calendar), one time with Yogiraj and another time at Srirampur, Hoogly District. [Translator's note: Srirampur is the literal transliteration of what has been referred to as Serampore, mentioned in several other English writings of Kriya saints.] At the Kumbhamela, Swamiji was walking on a path when suddenly, from behind, he heard someone calling him, "Swamiji! Swamiji!" Sri Yukteswar Giri Maharaj hadn't yet taken the vow of sannyas; he was living in an ordinary way. So he thought that even if someone was calling "Swamiji" towards him, the call might not have been for him. So, he didn't pay any attention to this and kept on walking. Again the call came, "Swamiji! Swamiji!" Then a Brahmachari approached him and said, "That Sadhuji is calling you. Please go and see Him." Curious, he went to the Sadhuji and the Sadhuji received him by saying "Swamiji, please have a seat." Sri

Yukteswar implored, "Maharaj, I am not a sannyasi. So why are You referring to me as 'Swamiji'?" Sadhuji said, "You know, no one puts down what I say; so why are you putting it down? The society that We live in—this is the terminology of that society." After conversing for a while, Swamiji found out that this was the renowned Babaji, the Guru of his Gurudev. Feeling blessed and fortunate, he then prostrated at His feet. He began to use the "Swamiji" prefix with his householder name from then on. Of course, he later took the vows of sannyas from Dashnami Sannyasi.

During their conversation, Babaji Maharaj said, "Since you're writing [an interpretation of] Gita at the wishes of your Guru, do something for me." Swamiji Maharaj was writing a spiritual interpretation of the Gita at this time. Babaji said that something had to be written about the connection with the essence of what the enlightened sages of India had said and the present Western spiritual writings. Swamiji was confused upon hearing this directive. He said, "Maharaj, what kind of order is this? I am just an ordinary man. How can I take on such a task!" At this, Babaji laughed loudly ("ho! ho!") and said, "Oh my child! Why are you doubting this? Who does whose work? Something came to my mouth and it came out. I ended up speaking it. So the work will also get done by the same impulse!" Babaji let out something about the Lord during the conversation, "Poor dear, His life is about to be finished." Later it was understood that this statement by Babaji was foretelling the passing of Lahiri Mahasaya. Empowered by Babaji Maharaj's blessing, Swamiji assumed the task he was given and petitioned, "I must see You after the writing is finished." Babaji said, "Once the book is finished, you will see Me." Hearing this, and with Babaji's blessing, Swamiji departed. He returned to his Guru in Benares, intoxicated by this extraordinary experience, and told his incredible story to Lahiri Mahasaya. Hearing this, Gurudev joyfully blessed him also.

The conversation was going along quite pleasantly until Swamiji Maharaj mentioned Babaji Maharaj's words, "The poor dear's present life is finished." Upon his saying this, Lahiri Mahasaya's body reacted as if struck by lightning and the ever ebullient Yogiraj became unbelievably serious and like a wooden doll, sat stern and rigid on his asana. His body became pale and wan. Swamiji was stunned and afraid. Never before had he seen this all-blissful being in this horrifying condition.

Total silence. Spending three hours in this way, the Lord returned to His normally blissful state and continued to converse as usual. Everyone breathed a sigh of relief. I have heard from Swamiji Maharaj that the Lord pulled Himself within at the eve of His leaving the body to cut Himself from the last bits of attachment to the world, and became absolutely Himself, totally free. Returning to Srirampur, Swamiji Maharaj began to think about the future treatise. He became absorbed with the research of the book during bedtime at night, when nature grew silent. Gradually, by the Grace of Babaji Mahatma, Swamiji collected the cream of Arya Darshan (high Indian spiritual texts) and composed Sanskrit sutras according to them and then gathered the proper passages from the Western Bible. Beautifully revealing that they both had the same vision, he created a book appropriate for the dawn of a new age where unity and its essence prevailed—a storehouse of knowledge called "Kaivalya Darshan" ("The Holy Science"). Swamiji Maharaj was expected to finish the Gita and a couple of other books but was not able to finish any of them, but somehow this "Kaivalya Darshan" was completed and published. Param Gurudev Babaji's order and directive were fulfilled. The publication evidenced His blessing.

The morning when the book was finished, Swamiji went to take his usual bath at the Ganges. Finishing his bath and coming out of the water at the Raighat, he was astonished and amazed to find Babaji underneath a banyan tree. Hurriedly, he did pranam, even though still in his wet clothes, and prayed to Him to come to his home nearby. Babaji wasn't agreeable about going to his house. "We are people of the trees. We like being under the shelter of the tree. We are fine here." After the denial of repeated requests for Babaji to come to his house, Swamiji hurriedly ran home, changed his clothes, and quickly put together some milk and sweets with which he returned to the banks of Ganges. But he saw that Babaji was not there. He searched for Him here and there, asking the people at the banks and nearby, people who were there at the time he was bathing, but Babaji was nowhere to be found. Those who were present the whole time of Babaji and Swamiji's meeting surprisingly said that they hadn't seen any man fitting Swamiji's description. Completely mystified, Swamiji returned home. Babaji's promise to meet him immediately after the completion of the book was fulfilled and realizing this, Swamiji's heart was filled with joy and gratitude. Yogiraj's great disciple Swami Pranabananda Giri Maharaj was sitting one morning in Benares with his Guru when he saw an ordinary looking man coming from the Ganges and entering Lahiri Mahasaya's home. Upon noticing this man, Lahiri Mahasaya quickly got up and fully prostrated at His feet. Swamiji also did pranam at the indication of the Lord. When he came to know that this was his Gurudev's Guru, the Supremely Divine Babaji Mahatma, he was taken aback. The three of them enjoyed a beautiful time that day, eating together and talking about many things. Out of curiosity, Swamiji asked about Babaji's age and came to find out that it was almost 500 years. It's possible by the power of yoga sadhana to maintain the body in that way and even though there may be some changes every 100 years, but old age never comes and makes the body infirm. Babaji also said that He would have to keep His body for another few years to complete His work. Paramgururaj Babaji Maharaj blessed Swamiji and happily encouraged him, saying, "You're on the right path. Keep doing sadhana. You'll get what you're looking for." Swamiji was grateful at having the blissful company of both his Guru and Paramguru at the same time. He had received Babaji's darshan once more at the 1300 (Bengali year) Kumbhamela. I've heard from Sri Sri Shankari Mata, disciple of Mahatma Trailanga Swamiji Maharaj, that once when she was sitting in Lahiri Mahasaya's company in Barrackpore, a simply dressed ordinary looking young man holding a staff arrived. Immediately, the Lord got up and prostrated at this man's feet. Mataji asked the Lord who this man was and found that it was His Gurudev, Babaji Maharaj. The great sage Sriyukta Ramgopal Babu spoke of his beautiful experience with Babaji Maharaj to Swami Yoganandaji. Once, at the end of the night, he came to the Dashaswamedh Ghat (a holy bank of the Ganges in Benares) at the instruction of his Guru. He sat and waited in the posture of a tapasyi (a meditator). Suddenly, he saw a brilliant and effulgent form of the Divine Mother. The beautifully radiant Lahiri Mahasaya rose out of the Ganges and stood next to Her; Ramgopalji was entranced. In this heavenly space then appeared the joyfully smiling Babaji and Ramgopal Babu was immersed in ecstasy. Only in the meeting of devotee and God is such infinite Bliss. Although there have been a couple of other things about Mahamuni Babaji Maharaj that have been heard here and there, there is nothing significant that we know. Some people have tried to figure out His real name, which we know is a useless endeavor. What importance is there in knowing the ordinary name of an immortal being? The greatest of sadhus, Swamiji Maharaj said that just saying the word "Babaji" draws the mind towards Him and it is completely purified and blessed.

CHAPTER FOUR

KARMAKSHETRE (in the world—karma: work, khsetra—field)
(as of Guru and the sheltered)

Soon after receiving initiation, Sri Sri Lahiri Mahasaya had to leave the mountainous province by order of His employer and come to Danapur. He immersed Himself fully in His duties after arriving at His workplace. No one at work knew what kind of immense transformation had taken place. His relatives and friends remained in the dark and beyond the unknowing eyes of the ordinary world, a huge spiritual occurring had begun.

The flower's perfume cannot be covered up. Immediately after blooming it attracts the senses of all [translator's note: it is also implied: "even the ordinary" or "even the unaware"]. The former work and domestically-oriented Lahiri Mahasaya's internal radiance slowly began to be recognized. Even the sahib (English boss) at His job noticed a certain manner about Him and affectionately began to call Him "Paglababu" (mad or ecstatic gentleman). At this time, we come to find out about an extraordinary occurrence. One day, Lahiri Mahasaya saw that the sahib was looking depressed and asked him about his troubles. His boss's wife was extremely ill back in Bilet (western country—in this case, probably England), and he couldn't get any news about her condition. Hearing this, Lahiri Mahasaya told him that He would get word about her. In solitude, through the power of yoga, He attained the information and let His boss know the good news that his wife had written in a letter to him in the very language of the letter. The sahib was somewhat consoled by this, having heard about the miraculous powers of Indian yogis, but he couldn't completely believe His words. In due time, he received the happy news from his wife in a letter and was astonished at how "Paglababu's" words matched her writing. His wife came to India after a few days and when she saw the Lord, she exclaimed that He was the Saint that she saw back home by her sickbed and it was through His Grace that she was cured. Realizing that he had personally witnessed the power of Indian yogis about which he had only heard before, he was amazed and stupefied.*

*From the "Sadhusamvad", article written by Sriyukta Narendra Kumar Bhattacharya.

Day after day, one or two people would come from here and there and receive Kriya Yoga Sadhana from Him. Irrespective of caste and creed, when He would find sincere seekers to be appropriate vessels, He would give initiation to them. After returning from Ranikhet, Lahiri Mahasaya worked for nearly 25 more years at His government job. He received a pension [from the government] after this time and began to live in His own house at Kashidham. Probably because He was unable to have much free time before His pension, only one or two people from time to time would have the opportunity to become initiates. It was after settling in Kashidham that Yogiraj came to have many disciples. It is heard that He once or twice visited Krishnanagar and Bankura district's Bishnupur at His second son in-law's home. Many people received initiation from Him in Bengal at that time, especially in Bishnupur. The Bishnupur area was blessed to have been the recipient of His special attention. It seemed that, due to the sadhana of many silent sadhakas, one could taste the flow of a profoundly deep spiritual ambrosia in that land. Sadhakas who thirst for such nectar would probably find it in the atmosphere there even today. In Krishnanagar too are there so many silent Kriyavan sadhakas who have kept the current continuously flowing behind the sight of ordinary people. It seems that the Lord's Holy Feet also graced the areas of Munga and Bhagalpur, because the presence of many secret sadhakas are found around those places.

Advanced sadhakas would view Lahiri Mahasaya as the very incarnation of God. We know about some supernatural events that occurred at that time. However, all was happening silently, out sight of the ordinary masses! Once Yogiraj saw His picture in the possession of a disciple and said, "Respect God or respect the picture." Sometime later, that same relative and disciple's house was under the threat of being struck by lightning. The Lord's daughter-in-law and another woman devotee, both frightened, threw themselves in full prostration in front of that picture, pleading, "Lord, save us!" Lightning struck that very house but the devotees were saved. They felt that as if someone was applying cool ice on their backs and protecting them from the heat. Another time, there was a woman who came to Him saying that she could not keep her children alive, no matter what. She took shelter at the Lord's feet and prayed to Him to please see to it that her next child lives. Overcome with compassion and mercy, He said, "Make sure that the lamp that is lit in the labor/birthing room remains lit all night; in no case should you let it go out." In due time, that woman became expectant of the birth of a child. So that the lamp would not go out, she even enlisted the help of another woman to keep watch on the light in the maternity room. Total attention was given on the lamp. As night was almost at an end, the mother-to-be and the woman in charge of helping her keep watch suddenly began to get sleepy and right about this time, the lamp also began to give signs of going out. The door was shut, but all of a sudden the lock crashed open with a loud bang. Everyone was roused from sleep. Still drowsy, they looked up to behold the ever-sheltering and affectionate Lord standing there and pointing toward the lamp. The sleepiness was abruptly broken. The flame was attended to and stabilized, and after that, the room was exactly the same as before. There was not even a sign of any other person. As His devotee had prayed, the child lived. I have heard from Sriyukta Ananda Mohan's mother that, during all types of disease and distress, many devotees of Bishnupur would take shelter and resolution in the Lord alone.

Beginning when He was still employed and continuing throughout His retirement, He gave initiation to gardeners, postmen, kings, maharajas, people considered to be of the lower classes, ascetics, sannyasis, householders, Christians (including Anglos), Muslims—hundreds of people from all walks of life, regardless of caste, religion or place in the hierarchy of society. Kashi Naresh Maharaj Ishwarinarayan Singha Bahadur and his son Prince Bahadur both received initiation from the Lord when the Maharaj recognized Lahiri Mahasaya, then his son's home tutor, as an enlightened master. It was learned from Yogiraj's advanced disciples that He used to speak in a lofty manner about the disciple Brinda Bhagat, an ordinary postman. One day, the Lord said in front of everyone, "Brinda is floating in the Ocean of Satchitananda." Through the power of sadhana, so deep was the inner spiritual sight of this unknown devotee from the "uneducated"* class of society, that from time to time he would resolve the most difficult spiritual and scriptural issues raised by scholars by his easy and simple words. It is also known about an advanced Muslim disciple of the Lord, Abul Gafur Khan. At that time, for a strict Brahmin to initiate anyone regardless of race, religion or position was thought of as an especially courageous act. Of course the Supreme Lord will destroy the sinful dogma of society in order to establish the True Ideal! Those that society labels as outcasts, that it mistreats and despises—it is especially for them that the Divinely Incarnated Beings come age after age to spread the message of hope: release from the illusory entanglement of the world.

Paramhansa Swami Pranabananda Giri Maharaj received initiation [from Lahiri Mahasaya] at an early age and, after attaining samadhi, he had wonderous experiences of the Lord's Grace. Later on, with the Lord's permission, he took the path of sannyas. If anyone expressed the desire for sannyas, Lahiri Mahasaya would not be so easily agreeable. Instead, He would seriously warn the person about the austere and difficult lifestyle and responsibility of the sannyasi. Pranabananda Swamiji used to say, "I couldn't find an to the expanse of this Immense Being. In wonderment, I wanted to test and find out whether His shadow touched the earth. But after pondering this, there was no space left in my mind to look for His shadow, although, both inside and outside, I have been with Him and traveled with Him so much."

Lahiri Mahasaya's venerable sons, Tinkori Lahiri Mahasaya and Dukori Lahiri Mahasaya, and Swami Sriyukteswar Giri, Maharaj, Swami Pranabananda Giri Maharaj, Srimat Keshabananda Brahmachariji Maharaj, Acharya Shastri Mahasaya (Swami Kebalananda Maharaj), Acharya Panchanon Bhattacharya Mahasaya, Acharya Brajalal Adhikari Mahasaya, Acharya Srimat Mahadev Prasadji etc. were among Yogiraj's advanced disciples in God-realization. Even after having spent time with so many of them, we can hardly begin to fathom the depth, enlightenment and power of these great ones. How much can we possibly understand about their Source, the Immense Being who was the Yogavatar?*

*[Translator's note: This paragraph had to be translated a little more liberally to make structure sense in English. Sincere apologies, because

this translator could not find a better way. The translator believes that the meaning and the intention of the paragraph is strictly maintained.]

I had heard from His Holiness Swami Sriyukteswar Giri Maharaj that one day, upon hearing seriously distressing news about the health of a friend who lived far away, he anxiously rushed to the Lord and pleaded in desperation for help. The Lord replied, "[Tell him to] go to the doctor." Swamiji expressed even more grief in his petition when the Lord said, gently laughing, "Oh! You want medicine! Okay, he'll be fine. Just take that medicine and feed him a couple-two-three drops." Saying this, He pointed to a bottle of Neem oil sitting by the window. [Neem is an Indian Margosa plant.] A true believer of Guru's word, Swamiji took that bottle headed off on a train towards his friend's place. Upon arriving at the destination, he was shocked to see that his deathly ill friend was waiting for him at the station! Swamiji asked how this could be, and his friend responded by saying that suddenly, at such and such time (the same time that Swamiji petitioned to the Lord), he began to be healed and as he was gradually getting better and better, he received word that his friend was arriving and decided to go to the station to welcome Swamiji himself. Swamiji was completely elated and grateful and he told his friend the entire story. He then fulfilled the directive by administering a few drops of the Neem oil.

We have heard that there was a devotee traveling from far away who was just about at the station to catch his train, when the signal for immediate departure sounded. In desperation, the gentleman focused completely on remembering the Lord. The train was mysteriously delayed for some unusual reason and the gentleman hurriedly and boarded his car. Just as he reached Kashidham and did pranam to his Guru, the Lord laughingly said, "Oh!! Such running around!!! Just leave a little earlier!" The devotee's heart was stunned at the omniscient Lord's Grace and he was completely filled with gratefulness.

We have heard from Sriyukta Kalikumar Roy Mahasaya that when he could come to Benares from time to time, he would stay at the Lord's house for periods of 5 to 7 days at a time and would even sleep in Yogiraj's room. He said that at night after everything became silent, many sannyasis in ochre colored robes could come to the Lord and spend the night discussing things pertaining to sadhana. Roy Mahasaya also said, "I have been there day and night for eight or nine days in a row and I saw that the Lord would not go to bed. Sometimes He might sit and close His eyes for a short while. Sriyukta Kalibabu mentioned one story where a certain gentleman came and the Lord instructed the 5 or 6 people present to close their eyes. When they opened their eyes, He asked, "What did you see?"

Everyone saw the same thing with their eyes closed: a woman whose features and colorful clothes that everyone described in the same way. After that, the Lord indicated to the aforementioned gentleman to beware of future associations with that envisioned figure. It has been heard that that gentleman actually did fall into disrepute in regards to that [which was addressed by Lahiri Mahasaya]. Once there was a photo taken with the Lord amidst His disciples. After the photo plate was treated with developing solution, all were astonished to see that everyone's picture came out but where the Lord's picture should have been was empty. Lahiri Mahasaya was particularly opposed to having His picture taken. One disciple named Gangadharbabu, taking pride in his own camera, took a photograph of the Lord at everyone's request. Gangadharbabu treated the plate with the developing solution and saw that there was no impression. But his tests showed that he had made no mistake. Seeing that the Lord was smiling, he understood that the vanity-destroying Lord obliterated his pride about his newly found knowledge. Then, at the devotees' humble plea, the Lord allowed the picture to be taken. In these ways, the Lord would demonstrate and make His disciples understand about the boundlessness of Knowledge and would arouse their thirst for Knowledge to grow ever more.

The great scholar Shastri Mahasaya (Swami Kebalanandaji Mahasaya*) spent time in the Lord's company for ten years in Benares before receiving initiation. At that time, he was studying Vedanta from the renowned Benarasi scholar Swami Bhaskarananda Paramhansaji. We have heard from Shastri Mahasaya that Bhaskarananda Swamiji one day became eager to receive initiation in Kriya yoga and invited Lahiri Mahasaya to his ashram. Yogiraj cryptically replied, "Does the thirsty man go to the well, or does the well move toward the thirsty man?" It was heard later that the two met at some garden and Swamiji received

Kriyayoga sadhana. The eminent saint Balananda Brahmachari Maharaj of Deoghar also received the Lord's Kriya yoga a long time ago.

*[Translator's note: It is possible that "Mahasaya" in this case was intended to be "Maharaj"; as it would be the usual term of respect for the title of Swami.]

It is also known that the great saint Trailangaswamiji and Lahiri Mahasaya were friends and used to meet and sit together. One day, as he was speaking about and praising Lahiri Mahasaya, Trailangaswami Maharaj responded to a curious disciple's question by saying that to get to the lofty level he had attained in the kingdom of sadhana he had to abandon everything down to even renouncing a loincloth.* That Man remained a householder and attained the same state. The jeweler can spot the true gem!!!

[Translator's note: Trailangaswamiji Maharaj had renounced even the wearing of clothes.]

A certain renowned disciple of the Lord first received yoga initiation in a dream and later when he directly [physically] received Kriya, he realized that he received the same instructions in the dream.

Knowing the plea of the petitioner before it is spoken and having resolved the issue already, pointing out and cautioning about the hidden, unclean thoughts of scholarly Brahmins, destroying the pride of disciples, saving people from danger etc. and many other supernatural events, and the accounts of the deep personal experiences of the Lord by Sadhu Kumar Nath Sudhakar, Swami Yogananda Maharaj and others—I won't go into recounting these things and thereby greatly increase the size of this book.*

*[Translator's note: the Bengali statement that Swami Satyananda Maharaj used here can be more poetically interpreted something like, "There are not enough pages to write of all the miraculous works." In keeping with the rest of the translation, it has been translated as close to the literal as possible.]

Lahiri Mahasaya had no desire to form any groups, and as such, He did not ask His disciples to change their societal norms, daily duties, performance of worship or ritual, or the individual's personal feelings for God. He would advise them to practice with respect and truthfulness, and through Kriyayoga sadhana alone, the Knowledge that revealed itself and the God-intoxication that manifested, would He attract the disciples' sights that direction. The Lord came here in the form of a human being. He attracted the people of the world through the way of living as an ideal human being. He would impart knowledge to His disciples through gestures, hints, conversation, jokes, and also in profound seriousness. Any questions by disciples in letter form would be returned to the questioner with the answer written very concisely by Him on that very paper. Sadhusabhapati Swamiji Maharaj [Swami Sriyukteswar Giri] used to say, "Sometimes I would come back after sitting around and having small talk and ordinary conversations with Gurudev, and suddenly I would become astonished to realize that I had unknowingly come back with a great deal of knowledge." By the fact that the Yogavatar's widely varied and advanced followers were non-dualist, dualist etc., it can be easily surmised that the magnanimous and Truth-seeing Lord, after revealing the path of the Soul, would allow the sadhaka to be free in his/her personal way. Lahiri Mahasaya basically lived in society as those in His family lineage would have normally done. He regularly followed the edicts of bathing in the Ganges, reciting the Vedas and other such observances. However, it is heard that towards the end, most of the time He would sit silently in asana, absorbed in yogic bliss. The suspension of heartbeat, the absence of pulse, breathlessness and an unblinking gaze filled with immense peace—this was His normal state of being. It was as if He had traveled beyond this smallness, and was now constantly living in the highest place of Brahman's Total, Undifferentiated, Infinite Consciousness. Up until the end, among observances, He would fast for the Shiva Chaturdashi, and would travel alone towards Sarnath on the day after the fast. Some disciples think that He used to meet Babaji on that day, somewhere around Sarnath.

CHAPTER FIVE

PROPAGATION

I have already mentioned previously that the Lord did not take up the work of propagation in the manner of forming any organizations, unlike the trend that it is today. But He came to resurrect the nearly dead path of yoga and propagation went on almost completely hidden from ordinary people. The fragrance of the flower in full bloom began to spread and attract on its own. It was through the devotees who were drinking the nectar of Kriya yoga that hundreds of men and women began to come to the feet of the Lord, yet there was no pomp around it. The neighbors of a Kriyavan sadhaka, in some cases even people in the same house, would not know about the sadhaka's initiation or practice. Leaving aside the ordinary householder disciples and sadhus and brahmacharis, there were disciples in the uppermost levels of society—high government officials, very wealthy and eminent devotees such as Paresh Kaviraj Mahasaya, Shyamadas Vachaspati Kaviraj Mahasaya, Kashi Naresh Maharaj, Jotindramohan Thakur etc. Even though He had disciples such as these from the highest positions and of the greatest eminence, He did not encourage anyone to do external propagation. The word spread in secret and in such a way that even today, I have witnessed great saints such as Swami Bholananda Giri Maharaj and other highly reputed sadhus and mahatmas pay homage to the memory of the Lord. It has been heard that Kashi Naresh's royal doctor became very enthused at wanting to spread the name of "Kashibaba," when the Lord stopped him from that endeavor. Towards the end, He gave permission to Yogacharya Pandit Panchanon Bhattacharya Mahasaya to discreetly form a place from where propagation could happen in as quiet a way as possible, with which directive Bhattacharya Mahasaya founded the Arya Mission Institution in Calcutta. Through the aid of this institution, the propagation of Kriya yoga began to expand in Bengal. Several books such as the commentaries of Lahiri Mahasaya on the Bhagavad Gita, books of spirituality* etc. were published. Some medicine was manufactured as well. The

Arya Mission also published a Gita with a Bengali translation of the Sanskrit, and Bengali commentary accompanied with footnotes from a spiritual viewpoint, which became a treasured part of Bengali literature and was a priceless boon to the God-thirsty Bengali seekers. As far as we know, there was no such Gita with Bengali commentary up to that point. Later on, this Gita was published in Hindi. In Deoghar, Bhattacharya Mahasaya also set up a shrine for the Lord in the middle of a large garden and set it up for proper worship.

*[Translator's comment: Satyananda Swamiji states this book to be "Darshan", which can mean general philosophy or spirituality or possibly the more specific, "Vedanta Darshan."]

Lahiri Mahasaya would not allow people to take charge of propagation. We know that even after the founding of Arya Mission Institution, He forbade one of His significant scholarly disciples from participating in that work. Lahiri Mahasaya used to prescribe a particular Neem oil for practically all illnesses. Many people knew how to make the formula for the medicine, but if someone didn't follow the Lord's instruction he would somehow find himself having to spend a lot more money and for some reason the solution would greatly decrease by itself immediately after it was produced, all of which would deflate the producer's enthusiasm and drive for proceeding further. But those that would follow His instructions would find the same process of producing the formula completely successful and thereby would continually receive the benefits of it.

To especially spread the wisdom of the Gita, Lahiri Mahasaya printed and distributed thousands of small Gitas (only the key passages/slokas)* in Bengali and Hindi. As far as we know, the Gita was a priceless book before that time. This anonymous and unpublicized way—what strange and unusual propagation! He would be absorbed in yoga and give spiritual commentaries on the Gita and other books of philosophy. Bhattacharya Mahasaya, Mahendranath Sanyal Mahasaya and other disciples would write them down. Some devotees in some cases would receive His concise and abbreviated commentaries on the scriptures via letter. These were writings that began to be produced as the aforementioned books. The explanations of the deep scriptural mysteries which were handed down by the oral tradition of guru-disciple succession were first brought out in book form to the ordinary people because of the power of the Lord's compassion. Half a century ago [from the writing of this biography], this Gita with spiritual explanation circulated mostly among the community of sadhakas. This beautiful body of literature became manifest during this transition of ages in the land of Arya—India—for the spiritual revelation of sadhakas, the progenitors of beneficence for all human beings. With Sriguru's support, His Holiness Swami Sriyukteswar Maharaj ji also began to publish an exquisite Gita, approved by the Lord, chapter by chapter, with his own commentaries based on his own realization. About the books that had Lahiri Mahasaya as the author, Swamiji Maharaj used to say, "That Gurudev Himself wrote any books—this is not correct, and to say so is to actually demean Him. He Himself did not author any book. What was written down of His words by His devotees while they listened to His spoken commentaries is what has been published in book form. Gurudev's language and manner from time to time were incomprehensible to many; it's not at all impossible that trying convey that language and manner in written form could produce some errors here and there." The Lord wrote to a certain disciple, "...the lord work Kriya good language grammatical correction up to you all—wish is print—my name should not be there—good if in secret."** We have seen manuscripts, in the possession of a siignificant devotee, of the early versions of the Gita with the Lord's spoken commentaries that were taken to Him that had extra "notes"*** written on them. Whatever the case may be, the erudition in these books of the experience of the fantastic kingdom beyond the senses will lead the Kriyavan on the path to Supreme Knowledge with the Divine Touch of the Yogavatar in this scriptural material.

*The parenthetical in this case is from the original text, translated.
**[Translator's note: The quoted text of the letter by Yogiraj is almost verbatim, without any attempt at interpretation.]
***The word "notes" is stated in English (although transliterated in the Bengali alphabet) in the original text.

When I was a boy, I was once in the company of the venerable Bhattacharya Mahasaya. I heard him say, "The Lord was Kabir," And Bhattacharya Mahasaya also said that the Lord Himself had stated this.

Special commentaries on couplets by Kabir were published by the Arya Mission. Whether he was thinking of the Lord as likened to Kabir as an incredible and beautiful yogi of the same lofty stature, or whether He was intoxicated with Kabir, was He born as a part of Kabir or did He incarnate as Kabir in a previous life—which of these Bhattacharya Mahasaya was trying to let people know I have not understood.

Some propagation has taken place through Acharya Sanyal Mahasaya and some other devotees of the Lord who founded temples and published other books. Presently, in Kashidham, the holy house of the Lahiri lineage, a beautiful marble statue has been erected. It is as if the Lord saw that the best and most natural way to spread the fragrance was by hiding in the woods. Ignoring the normal mode of propagating by the printing press, the Lord instead planted seeds in the best and most fertile soil. With His Divine Touch, in time His children of His Mind became trees and gave innumerable fruit. The teachings continued to be spread naturally and quietly. Whether it pertained to Kriya, discussing scriptures, the edicts of society, natural propagation, the most conducive methods—in all of these we find the same manner of instruction from the Lord. [Translator's note: it was difficult to ascertain an exact meaning from this previous sentence. There are flaws in the printing of the text in terms of punctuation. The printing mistakes have made the meaning ambiguous.] He was particularly interested in drawing everyone to the discussion and analysis of the Bhagavad Gita, the greatest of the Upanishads. [When it came to discussions of scriptures,] it is mainly the wisdom of the Gita that His devotees and disciples would gather to listen to, memorize and meditate upon. These gatherings used to be simply called "Gita Sabha." Supposedly, one day Lahiri Mahasaya said that 40 years later this easy path of sadhana, beneficent to all mankind, will spread and be instructed worldwide. And perhaps this is why He held in His own lap a child (Yogananda Paramhansaji)* of His dear disciple couple, blessed him, empowered him and prophesied, "This child will be an engine."** After receiving direction and guidance from the founder of Sadhu Sabha and Adi Satsanga Sabha, the Highest Acharya Swami Sriyukteswar Giri Maharaj, whose primary disciple—the founder of Yogoda Satsanga and the Sri Sri Shyamacharan Mission—Paramhansa Srimat Swami Yogananda Giri Maharaj's resounding message, giving initiation to thousands of men and women in the east and west, providing them with an opportunity to experience Soul, establishing ashrams and spiritual centers in many places and other world-conquering accomplishments surely attest to the infallible and peremptory blessings of Sri Sri Shyama Charan Lahiri Mahasaya.***

*The parentheses and the text within is as the original.
**Yogiraj used the English word "engine" in the prophesy.
***The last sentence has unusual structure but was maintained to represent the original.

CHAPTER SIX

DISAPPEARANCE

The current of propagation flowed along in its prescribed course—underground, steady and peaceful. The highest amongst men, the Yogavatar's reason for having a body was seeming to come to an end. We have already learned about Mahamuni Babaji's previous indication. Yogiraj's disciple Sriyukta Kalikumar Roy Mahasaya said that he and many other disciples received word in the month of Ashar that the Lord will leave His body when the month of Ashwin arrives. It is heard that Lahiri Mahasaya supposedly let His life-partner [His wife] know about His departure from His body six months before the event and told her not to grieve about it. The excuse for the event to happen appeared—a diseased boil on the back of that beautiful body. Supposedly, the Lord forbade surgery on the growth. But, surely enough, in time, whether it was because of someone's ignorance or for some other reason, surgery was performed. He no longer interfered. I had heard that He said that He wanted His samadhistha body [the condition of the body after one dies in Mahasamadhi] to be buried and not cremated. But when the time came, no one remembered those words either. Sriyukta Abhaya Charan once wrote about Yogiraj's wishes for [Maha] samadhi: "In one place in His diary*, it is written, 'Today I want to dissolve my consciousness in the Unstruck Resonance and remain from dusk today until dusk tomorrow. If I die, don't discard Me. Either bury Me right here or keep Me in this seated position. I will reawaken.'"

*The word "diary" is from the original.

On the 26th of September, 1895—Mahashtami of the Bengali year of 1301, announcing His desire to leave the body to those present in the land of Knowledge—Kashidham, the Lord turned to the North and sat erect, and by Yogic Power, exactly at the time of sacrifice at dusk—mahasandhi [great dusk], He was absorbed in Mahasamadhi. A desperate wailing went up among the devotees. Life became heavy with His departure. On the banks of the Bhagirathi River at the Manikarnika Ghat, the Yogeshwar's priceless and beautiful human body—the form of the One who captivated his devotees—burned into ashes and merged into the five elements. Some disciples were able to be present; some were preparing to come from far away. It is heard, that exactly at the time of His leaving the body, the Holy Form of the Lord appeared in the sight of His devotees in three different places at the same time. When Swami Pranabanandaji Maharaj was desperately trying to make preparations to come from a distant land to have darshan of Sriguru, everything had already finished on this side. Suddenly, Swamiji was taken aback by the appearance of His Guru in front of Him. He heard from the mouth of Sriguru's Form, "Why the rush? The physical body has been renounced." Consoling His deeply grieving devotee, the Lord said, "Why are you grieving? I'm always here."

Blissful memories of His physical existence come up in that room, on that bed, from seeing that beautiful oil painting of His form there. The transitory body disappeared but He remained in the hearts of the Kriyavan sadhaka devotees. Forever present. Even today, fortunate sadhakas are blessed by visions of His eternally pure, love-filled, Divine Form.

APPENDIX A

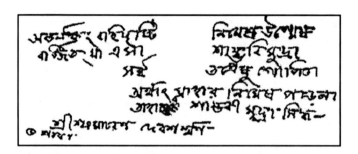

Handwriting of Yogiraj explaining Shambavi Mudra—from a letter of a disciple

APPENDIX B

THE LORD'S FIVE DIRECTIVES

(As told by Sadhusabhapati Swami Sriyukteswar Giri Maharaj)

1) Know yourself as very small—meaning service, worship and feeling of subservience (I am subservient yet I have kinship to all)

2) Always do satsanga—meaning the company of holy people or studying holy books

3) From time to time gather together and discuss

4) Do not disrespect any name of the Divine

5) Once a year leave the worldly duties and stay apart—1 month, or 1 fortnight, or 1 week or at least 3 days

APPENDIX C

KRIYA

The spiritual science bestowed by Yogiraj is usually known simply as "Kriya" and the practitioners are known as "Kriyavans". The mystery of Kriyayoga sadhana is of course imparted orally by the Guru and the many different and wondrous yogic levels of realization are dependent upon the sincere practitioners' depth of absorption in sadhana. We will only look at its aspects in an indirect way. This Kriya can be called "Kevali" inner pranayam, as mentioned in the scriptures. This technique does not use the difficult breath-holding methods of the usual types of pranayam., and as such, one does not have to fall into the dangers caused by those practices. This method uses a special technique by which the scattered currents of the nervous system are gathered, decay is prevented and the need of breath is dispensed; as in the gap of inhalation and exhalation, the restless breath within becomes still. The externally focused senses and mind turn inward; the agitated prana becomes more and more restful, resulting in the ayam of prana, meaning that from the true expansion of prana comes the state of pratyahara; the Light of the Soul in stillness is revealed and the path of the Great Ones is known. Along with pratyahara comes effulgence within, and the unstruck Voice of God is heard. Immersing in the dharana of Pranavashabda [Divine Sound], the yogi becomes absorbed in dhyana and then becomes samadhistha [in the Oneness]. The body, senses, mind, intellect and the dirt and restlessness of consciousness is gone, meaning that the fluctuations of consciousness cease and in the Light of Pure Awakened Awareness the Supreme Soul is known.

As new discoveries by science shed light on hidden truths of the physical world and show new and better ways, so does this Kriya yoga light the way in the world of spirituality, helping many sadhakas traverse the ages in immense speed via its scientifically founded process. The truth seekers and sadhakas of all types and all walks cannot have any objection to this type of disciplined sadhana. All types of Arya books speak about similar discipline. We have heard from a secret, advanced and lofty sadhaka, that he had see the great saint Srimat Vijaykrishna Goswami Prabhu himself practice this Kriya yoga sadhana in a mountain near Gaya. His yogi-gurudev is on the level of a brother to Babaji Maharaj in the yoga kingdom. The topsy-turvy conditions and our associations make these predilections by the universally beneficent sages seem impossible to us. That's why it is called prophetic vision.

Maharishi Patanjali's yogashastra [Yoga Sutras] is a great gift to the world. The compassionate Yogavatar made this shastra come alive. By His commentaries from a spiritual view on the yogashastra Gita [Bhagavad Gita] and many other books of philosophy, He was actually speaking about the different levels of experience through Kriyayoga sadhana. He followed those edicts according to the practices and restrictions of the present day, meaning yama and niyama. Instead of physically difficult postures for sadhana, He prescribed a steady and comfortable seating position. To bring about excellence in mind and body He instructed us with the Mudra, and to make human beings' Soul Work easier, instead of the "skillful"* way, He showed us the "easy" Kriya pranayam. He also revealed to us the mantra to liberate the mind in the same natural manner.

*"Yogahkarmasu kaushalam" [- from Patanjali's Yoga Sutras, referring to skillful means of yoga work. tThe bracketed part of this note is the translator's. The asterisk and reference is from the original.]

"Bhumaiva sukham nalpe sukhamasti"—When the entrapped soul's restlessness and dullness leave, a deep, peaceful state arrives. The dominant presence of that ppeace in the melody of the Infinite Unstruck Sound dissolves the borders that create smallness. The chains are freed. That is when the insignificant receives the touch of the Omnipresent, the experience of Brahma and the love of Vishnu. That is when spiritual surrender happens. In that surrender, Supreme Peace pervades the divine life in blissful yogic union. Within the human being is the endless current of bliss. Through the "easy" sadhana, the sincere sadhaka dedicates body, mind and soul and tastes the nectar of that bliss himself. This is completely and truly logical.

When one applies the strength of will and one-pointed love within and his gaze becomes still, then it becomes possible to fulfill all desires. Whatever we want to know or we want to understand; whatever desire we may have, all restlessness must be ended and we must take care to still the mind in order to attain Knowledge of the Soul. * Sadhakas should remember that the Lord instructed over and over to remain in the "Kriya paravastha" (after effect poise). [Translator's note: the parenthetical and the text within it in English is in the original.] He said, "Doing Kriya is Karma yoga. Remaining in Kriya paravastha is Jnana (Gyana) yoga. There is no resting in the Supreme Being if Kriya is not done first. The mind will become still on its own by remaining in the Kriya paravastha. When the mind becomes still, one can vanquish the most powerfully destructive desires." If one remains fixed in the state that comes after the proper practice of Kriya pranayam, the states of pratyahara, dharana, dhyan etc.—if one continues to be especially affixed in mind state after state, then, through Kriya, the true yoga, meaning samadhi, is attained.

* Te sarvagang sarvatah prapyadhara yuktatmanah sarvamebabishanti [reference note from the original]

Although He spoke about subjects relating to the Paramatman, the Lord did not call the world false nor did He tell us to close our eyes. It is inn the created world where He showed the path to salvation and in a way that related individually to everyone's particular being. Through this Kriya, it is possible to bring about strength and steadiness of the nervous system, mind and intellect, as well as peace in the daily work and existence in society. And that development further frees the being from the body and mind and it begins to be attracted in Soul. To attain the experience of Soul-Power, this is a properly controlled, beautiful, easy and complete way. This is proven by many living sadhakas in what they have attained through one-pointed sadhana. From the time I was a child, I received the affection and loving presence of a man who was the ideal householder—noble in society, scholarly, quiet, a sadhaka—a man who is like a father to me: the late Bhagabati Charan Ghosh Mahasaya. From his own experience, he always said this one thing, "You've received a priceless thing. Keep doing it. By this—physical, mental—everything will be better." Self Awareness is definitely attainable.

Uddharedatmanam natmanamabsadayet

Yogacharya Shastri Mahasaya

A Short Biographical Sketch of

Hansaswami Kebalanandaji Maharaj

by Swami Satyananda Giri

English Translation by Yoga Niketan

This translated book maintains that an almost literal translation of the Bengali words of the original author best serves both seekers and Kriyavans. No attempt has been made for the translations to be poetic or interpretive for the above-mentioned reason. If the reader notices irregular English grammar (including non-traditional sentence structure, punctuation, etc.), please understand that it is intentional. The translator has tried as best as he could to keep the work as close to the Bengali phrasing in the original without it being unreadable or incomprehensible.

Pranam, The Translator: Yoga Niketan

Hangsaswami Kebalanandaji Maharaj

"Yogacharya Shastri Mahasaya"

DEDICATION

tadviddhi pranipatena pariprashnena sevaya
upadekshyanti te jnanam jnaninastattvadarshinah

After the publication of Yogavatar Lord Sri Sri Shyamacharan Lahiri Mahasaya's short biography, certain friends requested the writing of some material through which we could come to know the Yogavatar's disciple, Yogacharya Shastri Mahasaya. Even though in later years he was from time to time addressed by the name of Swami Kebalanandaji Maharaj, a name given to him by the community of devotees, we knew and addressed him, as well as had his company as our own, by the name of Shastri Mahasaya. One obtains much beneficence in life by spending even a little time of reverent service in the company of realized sadhakas. We were fortunate to have had the opportunity to have received his company for a lengthy twenty-two years. But today, in the absence of his physical body, the more we remember his sadhana, the direction and order of his life, his instructions and guidance on the path of Knowledge, the more it seems that we were not able to act in quite the proper way while in his company. The reverence of heart with which one is supposed to present oneself when approaching an acharya [sage/scholar], the respect with which one should come as an inquirer—it is doubtful whether we—especially me—had that within us. So now, there is tremendous sorrow because of my disrespect, even though I had found a treasure trove. There is also regret. I have sinned by my irreverence to a pure current of the guru-parampara lineage. What the consequences of such sin is, I do not know. In any case, there is nothing to be gained by excessive repentance now. Whatever little I understood, if even with that little knowledge I can receive the company of his blessings from beyond the body, then I believe that I can still be bettered. The memories of the past appear: with a smiling face at examination time, he gave us courage, and by thoroughly demonstrating certain methods, he gave us the strength to be successful at making the impossible possible. When I was running around in the working world, even then this ego-less man of spare words affectionately drew my attention towards the essential purpose of life—Self-Knowledge. Today, while experiencing the blows and counter-blows of the torrent of work, when the Supreme Lord gives me the opportunity to feel His Mercy, turning me towards Him—engaging my mind to move to that Simple Bliss—then the holy memories of this acharya mahasaya awaken and his blessings are truly manifested. So while blaming my fate, I still feel that I am very fortunate to have had his holy touch.

I do not have the capacity to write biographies. And how many have either the ability to understand or the good fortune to be aware of the flow of life of realized beings? I do not know all of the exact dates for the course of events in Shastri Mahasaya's known life. It is doubtful whether I was able to even partially understand the significance or value of his life; still, I sit now to write. It is as if with inevitably incomplete threads I am trying to say a couple of words about him. Even if I cannot make it blossom in writing, that I might be able to have his holy company through words and that I might be able to present a little of the essence of the beneficence-filled portrait of his sadhaka-life to the society of everyday people—that these thoughts are giving me enthusiasm, this is also true. I am guilty of the incompleteness in the drawing of the portrait, but that I will receive forgiveness for this transgression from the appropriate place—I have this! belief as well.

The one—even before the emergence of the appropriate capacity for spiritual understanding—with whose affectionate friend-guru relationship I progressively received more and more spiritual illumination and thereafter had the opportunity to have the darshan and company of this great acharya—that this writer, who is devoted to him, is eternally indebted to him—that is needless to say. All of the devotees who gave their encouragement to write these few pages and those who helped in numerous ways towards the publishing of the book even in these terrible days—I express my deep gratitude to all of them. The blessings of realized beings are the blessings of the Lord manifested. Let it be that we all are able to receive those pure blessings.

Raspurnima, 1349 [Bengali calendar]

Swami Satyananda Giri

Yogoda Brahmacharya Vidyalaya
Ranchi

ABOUT THE THIRD [BENGALI] PRINTING

The third [Bengali] printing of the venerable Shastri Mahasaya's (Hansaswami Kebalananda Maharaj's) short biographical sketch is hereby published. The tendency to exaggerate the telling of life-stories of realized sadhakas—via excessive embellishment—is often seen, but in this case, that path has not been taken. Even so, feeling that it is timely, I mention part of a quotation read at the latest gathering in memoriam from a book written by the former student of Ranchi Vidyalaya and recent resident of the Sri Sri Bholananda Sannyas Ashram in Hardwar, Srimat Swami Sevananda Giri: "At that time, Shastri Mahasaya used to teach us Sanskrit in Ranchi. One day, we went to his cottage and saw that he was sitting in yogasana in the air above his meditation-seat and engaged in Kriya...we were stupe-fied...Infirm at old age, as he silently endured his physical suffering, I was at his bedside. Shastri Mahasaya sat up by himself and assumed asana; focusing his sight between the eyebrows, he gave up his body while doing pranayam." Seeing this happening, Swami Sevananda felt, "This ideal being is in paravastha..."

omityekaksharam brahma vyaharan mamanusmaran
yah prayati tyajan deham sa yati paramamgatim

In remembrance of the glory of India, may the spiritual traveler-sad-hakas' journey to the ideal be inspired by this humble, great saint's illuminated life. In benediction—OM.

Swami Satyananda Giri

CHAPTER 1

During the second half of the thirteenth century of the Bengali calendar, when India, particularly Bengal, was entranced by foreign ways of education and culture—even though certain wise beings would point towards the splendor of the glorious past of the sagacious land of India with her philosophies, ancient history etc.—when the inhabitants of the country at that time belonging to the "sophisticated high-society" condescendingly viewed the study of Sanskrit as a matter of charity, when ordinary brahmin scholars gained the infamy of being "frogs in wells" ["kupamanduk"—metaphor for being ultra-orthodox, or extremely closed-minded], at that time within such aggrieved society, among the certain families, even though somewhat guilty of being "frogs in wells," that were holding on to the pure, essential seed of the stream of Indian culture and conducting their lives according to such in the villages of Bengal—in that type of devoted householder family—in the village of Kharsangha in the district of Khulna, Ashutosh was born on the lunar day of Holy Sripanchami circa 1270 [Bengali calendar]. In that area of the Khulna district, there was also a reputation for spiritual atmosphere, along with Indian ways of life and culture. By the surrounding conditions and mode of life, the belief arises in our minds that the appearance and residence of the community of sadhakas touched that land with sacredness for many years.

The only child of his parents, Ashutosh was lovingly reared up, and at the appropriate time, following scriptural edicts, he received the ceremonial initiation for writing and reading and began his education at the local primary school. His father, the scholar Sriyukta Govindachandra Chattopadhyay was a highly erudite gentleman ["vidyaratna"—treasure of knowledge]. With the goal of raising his son as a strict brahmin, after the completion of primary-level learning, not being tempted by English education, he enrolled his son in a Sanskrit grammar school. In studies, sports, physical labor, etc., Ashutosh used to claim the highest position. He had a special keenness for physical culture and exercise during student-life; it is for this reason that his body was always strong and able.

Ashutosh became fatherless at a young age. The innocent-souled child, torn from paternal affection, continued his growth and maturation in the refuge of his mother's heart. An unshakable reverence and devotion towards his mother along with maternal blessings were treasures of his life. After finishing his learning in the village, for the sake of higher education, by his own effort he came to Calcutta and enrolled in the Sanskrit College. Thirsty for knowledge, the highly intelligent Ashutosh was in a short time able to draw the attention of his professor, the late great Ishvarchandra Vidyasagar Mahasaya. Through his proficient abilities, as he gradually excelled with eminence in the examinations of poetry and logic, he received a precious shawl from Vidyasagar Mahasaya as a present. The ocean-of-compassion-professor's fitting student Ashutosh, broken-hearted towards the suffering of others and disinterested in luxury, later found contentment by giving the shawl away to some friend who was stricken with cold and in need.

The intense longing for higher learning made Ashutosh restless. The possessor of the highest qualities, Vidyasagar Mahasaya, was pleased at this enthusiasm displayed by his dear student and arranged for his continuing study in Benares. Ashutosh, taking the blessings of the acharya on his head, arrived in Benares—the land of wisdom—and with inexhaustible enthusiasm, went on to take in more knowledge. In the highest Sanskrit university in Benares, he took the "Acharya" examination and gained the title of "Sahityacharya" [acharya—or scholarly authority—of literature [sahitya]], and later, he was decorated with the title of "Vedantasaraswati" [esteemed scholar of Vedanta] by the community of scholars there. At that time, as he became aware of the news that there existed a particularly good environment for Eastern education—perhaps the best environment—in Punjab, his thirst for knowledge grew even more intense. He left, and arrived in Lahore [now in Pakistan], the capital of Punjab. There, he excelled with exceptional eminence in the "Prajna," "Visharad," and "Shastri" examinations—divisions of "Prachya Vidya" [Eastern Studies]. We have heard that there had been no Bengali before him to have been present for this "Shastri" examination. During the time of stay in Punjab, to become acquainted with the thinking of the Western scholars who were present there who had an affinity for Eastern knowledge and wisdom, he began to study English. But instead of staying there for a very long period of time, he again returned to Benares. The intense longing for gaining knowledge continued to gradually grow. Because of this, he became engaged in learning many subjects via many ways in the land of Benares, spending his time in the study of astrology, ayurveda, philosophy, Puranas etc. He was also able to become proficient in Pali—a unique, olden language of India, and later, he aided the community of scholars by deciphering text from ancient books written in Pali. In this way, it was as if he always intently remained immersed in the discipline of study, maintaining the attitude of a learning student with a reverent heart.

CHAPTER 2

Spending time in the company of sadhus and holy beings in Benares, the land of knowledge, Sriyukta Ashutosh Shastri Mahasaya's dormant spiritual feelings began to awaken. Besides academic knowledge and the development of intellectual culture, he grew anxious for the attainment of True Knowledge within. He became very attentive to the practices of chanting, austerities, worship and ritual work, and being in the environment of sadhus and great saints, made sincere efforts to know about the important mysteries of sadhana. He felt himself to be fortunate for having received the presence and blessings of Sri Ramakrishna Paramhansadeva at an early age. He would try to quench his thirst for inner Knowledge by being in the company of the great saints of Benares such as Trailanga Swami, Bhaskarananda Swamiji and such others. Learning the methods of hatha yoga from sadhaka-practitioners of hatha yoga, he practiced all such techniques with reverent discipline and strictness. He was also proficiently able to proceed deeply into and realize the truths of the sadhana-mysteries of the pure tantric practices of the Kaulmarga. Even though he continued to progress and gain numerous types of divine experiences on the spiritual path in this way, he was not able to completely fulfill his longing. But the directive of the Lord came to fruition very soon. Through his wanderings about, Shastri Mahasaya eventually found himself in the presence of Kashibaba Yogavatar the Lord Sri Sri Shyamacharan Lahiri Mahasaya. The purpose for the strife and struggle of the road to finding Guru was fulfilled; the intense longing was quelled; Shastri Mahasaya had found his Sadguru. By the touch of sacredness, he understood that this was his God-directed place of refuge. At an auspicious time, Ashutosh was initiated. His doubts uprooted and removed, the disciple surrendered himself at Sriguru's feet. Seeking to realize Self-Knowledge, he found this saint-revealed Kriya Yoga sadhana to be in beautiful harmony with all sadhana practices. On one side he studied Vedanta Darshan at the feet of the renowned sage Bhaskarananda Swamiji, and on another side he received the sacred touch of spiritual essence from the presence of Sriguru. With these two currents, nourishing one and the other, it was if the one-pointed and aroused Shakti filled Ashutosh with renewed energy and pushed him forward in the Kingdom of Light. We have heard that at this time he would remain immersed in the performance of intense sadhana with a heart of complete non-attachment. With deep and reverent discipline, this practice of sadhana and the Grace of Guru bestowed upon him the immaculate ambrosia of the state of samadhi, and his life was filled with spiritual bliss. In this way, he remained in the company and received the blessings of Sriguru in Benares for ten years. The Lord Sri Sri Lahiri Mahasaya loved him dearly and would express His affection by addressing Shastri Mahasaya as "Pandit Mahasaya" [scholarly sir] and sometimes as "Rishi" [sage]. Shastri Mahasaya had immovable reverence and faith in Guru. He often said that the foundation of the kingdom of sadhana was "gurubhakti" [devotion to Guru]. One day, in a discussion about the acharya for the ages, Swami Vivekananda, he said, "I did not have the chance to know how far advanced Swamiji was in his spiritual life, but the incredible devotion to Guru I have seen presently is extremely rare. I think that perhaps it is through the power of this devotion he realized Shakti and thus was able to occupy the highest place in the world."

Having become aware of Yogiraj the Lord Lahiri Mahasaya from Shastri Mahasaya, the great saint Bhaskarananda Swamiji met Him and grew keen to know about the matters of Kriya Yoga. We have heard from the venerable Shastri Mahasaya that when, according to the dogma to which he previously adhered, Bhaskarananda Swamiji Maharaj announced the statement that he could not go to the home of a householder, and seeking to gain knowledge of Kriya Yoga sadhana invited Lahiri Mahasaya to his own ashram, it seems that then the Lord had cryptically said, "When there is thirst, does the well go to the thirsty or does the thirsty go to the well?" In any case, the Lord used to genuinely respect the sagaciousness and venerability of sadhus and saints. One day sometime later, in the presence of Shastri Mahasaya himself, these two great beings met and the knowledgeable, renown, revered by all, esteemed and highest among scholars Swamiji Maharaj seemed to become completely humbled by realizing the infinity of Wisdom and Knowledge, and received Kriya Yoga sadhana from this Rajarshi Janaka-like Yogiraj Lahiri Mahasaya. Age after age, the world has witnessed this manner of humility, thirst for true knowledge, modesty, reverence and the luminous vision of genuine love; it has read the story of Premavatar Srimanmahaprabhu and his begging for love, heard the legend of Maheshvar Shiva and Bhagavan Sri Ramachandra embracing and offering their utmost reverence to each other, and still our awareness does not awaken. Our useless vanity from the little knowledge we have does not go away. We just remain filled with arrogance and pride. And thus wisdom and devotion also move far away from us. The behavior of sincere, wise, loving saints is founded upon Truth, and that truly bestows the flowing Bliss of the Divine. But have we been able to renounce respect and disrespect, become inquirers filled with thirst, and thus be fit to receive the ambrosia of that Bliss?

The divine experiences from sadhana increased the flame of renunciation within Shastri Mahasaya. The desire to become a householder had left and was far from his mind. His mother, seeing her only son in this condition, became restless and began to make concerted efforts to make her son a man of domestic life. At this time, although the scholar Ashutosh—obsessed with sadhana—had had opportunities to serve as a teacher in certain educational institutions, he did not join them. On this matter, the view of his Supreme Benefactor, the Divine Visionary Sri Gurudeva was also in agreement with his feelings.

Sri Sri Thakur [Sri Sri Shyamacharan Lahiri Mahasaya], determining the appropriate time, eventually advised him to become a householder. His mother's wish was fulfilled. At a late age, Shastri Mahasaya was married. But it was never possible for him to act quite as a householder in domestic life. Enraptured by spiritual inspiration, it seemed that conducting domestic living in a non-attached, non-desirous, easy and simple manner, as well as with a vow of poverty, was the special way of his life. In financial stress, facing difficulties in carrying out requested tasks, the death of a child, and in numerous types of unfortunate occurrences, not for a single day was he seen to have been depressed or to have turned away from his duties. Observing his behavior, it seemed as if he had given all responsibility of householder life to the Lord and was at complete peace. The unthinkable ways we saw by which challenges such as the wedding arrangements for his daughter and other needs of domestic life were resolved—by such events our belief of that [that he had relinquished all to the Lord] seemed to be greatly and strongly confirmed. Eminent, wealthy and noble persons such as Maharaja Manindrachandra Nandi honoring their invitations and being present on the wedding day of the daughter of this poor brahmin scholar is certainly a bit surprising in the eyes of society.

In any case, having taken up householder-life, he began work in a Sanskrit grammar school in order to earn money. For him, the mantra of domestic living was to lead life unostentatiously. As such, he seemed to be reticent even in the job of a teacher in an institution. For a time, he joined the scriptural studies group of the renowned Pandit Jivananda Vidyasagar Mahasaya in Calcutta, and helped significantly in the writing of many higher level books. He had served the nation by deciphering text from rare books written in the Pali language. He had also prepared manuscripts of several books himself. Established scholars of Bengal respected him. They would show Shastri Mahasaya books and writings that they had composed and sometimes would correct errors, after which they published such works.

Even though we spent a span of twelve years in his company, we did not know that he was this great a scholar and the possessor of this many titles. We came to know about his unfathomable erudition suddenly one day from Mahamahopadhyay Pandit Sriyukta Bidhushekhar Shastri Mahasaya of Shantiniketan. One day, upon seeing a portrait of Shastri Mahasaya [in this case, Kebalanandaji], Prabhupada Sriyukta Atulkrishna Goswami Mahasaya said, "Oh! This is Ashutosh's picture! Ashutosh was our companion-student. He is the most elevated of persons in every way." Even though he kept himself hidden, the late Lion amongst Men and Patron Ashutosh Mukhopadhyay Mahasaya requested him to take the job of a high level professor after coming to know about his talents; but he did not accept that [job]. At one time, Shastri Mahasaya was engaged in the work as a Sanskrit professor in a certain college. For some unavoidable reason, he had to be absent from work for a few days. Arrangements were made for a temporary professor to take his place at that time. When Shastri Mahasaya returned after his leave and saw that another professor was at work in that position, and that there was a need for that person to do that work as well, the very caring Shastri Mahasaya, determining that professor's necessity to be greater, left that position. Yet he did not worry about how he was going to manage the days.

Even at the time of domestic need at such a mature age, he did not agree to take the job of professorship in Baharampur College at the request of the late Maharaja Manindrachandra Nandi Bahadur. How many persons of such powerful conviction to ideals and discipline are seen?

He had become a householder; therefore, he had to understand and manage the pressures and needs of domestic life. For that reason, he took up the work of tutoring in private homes and later accepted a job as a teacher in the Metropolitan Bahubazar Branch School. The special purpose for working in this school was to build up this insignificant school into a high level educational institution which would be imbued with an atmosphere of Truth. Because earning a living was accompanied by the feeling within him to do this service, he felt some-what at peace about it. Improvement of the school was seen during his association with it. At this time, he lived with his entire family at a rented house in the Amherst Street area of Calcutta. Later, he moved to the Kasbar area of Baliganj.

He offered himself for many types of beneficent cultural works of soci-ety, and it was behind the eyes of the people of the world that he engaged himself in all of these things. This was the exceptional quality of his character. Shastri Mahasaya was a particularly enthusiastic sup-porter among those leaders who wanted to prove and establish the Kshatriya-ness of Kayasthas [a general type of non-brahmin caste], as well as confirm the right for them to perform the "upanayan" [sacred thread] ceremony. The wish to have [greater] education of scriptural wisdom and the elevation of society was at the root of this effort of his. Shastri Mahasaya believed in the edicts of "varnashram" [societal cate-gories] and was a reverently disciplined brahmin. He had respect for lineage and the divisions of "varnas" by quality of work. We have also observed him to reason that one can excel and improve to the behavior of a higher varna from another varna through sadhana. He believed that Kriyavan sadhakas from any varna could ascend the highest steps of spirituality and attain the highest state. He perceived Kriyavans as members of the same family, and even if a person who was a Kriyavan was from another varna of society, he did not hesitate to partake in meals with that person. Citing the reasoning of the scriptures, he made us understand that through the cultivation of a special scriptural mantra, and leading a disciplined life in accordance with the essence of that mantra, the possibilities of corruption by associating with and eating with people of different varnas—as dictated by prevalent dogma—could not remain. Although he had unshakable reverence for the "Sanatan Hindu" religion, we have seen that his heart was magnanimous and that he was a seeker of Truth. As the late great Vidyasagar Mahasaya taught us to be liberated from the snake-like grasp of societal dogma, as well as showing us the truth of the ancient sages and teaching us how to be open-minded, all while staying true to scriptural wisdom, the student of Vidyasagar, our Shastri Mahasaya, was inspired by the magnanimity of his teacher, and was also able to have his own hand in the customs and injunctions of societal life. But he became disappointed if he saw norms being destroyed with the excuse of [accusations of] dogmatism or because of the delusion of modernism. If there was no appropriate philosophical reasoning, he did not like deviations from the prevalent set of societal injunctions. In the flood of people following blindly like sheep as we find today, the venerable Shastri Mahasaya's devoted discipline, as well as his open-heartedness, is drawing people's reverent attention towards the sadhana and culture of India. What doubt is there that the current of this essence—in the middle of the whirlpool of the present day—is for our beneficence?

CHAPTER 3

The Christian year 1907. Srimat Yogananda Paramhansaji was a student at that time. During that period, his madness for Truth brought about an intense feeling of renunciation within him; he could not keep himself bound up with home-life. He had already received initiation into Kriya Yoga sadhana from his father who was a disciple of Yogiraj [Sri Sri Shyamacharan Lahiri Mahasaya]. Once he [Yoganandaji] even left his home and ended up in Hardwar. His elder brother was somehow able to catch him and bring "the boy from home back home" with considerable effort. At that time, he had a private tutor in the house. He [the tutor], along with academic learning, used to give his student spiritual advice and encouraged him in many ways. Everyone in the household, especially the elders, thought that if they wanted to keep the young one at home, it was not safe to have the influence of this spiritual-advisor tutor mahasaya around. So, Yoganandaji no longer was availed the opportunity to have the company of that tutor mahasaya. But who can destroy what the Lord has destined? The great ones say that for the devotee, God comes to his/her door. After a few days, the guardians searched out and engaged Shastri Mahasaya himself to take the role of private tutor in the house. Having found a new pandit [scholar] mahasaya, when the curious Yoganandaji came to know more about him—that the man was erudite in all scriptures and was a yogi as well—he felt himself to be fortunate. Within a short time, he realized that the pandit mahasaya was an advanced disciple of Sri Sri Lahiri Mahasaya. His longing for sadhana intensified even more because of this, and drawn to the spiritual nature of the pandit mahasaya, he came to find out about many hidden mysteries of Kriya Yoga sadhana at his [Shastri Mahasaya's] feet, and began to attain more and new illuminations on the path of spiritual ascension. During the lessons, spirituality was the principal topic of discussion for Yoganandaji. He became eager to study the Gita scripture from Shastri Mahasaya. The ideal teacher had found the model student and was very pleased. Fearing that the fact of neglecting academic studies and favoring scriptural discussions could be detrimental if noticed, permission for the extensive recitation and study of the Gita was obtained from the guardians. This writer, through having had Yoganandaji's companionship and affection, had already received Spiritual Light previously and had followed him; thus, for [the writer] too did this fortune of having Shastri Mahasaya's sacred company manifest at this time.

Having found a divine being while sitting at home, the young Yoganandaji, ecstatically in Bliss, did not very much feel the problematic need to leave home for a while. Gradually, during his intermediate years, many educated youth from the University as well as other inquiring men and women came and received initiation from Shastri Mahasaya. At that time, a wave of Bliss was seen to flow through the community of all these Kriyavans. It seemed that there was a deep belief in the minds of everyone: "We have been initiated with the holy thread [symbolic] at the feet of an ideal acharya, so what fear is there in this worldly life?" All of the Kriyavans who had come together at that time under the leadership of Yoganandaji—in them there was truly a divine feeling that one could observe. Everyone was inspired by the ideal of spiritual realization. The central power in all this seemed to be the blessings of Shastri Mahasaya. His teaching was simple and easy, but that itself transfused power in everyone. Several times, we saw that when there was an inability to determine dutifulness in the working field, he would clarify such issues extraordinarily through one or two very ordinary comments. From time to time, we thought that perhaps this was exemplary of the presence of his supernatural powers. Some people disciplinarily learned from him the different types of sadhanas regarding mantra-power as well as practices of hatha yoga. The atmosphere of sweetness and quietude present in his character brought reverence and belief in the hearts of unbelievers. Approaching to test him suspicious-mindedly and irreverently, the scenario has been seen where such people would become filled with excitement, their hearts enraptured, and feel blessed to take refuge at his feet. Even from a certain highly educated luminary of the University—a proud youth who had vowed that he would not lower his head to any person connected with religion or spirituality—we heard after he bowed at the feet of this egoless acharya, "Being in the presence of this person—the head bows by itself."

CHAPTER 4

In the month of March in the Christian year of 1917, at the time of the transiting of the holy great equinox,* through the patronage of the sage-like king, the lord of Kashimbazar, Manindrachandra Nandi Bahadur, Swami Yoganandaji established the Brahmacharya Vidyalaya. He became especially eager to have Shastri Mahasaya teach at this ideal ashram-school. Although at Yoganandaji's request he would be a director at the school, thinking upon the fact that he would have to join up in a new place of work [relocate], Shastri Mahasaya did not accept the proposal at first. But later, because of his student's overwhelming zeal, as well as feeling the need for that type of an ashram-school, he joined the school only a few days after its founding. The residents of the ashram were elated to have the fortune of having him as the principal dharmacharya. Because of his blessed arrival, the school assumed the form of the brahmacharya ashrams of the rishis [sages]. It seemed that he surrendered the weight of looking after his family to the Hands of the Lord, and it was from this time onward that he began to lead his life as a "banaprasthi"** sannyasi. At the side of the blessed is God—his disciples became the caretakers of his domestic life. When the school was in its infancy [beginning conditions], his presence and advice were immensely beneficial when encountering troubles and problems. He began to bring about an atmosphere of pious conduct throughout the newly founded school. His meditation and austerities continuously brought new life in this institution in the midst of the many ups and downs. The founder-acharya Yoganandaji was also filled with ardor at this beautiful opportunity, and with help of colleagues, he endeavored to actualize many new plans. Although there was an entrance examination set up for the school, that the students would carry themselves with the virtuous conduct of brahmacharis and study a great deal of Sanskrit—this was his particular intention. While maintaining modern educational methods, his sole desire was for the ashram to be filled with an atmosphere of sacredness through the practicing of Vedic recitation-song, hymns glorifying the Lord, oblations, worship, reverent approach to acharyas etc. He used to give children initiation into mantra sadhana, and if appropriate, into Kriya Yoga sadhana. Among the teachers, some of them taught scriptures such as the Upanishads in his presence. With these kinds of sensibilities and feelings, through Yogananda Swamiji's spiritually-intoxicated madness and Acharya Shastri Mahasaya's intense sadhana, the school had become a place of tapasya [profound virtuous and spiritual practice].

*[Translator's note: This asterisked note is in the original Bengali. The footnote accompanying this asterisk is translated as follows: "Yoganandaji had decided upon this auspicious day for the founding of the school through the instructions of his Gurudeva, Sadhusabhapati Srimat Swami Sriyukteshvar Giri Maharaj."]

**[Translator's note: "Banaprasthi" is a stage of life prescribed in the Vedas, at which time a person, having fulfilled his worldly duties, goes on to lead a simple life of sadhana.]

As the work of the school continued to grow, Shastri Mahasaya took a personal leave of absence from the tutorial work of the school. The lord of Kashimbazar, Maharaja Bahadur bore his daily expenditures. When the school was properly founded in an expansive garden-estate in Ranchi, he then went on to live in the Brahmacharya Vidyalaya's original place of founding, in the tranquil environment by the Damodar river. It seemed that the quiet sadhaka Yogacharya Shastri Mahasaya had built himself an ashram for yoga sadhana in the miraculously beautiful nature by the shores of the river Damodar, in a land silent and free of commotion, hidden from the eyes of the people of the world. His view was that if the Brahmacharya Ashram was established in that place of solitude, it would have been easier to impart the ideal type of education at the school. Because of many obstructive occurrences, that did not happen. The Brahmacharya Vidyalaya continued on its path of growth in Ranchi's lovely and mountainous land. From time to time, Shastri Mahasaya graced us by visiting the ashram in Ranchi.

Some time before, a certain head of a temple in Benares bestowed upon Shastri Mahasaya the very sagacious name of "Hansaswami Kebalananda." When he began to lead his life like a sannyasi in this way, then his devotees, after receiving his permission to do so, started to introduce him as "Swami Kebalanandaji." In the Christian year 1924, several of his devotees founded a spiritual institution named "Satsangha" at Raja Dinendra Street in the Gadpar area of Calcutta. Hansaswami Kebalanandaji Maharaj, in the role of acharya, directed the work of that institution. Persons of distinction as well as highly educated professors were seen to come and spend time with him for the purpose of listening to his the scriptural recitation and commentary. Each of the Sunday spiritual meetings would become illuminated by his presence. Shastri Mahasaya himself carried out the performances of everyday worship, japa, oblations, yajna and other such rites with reverence, and advised everyone—according to one's own nature—to be respectful toward such things. Although the performance of these rituals aroused feelings of devotion—that all of these acts were symbolic of inner acts, and that it was within where the true essence of all these acts were nourished, which further elevated the sadhaka on the path of sadhana—this he would express and explain very clearly. Among these activities, he gave a tremendous amount of attention to elucidate on the subjects of dhyana, dharana etc. as they related to Kriya Yoga sadhana.

A while after this period of living like a renunciate, he [again] became a resident of Benares. Benares was the land of his Guru and his place of learning. This ancient pilgrimage site that was graced by the sacred dust from the feet of realized sages and great beings was forever glorious for him. Yogiraj's grandson Sriyukta Ananda Mohan Lahiri made arrangements for Shastri Mahasaya to live at his own house; although a few years later, he lived elsewhere. Ananda Babu says that during their time of residence at that house, certain great beings close to the Lord Lahiri Mahasaya would grace the place by coming there, and sometime before the construction of the house was finished, Mahamuni Sri Sri Babaji Maharaj also blessed that place, seen by the trunk of a tree on that compound. Thus, this was a great place of sacred pilgrimage for him. His days passed in Bliss. The practice of sannyas went on to take him into even higher levels. At this time, advanced sadhakas from our Guru's place also used to come to him to know about the loftiest mysteries of the spiritual world. Sometime afterwards, the memory of his mother came upon him, the one for whom he had had everlasting devotion, and whose blessings were ever working on his behalf. He brought his mother to Benares and began to take care of her. Despite his not wanting such, his wife and daughter [also] came to him at this time. But he did not pay much attention in that direction and continued to serve his mother in all ways by his own hands. How often does one find this perspective today! It was in Benares that his mother left her body. The student of the beautiful mother-devotee Vidyasagar, the mother-devotee Ashutosh—though having taken up sannyas-life—stayed at his mother's side until the last day and nursed her, and thus was contented in his soul.

After the loss of his mother, he decided that he would go towards the Himalayas. But who knows why, obstacles started to appear in the way of this happening. He was nevertheless unrelenting and continued to cut through all of these barriers. Just at the became anxious to be completely free of the karmic grasp of worldly life, right at that time, by the Lord's design of destiny, he suddenly became sick. People wanting to take care of him came from numerous places but it seemed that the great sadhaka whose being was free of material ties and who had attained the Stillness of paravastha became rather annoyed at accepting any kind of service towards him. After going through all of the physical suffering in silence for some days, this ideal person, on Wednesday, the 24th of Chaitra, 1338 [Bengali calendar], during the full moon, he discarded his mortal body, leaving devotees, friends, disciples and all such others afloat in an ocean of grief, and becoming liberated from all enchainment, attained Supreme Union. On the banks of the Bhagirathi, at the holy pilgrimage site of Manikarnika, in the presence of sannyasis, brahmacharis, householders and others—disciples and devotees, [his] material body dissolved into the five elements. The acharya remained ever awake in devotees as a sense of divine touch.

Through his simple and easy method of leading life, he became our own as a simple and easy person. He was a true brahmin and a Veda-illuminated, intellectual scholar. He had taught works of literature, philosophy, astrology, ayurveda and many such subjects, and among his students were the wealthy, the poor, residents of different lands—we have even seen practitioners of Buddhism from distant Sri Lanka! But we never saw him to have any desire for fame from any of these happenings or from the performance of any acts. He abided in an ever-blissful state, knowing all situations to be the will of the Supremely Compassionate Lord of Lords.

Certain disciples have made arrangements for the preservation of his memory. This is natural. They deserve the gratitude of everyone. Seeing the picture of a beloved holy one or seeing his memorabilia causes reverence to rise in our hearts; thus, those material things also become articles of our worship and help to awaken spiritual feelings. May we be able to remember that thinking or meditating upon his saintliness, sweet behavior, friendly nature, meditation-absorption and unperturbed state of being is what will truly preserve his memory within us. It is in the sadhakas and great beings that we find the scriptures in living form. As such, when the profoundly tranquil image of the great acharya Hansaswami [Kebalananda] Maharaj awakens in the place of memories, it comes to mind—

duhkheshvanidvignamana sukheshu vigatasprihah
veetaragabhayakrodhah sthitadhirmu niruchyate

[not distressed with sorrow, not desirous with
pleasure unaffected by fear and anger, such a sage is said to
be in the state of silent abiding in Stillness]

Swami Sri Yukteshvar Giri Maharaj

A Biography

by Swami Satyananda Giri

English Translation by Yoga Niketan

with special thanks to Swami Vidyabhaskarananda Saraswati
for translation of the Sanskrit slokas

This translated book maintains that an almost literal translation of the Bengali words of the original author best serves both seekers and Kriyavans. No attempt has been made for the translations to be poetic or interpretive for the above-mentioned reason. If the reader notices irregular English grammar (including non-traditional sentence structure, punctuation, etc.), please understand that it is intentional. The translator has tried as best as he could to keep the work as close to the Bengali phrasing in the original without it being unreadable or incomprehensible.

Pranam, The Translator: Yoga Niketan

Swami Sri Yukteshvar Giri Maharaj

DEDICATION

One Saturday at dusk, in the Bengali year 1318, in the company of the most revered Swami Yoganandaji at the Simla neighborhood in Calcutta, I received darshan of the one that Yoganandaji had called beforehand his "Jnanagurudev": Srimat Swami Sriyukteshvar Giri Maharaj. On that very day that tall, athletically built man with a regal stance, long arms that came down to his knees—a man amongst men—completely captivated my heart. After that, day after day, in different organizational work, in the Satsanga Sabha and other places, I was fortunate to have his company and gained the wisdom to resolve so many types of issues in my life. In our discussions, because of his indulging me with his attention, and due to my limited intellect and carelessness, I argued with him about so many things and, consequently, I was reprimanded by him. Still I would count every fortunate day in which I would have his presence, his divine company, hear a couple of words from his mouth, listen to his humorous stories and be able to enjoy his joking and kidding around. Sometimes I was guilty of being critical and spoke unfavorably about the direction of his work, yet upon receiving a momentary touch of this great man's inner light, I became enchanted and collapsed at his feet. The sinner's sin vanished in that Holy Touch. Even if I, as the perpetrator, came to him with trepidation, so many times I would be relieved of any fear in his affectionate welcoming. Supposedly, I am known as being an emotional person and the holy Maharajji's reputation in society was as an emotionless, logical man. Yet it is from sitting at this yoga-united man's feet and listening to his seemingly dry yet deeply knowledgeable, scientific and mind-gripping talks that so many times I would become overcome with divine emotion. Penetrating the veil of logical analysis, I tasted the delightful nectar of bliss. Sometimes, away from him, for some reason or another, maybe I would become annoyed, afraid or confused. I would come to him and argue with him too, but in a moment of his company those feelings would disappear somewhere. It was from his affection that my vanity was annihilated at the feet of this Divine Incarnation of Knowledge.

In Puri, being there as the ashramswami of Sadhu Sabha's Karar Ashram, he gave an insignificant person like me his respect and love and graced me by allowing me to live near him for some time. Although sometimes I failed under his rule, the memory of this, the most precious time of my life, is permanently and radiantly etched in my mind. In the battlefield of life, whether in the running of the ashram, teaching people, and later, with the teaching system and management of the Ranchi Brahmacharya University, who knows in how many ways and how much wisdom he gave this little being, building me into a new person. Almost every day during ashram life, he would bless this weak, skeptical man, showing me with the greatest care the power and equipoise of Kriyayoga sadhana, endowing me with the strength of sadhana and a disciplined life, for which I was bound to him in deep gratitude. A sick man misbehaving in his sickness and then begging for safety, this Satyananda received mild reproof, and later was affectionately blessed by this venerable and great teacher by his visitations, timely and untimely, and his amazing cures for these behavioral ailments. Mental courage, hope, and a steady and full reliance on Providence were some of the endowments of wisdom, and these sacred memories are forever alive in this servant's mind.

In one moment of his company, I found the boat to cross the ocean of this world and then spent my days intoxicated in bliss and joy. At that time, I could not even imagine writing about the life of this great, enlightened Acharya of the Age. A couple of friends hinted at this but I did not pay any attention. Whatever I learned from conversations in his holy company and whatever I learned of his immense nature through being his initiate, that is what is floating in front of my mind even in the absence of his physical body. Seemingly unconnected, every incident is presenting itself in front of me as having had great significance. This writer is not capable of properly capturing those things on paper. The one from whose blessed presence hundreds of ordinary sadhakas were able to easily and magnificently progress on the path of Kriya yoga and were lifted by him to lofty levels, the one in whose holy company ordinary, barely educated people became writers and poets of Essential Knowledge, the one through whose beautiful words of logic, irreverent and negligent villagers became respectful, thoughtful and effective members of community, the one with whose slightest reproach the most touted and proud person would instantly cower—how can I paint a picture of his colossal character? One reassuring fact is that he lived with us as if he was our own kind. In all his teaching and in his behavior he taught us to know human beings in a simple way rather try to see beyond them.

While doing the supreme, higher than the highest, His Holiness Guru Sadhusabhapati Maharajji's work through the Sadhu Sabha and Satsanga Sabha and the spreading of Kriyayoga sadhana initiation, and also when, under the direction of the revered Swami Paramhansa Yoganandaji Maharaj, I traveled to many places and became close to different Kriya yoga sadhakas and devotees, I found many of them also greatly desired that a biography of Maharajji be written. After the two short biographies I wrote of Adiguru Yogiraj Lord Sri Sri Shyamacharan Lahiri Mahasaya and Yogacharya Sri Shastri Mahasaya (Hansaswami Kebalanandaji Maharaj)* were published, it seemed that these requests increased a hundredfold. But when I would think about this superman's huge personality and his fathomless ocean of knowledge, I would become overwhelmed. Waves upon waves would come and take me over and I could not capture anything properly, and I did not have the courage to write anything down. I did not have the fortune of seeing the Incarnation of the Age, Yogeshwar Lord Sri Sri Lahiri Mahasaya. Whatever I heard through the lineage, whatever little I could understand, is what I digested, and only with that was I able to make a simple and small offering at the feet of the Lord, based on the words of the successors about Him. It is not out of place to say that that book is not a real biography or even an abbreviated one. But in this case, I have been directly in the company of Greatness! Whatever I would think about—I would begin to wonder if any of that is exactly right. The huge fireball of Cosmic Light totally flooded my limited vision. I received True Holy Company; I was thinking: who knows what I will end up saying trying to say something else—I felt fear and trepidation in my mind about this. So, even though I wanted to from time to time, I could not summon up the courage to pick up the pen. Then, through the good wishes of noble devotees, a little light seemed to appear in the darkness. With their holy encouragement I became enthusiastic and sat down to write. Whether the sequence and order of events and the instructive words etc. are properly organized, I cannot say. I have written whatever came up, with whatever feelings came up, in my mind at the time I was writing. Whatever little I tasted is what I have presented to the devotees and seekers. If they are able to overlook the mistakes and imperfections in the few lines of reading here, and if they like the material in this book even a little bit, and if some reverence is awakened from the wisdom of this great teacher, then the writer will have received their silent blessings and felt that this little effort was a success.

*The parentheses and the text within are in the original.

Everyone is aware of the troubles involved in publishing even such a small book. The same fate had also befallen this insignificant book-writer. But I was able to traverse this problem because of the efforts of many friends and dear ones, and I am indebted to all of them. I pray that they receive the beneficence of this Great Being's blessings. I offer my praise and thankfulness to my beloved student, the founder of the Jhargram Sevayatan Ashram and its trustees for taking the responsibility for the proper management of this book. The one by whose spiritual help and encouragement we are gratefully able to have this small biography of the enlightened and awakened life of the Divine Visionary Paribrajacharya His Holiness Jnanagurudev, completely beloved in my heart, Paramhansa Yoganandaji is, of course, always there.

We are certainly tremendously fortunate to have brushed with such holiness. But still I think about all the times and opportunities that I wasted. I did not understand very much at that time. If I had the Beloved One for another few days near me—how much more I would have benefited. I was unfortunate to not have been present during the last moments of his being in a body, but I was fortunate that in his last days in the world he remembered this petitioner of grace and graced me with his Divine Blessing. What he revealed of the direction to go in life and the wisdom that he gave on everything in many different ways—I have been neither able to do any of that, nor have I been able to absorb in my heart the deep meanings of all that he taught. Thus, in this auspicious and holy day, in purest sincerity I offer my reverence-filled heart to the Supremely Beloved Lord of Acharyas, and praying for his eternal blessings from beyond, I say:

Karpanyadoshohapahataswabhava
Pricchami tvam dharmasammudhrchetah
Yacchreya syannishchitam bruhi tanme
Shishyastehaham shadhi mam tvam prapannam

"My being is overcome by the flaw of faint-heartedness
and my mind is bewildered concerning what is duty.
Hence I beseech Thee: reveal unto me what is
proper. I am Thy disciple. Teach me who have taken
refuge in Thee."

Signed,

Satyananda Giri

Mahalaya, 1354
Sevayatan-Yogamandir
Jhargram (Medinipur)

BIRTH—EDUCATION—LIFE IN THE WORLD

By the will of the Supreme, who is the Cause of Everything, in whose nineteenth century India—the second half of which beheld a scenario of societal, political and spiritual transition and transformation—the Acharya of the Age, Srimat Swami Sriyukteshvar Giri Maharaj was born in the form of a son to the middle class family of Kshetranath Karar—father, and Kadambini—mother, on the 10th of May in the Christian year of 1855—the last Friday of the month of Baishakh—in the city of Srirampur of the Hoogly District, on the banks of the holy river Bhagirathi.

The only child of his parents, in due time and according to edicts, he was given and known by the name Priyanath, and began to be reared in tender care and affection. His father, Kshetranath Mahasaya was a minor land owner and he also earned money from another business which he owned. The environment of western civilization in the city of Srirampur influenced him as well. Mother Kadambini ran her household as a proper wife and ideal mother, firmly observant of the rules and norms of Hindu family life. At the suitable time, Priyanath was given the "literary initiation" and enrolled in school.

Priyanath's sharp intellect and intelligence caught the attention of his teachers and he became a favorite pupil. Besides other subjects, he was naturally adept at mathematics. He used to say that he could not remember a time when he did not receive full marks [100% correct] in mathematics tests during his days at school. From his very childhood, he had the inclination to study his schoolwork and everything else in depth. He could not accept with satisfaction any unscientific conclusion. The tendency to cultivate and study as well as enquire into the Essential Matters seemed to emanate as an inborn characteristic of the child Priyanath.

Being the child of a well-to-do family and an intelligent student, from his young days he became close to certain important and noble families of Srirampur, especially the Goswami family. The elders of the Goswami family doted on him. They were very happy to see him participating in discussions in events where the children and youth were expressing their intelligence and knowledge, and these elders would strongly encourage him at the appropriate times. From a young age, Priyanath used to enjoy listening to scriptural discourses and would thereafter be inspired to analyze the matters with his own intellect and flow of thought. In his childhood days in school, he could not take anything to heart that was not scientifically sound or meaningful, whether pertaining to normal subject matters, scriptural issues, or even music and drama. He become annoyed and perturbed when he would analyze some high philosophical perspective by some eminent scholar or elder and find that there was no logic behind it. When Priyanath was a student in the second grade (at present in ninth grade),* a scriptural scholar came to the Goswami house and was lecturing to everyone about many subjects related to the shastras. At that time, Priyanath went there and listened to the deliberations with full attention. Different people asked the scholar various questions on numerous subjects, to all of which he answered by giving scriptural examples. Without giving much explanation to make it understandable, with every precept he would say, "It's in the shastras; therefore this precept should be followed." He carried on this way for quite a while. The smart youth Priyanath was able to easily get the pundit's attention. Along with everyone else's questions, he put in a couple of his own. But instead of elucidating, the scholar would give his scriptural quotations over and over again, which finally annoyed Priyanath to the point when he turned to some friends and said in such a way that the pundit could hear: "Mahasaya, the other day, about......subject, I discovered a special quote from the shastras. It was an amazing proof! The sloka was '......labhet pathi ghurna prasrabane.'"** Saying this, he quickly left the place and laughed hysterically with his friends, and then said, "He doesn't make any effort to help us understand anything; even when ask him, he won't answer with any logic. Just a bunch of incomprehensible mumbo jumbo from the shastras and then yelling at us, trying to make us feel stupid—I couldn't tolerate it any more. So, I composed a sloka of my own and said it. It means, 'You will attain that thing when you go around urinating on the road.'" His companions were rolling over with laughter. Over in the gathering, the scholar was quiet for a moment and then suddenly said, "What did you say? What sloka did you spout? Trying to make a mockery out of me! Why you little rascal...I'll show you...!" By that time, Priyanath was out of reach. Later, when some people in the Goswami house would scold him about that, he would say, "Just a bunch of stupid scriptural exhortations—I was annoyed. Whatever it may be, shouldn't he try to explain at least? The Sanskrit sloka that I composed is also a scriptural precept. What's the point in explaining it? I said something from the shastras. That's all, nothing more to be said!!" Although the elders gently rebuked Priyanath a little bit in the beginning, they gradually became attracted to his analytic ability and later, when there would be discussions on complex matters with distinguished people, they would consult him also.

*The parentheses and text within are in the original.
**The ellipses (...) are in the original quotation.

Priyanath lost his father when he was a child. Although his mother was the legal custodian of everything, his father's household, the land ownership and management, and the business—all were attended to by him. He did not have much of a mind for business and consequently, the his father's small business went defunct. But because of his sharp intelligence, he became adept at other things. People such as those dealing with law in the houses and courts of provincial kings and landlords would consult him from time to time for his analysis and insight on problematic issues. Once, he caught the attention of the Maharaja of Susanga, who offered him a high-paying position in his land ownership. We have seen that in some situations people would consult him on some complicated matter, write down his easy resolution, and leave, to which eventually the lawyers would say, "This was the view of a prominent barrister in Calcutta." When Swamiji Maharaj would hear of this, he would explode in his patented belly laugh, enthralling us with this and so many other stories. Through these discussions he used to try to make us understand that for a human being to attain his humanity, meaning in every kind of thing—even the spiritual world—to become great, one has to be attentive to whatever situation one may be in. Only in this way can human beings' behavior become excellent, easily and freely, the kind of intelligent behavior that can especially help even knowledgeable people. Thus he would say, "If there is some work that must be done, then one should not be disrespectful and careless towards that work, because that disrespectful attitude can plant a seed of disrespect in the mind. The religious path or path to truth is not just meditation and concentration. Without regulating the entire life properly, it is not possible for a normal person to realize the highest ideals." That is why he instructed to pay attention to [such things as] cleanliness, orderliness, maintenance of the body, lawfulness, civility, simple behavior, self-sufficiency etc.

In due time, Priyanath successfully passed the entrance examination and enrolled in the Srirampur Christian Missionary College. During his studies, he became deeply interested in the Christian Bible, and besides the usual life story of Jesus Christ, he would explore the book of Revelation (the experience of Spiritual Knowledge and the revelation of the Supreme) and other such subjects, which captivated him and became a deeply significant part of his spiritual life, sadhana and realization, where he would become able to reveal the connection between the beautiful inner spirituality of the Christian religion and the mysteries of yoga. Later, this experience would express itself in his spiritual work in a special way.

In college, he became even more driven to investigate these things. He had a natural affection for scientific matters and along with studying ordinary science, he also began to feel attracted to the sciences of anatomy and physiology, as well as medicine. One day, he was listening to some scientific lecture from a professor. The subject of anatomy and physiology somehow crept in, although the lecture was about a another science. Priyanath took this opportunity and began to ask detailed questions in order to learn more about anatomy and physiology. The professor sahib was not that versed in that field and thus was having trouble giving complete answers to the student's questions. Finally, the teacher became irritated and said, "First go to the Medical College; then come to my class."* This reproof became a blessing instead of a curse for Priyanath. He stopped going to that college and enrolled in the Calcutta Medical College instead. After wholeheartedly studying the science and essence of anatomy and physiology, he left the medical college before the end of the second year. He did not go back to study in the Srirampur college either. This was the end of his ordinary student life, but he was overcome by his thirst for knowledge on many different things. His mother tried to reengage him in the field of his father's business. But that only yielded some money; her son's mind was not in it at all. In the course of time, Priyanath married, and for a little while he became employed in an office as an accountant. He used to say, "At that time, I saw that those who were doing that work were laboring almost all of the time, but that job was so easy for me that I would finish the needed work in a short time and then I would just chit chat." Even though he was well paid, the job did not satisfy him. He left his job and felt relieved.

*The words in quotes are written in English in the original.

The thirst for knowledge remained as a constant companion. He became interested in studying homeopathic curative methods and after learning about the fine and fundamental points, he was solidly convinced of the supremacy of this science. At this time, he was introduced to the naturopathic experiments of the German luminary Dr. Konn, and establishing himself in the truth that natural medicine was the solution for all types of illnesses, he became immersed in cultivating these methods. It is from these insights that he was able to postulate about physiological matters such as the structure of the body and mind and other such things, and through experimentation and scientific analysis, his conclusions agreed with the prominent naturopathic physicians that eating meat and fish was unnatural and harmful. But he admitted that sometimes, especially under the consultation of a physician, it might be necessary for some ill persons to eat non-vegetarian food in order to regain strength. He also used give advice that one should be simple and natural in respect to clothing and hair. Through extensive experimentation and penetrative observation, in order to formulate curative processes, along with spiritual practices—such as those in the field of Kriya, he eventually would demonstrate and enlighten people on the beauty and effectiveness of natural medicine, which would become of great service to the sick and diseased, making it possible to obtain simple and easy methods of cure.

Besides pursuing the knowledge of many different subjects, he was also interested in physical culture. With his naturally athletic body, he was able to excel in sports such as horseback riding, hunting, weapons' sports etc.

His closeness with the Goswami family brought him in contact with numerous accomplished, respected and wealthy persons, through whom he gained the experience of the many different aspects of human character. He would look back in his own life and freely admit that the company of these people profited him in the proper building of his mind and temperament. The late Pandit Iswarchandra Vidyasagar Mahasaya's work in progressive reforms while maintaining the Indian ethos had an influence on him. He was able to have the company of the Emperor of Literature, Bankimchandra, whose books and writings would bring light to his views on nationalism, freedom of thought, logical and analytical methods, religion, morality, society and other such things. Instead of the imaginary mindsets of scriptural and religious thought, the priceless philosophy of "the truth of Man is higher than all else" gave him a new perspective which seemed to give him a feeling of freedom to be his natural self. I have heard him say in conversations, "Bankimbabu is the one who is our guru."

I have heard from Swamiji Maharaj that the publisher of the periodical Bangadarshan requested the newly composed profound song "Bande Mataram"; Bankimchandra replied, "What good will it do to print this now? There are still twenty-five years to go before this mantra-song's meaning will be understood." Bankim's foresight and prophetic words would be realized in due time by the children of Bengal.

He used be enraptured by the art of music, particularly instrumental music. It is not that he was very knowledgeable in music theory, nor was he skilled at many different types of music or adept at different instruments. With the aid of his natural ability to learn, whatever he learned was precise and somehow that itself made him excellent in the musical domain. He learned a few compositions on sitar from his master [of music], which was enough to distinguish him. When people would come, his master would ask him to play, and the audience would become enchanted. He used to encourage everyone to study and cultivate the art of music. He would emphasize that music should have its own place in the systems of education. He became perturbed whenever anyone would sing without paying attention to pitch, melody or rhythm, regardless of how or whom, whether they were children, youth or elderly, and he cautioned that to not pay attention like that could allow the possibility of becoming inattentive in character. He was in favor of proper education in music, dance and theater for students in school, and he would give amazing advice on very subtle elements regarding what may or may not be improper or unsuitable for the children.

The usual entanglements of worldly life were not able to bind him for very long. In just a few years, he became a widower. Later, his only daughter left her body after a battle with illness. Only his granddaughter remained as the sole blood connection to the world. As if to give Swamiji freedom from the ties of ordinary societal life, she married and went off to her husband's house. No one saw him unnerved by any of these changes. The feeling that he had fulfilled and been freed from prarabdha [results from past lives] became firmly established in his mind. He used to say, "God made me a sannyasi through an easy way." Before his daughter's illness, he made preparations to travel the world to gain knowledge about many things, but the obstacles of life did not allow that desire to be fulfilled. In this first stage of life, the virtues of subtle insight, clear analysis, deep research, steadiness of character and non-attachment began to reveal themselves as what would comprise the immense personality and radiant life in the future for the Acharya of the Ages, His Holiness Swamiji Maharaj. Whoever may have been touched by the rays of the dawning of this life are blessed. UNFOLDING OF SPIRITUAL KNOWLEDGE

sadrisham ceshtate svasyaah prakriteh jnaanavaan api

Even a man of knowledge acts according to his own nature.

INDICATION OF PATH—
FINDING GURU—
INVESTIGATION OF TRUTH—
SELF SURRENDER

The types of moods or behavior, a madness for spirituality—the outward signs that we would normally imagine—were not evident in Swamiji Maharaj's early life as far as we know. However, he used to participate in the usual occasions such as the Holi festival and Durga festival, and would be involved in going to pilgrimages with his mother along with doing other beneficent works; if he would meet any sadhus, sannyasis or some significant sadhaka, he would become keen on being in their company. Penetrating the immense mysteries of God's creation, Soul enquiry, and the application of astrology in spiritual work—it seems that these were the types of matters that were naturally endearing to him. If he would hear of an eminent sadhaka, he would be attracted to that person, but if he found evidence of a sadhaka having supernatural abilities, he would actually go to them to satisfy his curiosity. He believed that most of those supernatural stories were nonsense and insubstantial advertisement. Later, he used to say that experience showed that the extreme zeal and emotionalism of the devotees of realized sadhakas—rather, emotional transgressions—spreading a bunch of ridiculous stories about them, brought their gurus down to a lower level instead of glorifying them He said that it is true that beyond human understanding the impossible can be possible through yogic miracles, but even if those things happen, it is better not to reveal them out of emotionalism and without any understanding. Lacking the comprehension of those types of events, exclamations with restless zeal take place, destroying seriousness and creating disrepute. Because of this, he would caution over and over about it and forbid paying too much attention in these directions. He used to say, "In earlier times in my life, even though I enjoyed hearing about sadhus, sannyasis, sadhakas etc., when I would hear extremely unusual stories about them, it was as if rascally ideas would come to my head, and however I could, I would employ many different methods to prove those stories as false." He told us a humorous story about some well-known yogi sadhaka of that of that time: "I used to often hear from this yogipurush's devotees and disciples that every night, their gurudev would sit still in yogasana in mid-air. After arguing back and forth, when those devotees began to spread the word of that event even more, one evening, being extremely careful, I silently lay down under the bed of the yogi sadhaka mahasaya. From time to time I thought that, it could be—maybe his supernatural work was true. But since it was not possible to prove it in the normal way, let me satisfy my curioosity in hiding. At the proper time, the yogibara entered the room, closed the door, and lay down. Time passed on. Staying completely quiet under the bed, eventually I became restless. Finally, I lost my patience and said, 'What? You didn't float up in the air?' The yogibara hurriedly got up and said, 'Oh! You are under the bed, you punk! No wonder my samadhi wasn't good tonight!' After that, laughter exploded inside and outside." The devotees do not pay attention to what the sadhakas say, and how much excessive bragging and boasting they do with those words! When we would ask about the supernatural abilities of certain realized sadhakas of that time, about which we heard through public hearsay, he would tell us of his experience and many times would deny the validity of those things. But he would accept the truth of sadhakas' evidence of exceptional strength, amazing dedication, extraordinary temperament etc., while forbidding us to believe exaggerated and illogical stories, following blindly like sheep.

At this time, in the Goswami household and in houses of other noble families, the influence of Yogiraj Sri Sri Lahiri Mahasaya was becoming evident. Priyanath saw that they would regularly do some kind of sadhana behind closed doors. Eventually he heard that they were disciples of a renowned yogipurush from Benares and practiced yoga. He had knowledge of numerous sadhus, sannyasis, sadhakas etc.—many such gurus; some he even saw. But the word about this guru, about whom he had not been previously aware, attracted him in some unknown way. Leaving aside other sadhus and mahatmas, he became eager to meet this realized being. No reason, no relation to any events, what kind of a strange attraction is this?! How can the mind of such an analytical man like Priyanath become overcome with such longing? Who is this Mahapurush from Benares whose wondrous touch came through some everyday people in Srirampur and inspired him so? In any case, he began to make great efforts at finding more information about this Yogiraj as well as trying to get his address, but no one would agree to let him know anything. His eagerness ripened; he became restless. Then, in the middle of some conversation, he caught a whiff of information about the address and without wasting a moment, he headed for Benares, saying, "I'm coming back after an excursion." Although after he arrived in Benares he became a little exasperated by difficulties, he was eventually able to locate Sri Sri Lahiri Mahasaya's house, finding which he was able to dispel some of his suspense. When the devotees departed, he felt as if the longing of many lifetimes had found the chance to be fulfilled in the presence of this Man, and prayed to the God of his Heart to receive initiation in Kriya yoga. On the day prescribed by the Lord*, after bathing in the Ganges and dressing himself in pure garments, he arrived at his Guru's house and on the Suklapanchami of Ashar 1290 [Bengali holy day, month and year], received initiation in Kriya yoga for which he had prayed. The fortunate disciple took his Guru's blessings and came back to his house in Srirampur. Returning home, with great devotion he became deeply immersed in sadhana, and practicing day after day, began to attain blissful ecstasy from the work. As he progressed on his path of sadhana, captivated by the beauty of ever-new divine experiences, his naturally analytical foundation became illuminated by the Light of Self-Awareness. When complexities would arise on the path, he would get his answers through letters to Sriguru. From time to time, he would also travel to Benares and resolve many issues in person.

*[Translator's note: As also explained in the translation of Swami Satyananda Maharaj's biography of Sri Sri Lahiri Mahasaya, in the original text, the Bengali word "Thakur" is used throughout to often address Sri Sri Lahiri Mahasaya. The closest meaning is "Lord" in the divine and deistic sense of the word. God is addressed as "Thakur" in Bengali culture, as well as God-humans. Sometimes "Thakur" is also a family name, but that does not have the same connotation.]

Priyanath's truth-seeking, forever enquiring mind became ever more inquisitive about knowing the vast mysteries of the universe.

"Wherever you see ashes, throw it up, you might just get the priceless gem"—with this motto in his mind, he traveled around to many places. If he would find the whereabouts of luminary philosophers, scientists, sadhakas, scholars, astrologers and other practitioners of such fields, he would go to them and candidly ask to learn from them. Through the close company of persons such as Benrares' eminent Trailangaswamiji, Jnani Vaskarananda Swamiji, the guru of Agra's Radhaswami sect and many other sadhakas from other communities, he even practiced many of their methods of sadhana which he received from them. He went to Dakshineswar to have the divine darshan of Sri Ramakrishna, but the Lord* was not there that day for some reason, and Swamiji was not able to see him.

*In this case, "Lord" refers to Sri Ramakrishna.

His desire to gain knowledge through different means became so acute that upon hearing the words of a Santal* sadhaka, he traveled deep inside a mountain jungle to the sadhaka's hut and expressed his desire to become his student. As far as we know, he was able to progress well in almost all of these paths of sadhana and became dear to the gurus of these teachings. Because of his reverence and discipline, even the Theosophical Society enthusiastically made him an honorary member.

*Santals are an aboriginal people in Bengal.

He received instructions in sadhana from the aforementioned Santal guru, and was given permission to be present at the wondrous devotional and mystical dances to Krishna by his disciples in full moon nights, which were usually done in extreme secrecy. Swamiji Maharaj used to say, "In the deep jungle, with a serene full moon, in a frightening yet enchanting atmosphere, children, women and men in small groups would dance ecstatically. It seemed to conjure up the scenario of the supernatural dance of bliss on the rasamandali.* I saw evidence of the amazing power of their sadhana in the extraordinary restraint, focus and discipline with joy in that wild state. The strength of their guru's sadhana, spiritual supremacy and stern adherence to rules were at the root of this disciplined ecstasy."

*[Translator's note: This refers to the dance of the gopis and Krishna during His incarnation. "Rasamandali" is the stage where the "Rasalila" (play of Krishna and the gopis) took place.]

Discussing the fundamental elements of sadhana methods with tantrics, vaishnavas, bauls etc., he was able to discover the inner similarities of all paths. If we try to respectfully understand that the sadhakas and high beings of all sects teach spiritual elevation by turning the attention inward, then the commonality all paths becomes revealed and the sectarian differences disappear. We received glimpses of this truth in his teachings. By going to the feet of the different mahapurushas and teacher-gurus, he was able to know the mysteries of sadhana and excelled at the practice of spiritual knowledge. However, he had to remember and be cautious, knowing that even while staying true to the ideals of Soul Knowledge, disciplined in Truth and respectful, only loitering in the ordinary company of sadhakas of different sects one could lose the way as well. When it was pertinent, he would say, "Sit with everyone, listen to everyone with respect, remember that a gem could be hidden even in ashes, but your own seat—meaning, your own particular spiritual foundation—be very aware of that. Losing your own post and being five different ways from following the words five different people won't get you anything—meaning, one must believe in and be firmly established in the guru-given sadhana. Only then can one taste the nectar from different flowers and create a chakra-garland of nectar."

In the multifarious, divine play of the world, the knowledge-enquiring sadhaka Priyanath, through obedience to sadhaka mahapurushas of many holy places, dispelled all doubts in this way about the unity of the root substance of the appropriately various settings of different paths. But he remained unmoved from his seat of the sadhana given by his Guru. The steady discipline and practice of Kriyayoga sadhana filled his inner being with Effulgence. Day after day, his consciousness became more and more pure and radiant. Attaining the beatitude of the Bliss of Brahman in the land of samadhi, the river of his life united with the Absolute Ocean of Satchitananda-substance. The blessings of the Guru now became evident in the natural and divine transformation of the intellect and intelligence of the reverent sadhaka. Being absorbed in this Grace, the disciple—with illuminated consciousness and filled with gratitude—surrendered everything to the feet of the Incarnation of All—Sriguru, and thus became sanctified. Seeing the Light of the Knowledge of Brahman in the divinity of His disciple, the Truth-Seeing Sage Guru joyfully and proudly gave him Shelter. The One who brought back the lost Yoga-science for this age, Yogavatar Lord Sri Sri Lahiri Mahasaya seemed to now be building this dear disciple as an Incarnation of Knowledge, adorning him with the Knowledge of Brahman for the good of so many. In the Court of the Lord of the Universe, in Benares—the land of knowledge, the Supremely Divine Yogiraj Maheshwar's blessings in the Light of Knowledge became manifest.

Pashabaddho bhavet jivah pashamuktah sadashivah

The individual soul is bound by fetters; freed from them is the eternal Siva.

COMPANY OF SADGURU AND SCRIPTURAL CULTIVATION

Having ended all conflicts in his mind and full of Sriguru's Grace, sadhaka yogi Priyanath returned to Srirampur and became absorbed in deep sadhana, and day after day, while ascending through and attaining knowledge of different levels of yoga-samadhi, throughout this part of sadhana he would exchange letters with Sriguru, in which he would present many questions about his experiences, seeking their resolution. Sometimes his mind would pull him to go to Benares and he would show up at his Guru's feet. Immersed in his Guru, in the course of discussions on spiritual sadhana and such matters, he also prayed for answers and other help on the many problems, dangers and pitfalls, sorrows of dear ones, obstacles etc. of ordinary householder life, and was blessed to witness the breadth of the supernatural powers of the Lord Sri Sri Lahiri Mahasaya in all things.

When he would come to his Guru, he would usually not mingle with anyone, nor would he say very much. If there were people present, he would sit quietly on the side of the room, focused on his Guru. When everyone would leave, he would ask a few questions or show Yogiraj some writings. He used to say, "In the Presence of Gurudev, many problems would be resolved in ordinary small talk. Sometimes there was so much chit chat and even jokes and laughter, it seemed like— wait, we didn't really talk about anything important! But, when I would return and think a little bit after having settled down, I would realize that it was almost as if I had received Divine Knowledge in those conversations." Gurudev Sri Sri Lahiri Mahasaya would at times speak with seriousness, or in an ordinary manner, or sometimes with signs and gestures; this was at times difficult to comprehend for those present. But quieting oneself a little bit and thinking about that which had transpired before, the meaning would clearly reveal itself. Fortunate with the Grace of Guru, the disciple was now living the "Soul incursion" ideal.

The Lord Sri Sri Lahiri Mahasaya would from time to time discuss philosophical literature and the Gita scripture with His disciples. He was particularly attentive to the deliberation and understanding of the Srimad Bhagavad Gita, the supreme shastra. Drawing out and explaining the hidden mysteries of the esoteric books in light of the glorious experiences and wisdom of sadhana was the specialty of his discourses on scriptures. The perfect student—the scientifically enquiring, samadhi-attained, great sadhaka Priyanath would drink the nectarous words from Sriguru's mouth to his heart's content. The Light of Divine Knowledge flooded him within. He became genuinely studious of the scriptural works.

Sri Priyanath's knowledge of Sanskrit was ordinary, if judged by the standards set up for comprehension of the shastras. Of course, his English was college-level proficient, and previously he had learned French. He also knew ordinary Hindi. According to custom of the time, he read the Ramayana, Mahabharata, Puranas etc. and also attended extensive lectures by pundits on Puranic subjects. He enjoyed the inner, sadhana oriented commentary of the Vaishnava scripture, Sri Chaitanyacharitamrita. He examined books from numerous different sects, and even had some discussions on Islamic matters. He studied the Christian Bible with the deepest respect.

With his analytical and logical mind, he was particularly attracted to philosophical treatises. Detailed discussions of Samkhya philosophy, the cultivation and practice of the Patanjali Yogashastra, and understanding the Mimamsa Vedanta's essential subject matter via pure logic were things that seemed to be easy for him—meaning, he was effortlessly able to always come to the non-dual conclusion, "all is Brahman". With this philosophical cultivation and the divine experiences of sadhana, he began to explore the Srimad Bhagavad Gita. He saw that revealed in the Gita's eternal truths was the fundamental commonality of philosophic theory, the knowledge of the Upanishads, the significance of the Puranas and the conclusions of science. The book that expressed the incredible experiences in the Kutastha of sadhakas on the path of sadhana, that Paramrishi Vyasdeva presented as a dialogue between Sri Krishna and Arjuna, that Gita became his highest scripture. For the regular study and discussion of the Gita, he established a "Gita Sabha" [Gita fellowship] with some Kriyavans and devoted people. He kept a written record of the regular recitation, commentary and interactive talk on the wisdom of the Gita that took place in this sabha. When a complex question would arise, he would resolve the issue via letters to his Gurudev. Sometimes he would actually go to his Guru's abode. Even though he deeply studied the commentaries on the root meaning of the Gita by the His Holiness Lord Sri Sri Lahiri Mahasaya, he took the timely and appropriate scientific perspective of the eastern and western luminaries, and extracting the inner meaning of the mysteries of the Gita in this way, began to print his own commentaries part by part. As each part would be printed, he would take it to his Guru every time, and would receive his Guru's support of this essential writing, and taking his Guru's blessings upon his head, would return with new enthusiasm. In this way, he was able to publish up to the ninth chapter.

He had a special keenness for astrology. To learn to be an astrologer, he used pay the traveling expenses of scholars from many places and bring them to his house to discuss the subject with them. If he heard of an renown pundit, he would sometimes even travel to places far away to go to him.

According to Maharajji's calculation, in the month of Magh, 194 Dwapara Yuga (1894 Christian Era),* sadhaka Priyanath went to the Prayag Kumbhamela to see the great gathering of sadhus and high beings as well as to be in their company. Arriving at the Prayag pilgrimage, he began to spend time with sadhak-purushas from different paths. During the festival, one day on the other side of Allahabad's road to Jhusi, while walking by the sadhus' camps he suddenly heard someone with a familiar voice calling him: "Swamiji, Swamiji!!" He was not a sannyasi at the time; and who would be calling him like this—especially in this place where he was an unknown person? Suspicious of this, he ignored the call and continued to walk. But, out of the unfamiliar residence of a sadhu, a devotee came out, called him and took him to the sadhu's place. Arriving there, Priyanath saw a divinely radiant Man looking at him and gently laughing. He was awed, stunned and stupefied by the Sadhuji's holy presence. His mind bowed itself in reverence. The Sadhuji told him in Hindi, "Swamiji, rest here. We have to talk." Priyanath answered, "Maharaj, why are you calling me 'Swamiji'? I am not a sannyasi!" The Sadhuji then said, "Swamiji, why are you denying My words? No one denies Our words. The land from where the people come, they speak the language of that land; so I also called you in that type of language. Why be so displeased?" (Some time before this event, because of the deaths of his wife and daughter, Priyanath was freed from the ties of worldly life.)** He began to delight in conversing with this unusual Sadhu, and, in the noble attitude of His speaking, His excellent logic and beautiful manner, he was amazed to find an amazing similarity with his own Guru. When the subject came up and Swamiji came to know that the Sadhuji was Guru Sri Sri Lahiri Mahasaya's Gurudev, Sri Sri Mahamuni Babaji Maharaj, he became completely overcome, and with a grateful heart prostrated at the Feet of his Paramgurudev. Satisfied with his humility, thorough enquiry and service, the Wise, Knower of All Things Mahavatar Paramgurudev blessed him and said laughingly, "So, you wrote the Gita because of your Guru; now write a little something because of Me." Astonished, and wondering how it was possible that He would know about the fact of the Gita publication, Swamiji asked what it is that he would have to do. Babaji Maharaj said, "Write something about the unity of eastern and western philosophy, so that especially the people living in the West can become aware of that matter through that book." Hearing this directive, Priyanath seemed to become a little daunted and said, "Maharaj, I didn't study all that much and I don't know very much. How can it be possible for me to do this heroic work?" Immediately upon hearing his words, the Blissful Babaji Maharaj loudly laughed and said, "Hey, who can do what? Why this feeling of being so responsible, or why so self-concerned? The feeling came to my mind—it expressed through my mouth—you heard—the work will also happen—Whose work it is, He does." His Holiness Paramgurudev's beautiful explanation filled Swamiji's mind with wonder, belief and enthusiasm. With a reverent heart and head bowed, he received Guru's directive with his whole being. Then he asked, "I have to see You after I finish the book. Where will I find You then?" With affection towards His devotee, Babaji Maharaj said with His usual gentle laugh, "We will meet." When the discussion on the matter was finished and as Priyanath prepared to leave, Babaji Maharaj hinted at something particular—in a kind of riddle—about His disciple, our Supremely Holy Lord Sri Sri Lahiri Mahasaya. Although Priyanath could not take the meaning of that to heart, he put it in memory, and taking the blessings of Paramguru upon his head, came to Sriguru's house in Benares, his consciousness overflowing with ecstatic bliss.

*The parentheses and the text within are from the original.
**The parentheses and the text within are from the original.

Paying homage to Sriguru's Feet, Priyanath related to Yogiraj his story in joy and enthusiasm about his experiences at the Kumbhamela, including his meeting and talks with His Holiness Sri Sri Babaji Maharaj. He expressed the hint-statement that Babaji Maharaj had made (the gist of which was: "this life is finished..."),* as the subject came up. Immediately after hearing this, the ever-blissful form and beautiful body of the Lord instantly became a stern and stone-like figure. The entire body became pale-gray; there was a terrible silence. The current of bliss among the devotees present stopped. All were gaping with tremendous suspense. The Guru-surrendered Priyanath, afraid, anxious and at a loss for what to do, began to blame himself. Those who had not for one moment ever seen the Lord out of His blissful demeanor, seemed to have a horrible desperation well up within them. And there was no one to give peace or courage. After three long hours passed in this way, His Holiness the Lord returned to His normal Self. Everyone breathed a sigh of relief. The devotees present once again became enraptured by the Beloved Lord's easy and beautiful manner, conversation and teaching, as if nothing had happened. It was known later that with the help of that hint, the Lord understood the directive for His imminent departure from the body. The pull of physical existence can, if only for a moment, temporarily arrest the attention of even jivamukta (fully liberated while in the body) beings. That is strange indeed! Swarasvahi bidushohapi tatharudhohavinabeshah. In any case, the unwavering Yogibara Munibara Lord was once again in samadhic absorption in the Ocean of Bliss, and returned to His natural, death-vanquishing state of Grace.

With the blessing of Paramgurudev and having possessed the title of Swami, Srimat Priyanath Kararswami returned to Srirampur and, as per Babaji Maharaj's instructions, began to think about composing the new spiritual treatise. He previously had a desire to go to Paris for an exhibition. He began to study French for that and acquired skill in the language in only six months. Thinking about the glory of India and feeling himself to be an ordinary representative of India, he wrote a book in French based on his study of the essence of the Christian religion. In order to learn French, he used to often mingle with the Christian missionaries of Chandannagar. One day, he took the manuscript of the book and showed it to a missionary. That Christian missionary looked through the book and saw that in it there was a new understanding and perspective of their religious scripture, the Bible, as it pertained to the arrival of Lord Jesus, His sadhana, education, the wondrous experiences of His companions etc. and in the fundamental, spiritual elements. The missionary sahib felt that these conclusions would cause harm to the ordinary, sectarian belief of the Christians. The sahib said that he wanted to look at the manuscript in more detail and kept it. And he said, "This will cause an upheaval in the Christian world." Because of circumstances, Swamiji Maharaj could not go to the foreign country; he also did not try to get that manuscript back for a long time. Later, when he went to get the manuscript, the sahib said in circuitous ways, "I've lost it somewhere. I can't find it." It is our misfortune and a loss for the world that we had to be deprived of such a magnificent discovery of truth. Some time later, we tried but could not find any of the papers on that matter.

One night at an auspicious time, he meditated upon the blessings of the spiritual lineage, especially the beneficent wish, directive and encouragement of Paramgurudev, and while going through the process of analyzing the essence of the spiritual treatises of the east and west, he arrived at a framework of the substantial elements for the composition of the new book. He began to create Sanskrit sutras based on the unifying conclusions of eastern philosophy and sadhana, and alongside those sutras, he wrote down the corresponding western spiritual material that expressed the same understanding, using quotations from the Bible and explaining their underlying meaning in English. Swamiji Maharaj's disciples, Howrah's prominent barristers Sri Narayan Chandra Ganguly and Sri Nilananda Chattopadhyay Mahasaya especially helped in the writing of the English part of this book. The name of the book became "Holy Science" or "Kaivalya Darshanam." From having had discussions with His Holiness Swamiji Maharaj, I came to know that some of the gist of the previous book in French was in this "Kaivalya Darshanam." The publisher of "Kaivalya Darshanam," who was a disciple of Maharajji and an executive of Sadhu Sabha, as well as a landlord of Bhandarhati and a native of Khidirpur, Roy Atul Chandra Choudhury Mahasaya wrote in the dedication section: "This Book is the true Philosophy of Religion. It was compiled…to establish the truth that there is an essential unity in the basis of all religion,…the teachings of the Bible itself…are perfectly non-sectarian. To show that the Holy Bible wholly teaches pure Sanatan Dharma, the Eternal Religion of the Indian Sadhus, I have collected these parts and published it in book form so that the religious public may not be misguided by the mistaken ideas of sectarianism which we think is the curse of Religion in its true sense.

"The Sanskrit sutras of the book, having reconciled all the different schools of Indian philosophy, will be also a great help in the study of Bhagabat Gita, the highest book in philosophy and theology in the present world."*

*The quoted material is written in English in the original book of Swami Satyananda (probably copied from the "Holy Science" manually), followed by a Bengali translation. Only some spelling mistakes of English words (the Sanskrit untouched) have been corrected and some commas have been added. The ellipses were indicated in the original by asterisks. Otherwise, the text is literally the same as what is in the original, including the capitalization of words etc.

The author Swamiji Maharaj wrote in the beginning of the book:

Chaturnabatyuttarashatabarshe gate dwaparasya prayagkshetre
Sadarshanavijnanamanvayartham paramgururajasyajnantuprapta
Kararbamshya Priyanathswami Kadambini Kshetranathatmajena
Hitaya vishwasya vidagdhatrishnaih pranitam darshakaivalyametat

In the 194 year of the Dvapara-Yuga, in the Prayag, in order to analyse the teaching of the six systems of philosophy, having obtained the permission of the Lord Parama-Guru, Priyanatha Svami of the family of Karar, son of Kadambini and Kshetranath, presents this `Darsha-Kaivalya' for the welfare of the world.

One morning when the writing of the book was completed, upon coming out of the water after bathing in the Ganges at Raighat, he was amazed and greatly delighted to see Paramaradhya Babaji Maharaj by the trunk of a tree next to the riverbank. After paying homage to His Feet, he humbly invited Paramgururajji to grace his home nearby with the dust of His Feet, to which Babaji Maharaj replied, "We are under-the-tree people. We like to sit under trees." When all forms of petition were to no avail and Paramgurumaharaj did not comply with Swamiji's request to leave His seat by the tree-trunk, Swamiji hurried home, changed his clothes and obtained some milk and sweets with which he came back to the bank of the Ganges. But not seeing the Sadhuji by the tree trunk or anywhere nearby, he was surprised and hurt. He tried to enquire and search numerous times by the riverbank and in places beside it, but all attempts were fruitless. Those who were at the bank before said that they had not seen anyone who fit that description whether by the tree trunk or anywhere nearby. In a short while, Swamiji remembered Paramgurudev's words of assurance. His Holy Appearance occurred on the very day of the completion of the book that was done under His direction. Momentarily overcome with disappointment, discouragement and sorrow, after a while it dawned on Swamiji that this was the Knowledge-bestowing, devotee-loving Paramgururaj's supernatural method of teaching His yogic wealth, and immediately upon realizing this, the grateful devotee, speechless in his understanding, reverently received the full power of Guru's blessing.

Guroh kripahi kevalam

The Guru's Grace alone is (sufficient).

ORGANIZATION AND PROPAGATION

When Munibara Sri Sri Shyamacharan Lahiri Mahasaya was no longer present, His significant disciples began to attend to the spreading of the priceless method of Kriyayoga sadhana in ways that would be according to His wishes. Our His Holiness Sri Guru Maharaj was also thinking about the proper way to propagate the Guru-given method of sadhana. At first, he gave Kriyayoga knowledge to his close friends in a friendly manner. It has been heard that Srirampur's eminent barrister, the late Akshay Kumar Bhattacharya was his first friend-disciple. While doing Gita recitations and commentary, in order to propagate the Guru-given words of Truth he began to think about forming a Gita sabha (Gita fellowship). In those days, even some important and respected orthodox Brahmins of Srirampur were interested listening to his commentaries on the Gita, having heard in various situations about his credibility. But because of the narrow-minded, suffocating, snake-like entanglements of the prevalent societal attitude, they were not courageous enough to break the rules of the set ideas of that time, including the impropriety of attending discussions on sacred subjects at the house of and by a man—although knowledgeable—from a non-Brahmin lineage. At a time of untruth in a society devoid of sadhana—in this pure and sagacious land of Truth seeking sadhakas and divinely visionary sages—what lameness this was from such subjugated mentality! It is when repentant Indians want atonement according to God's will and become practitioners of Truth and discipline can this sin be dispelled and beneficence manifested. Later, we saw that in that same Srirampur, the Brahmin community in the Sanskrit school called him "Dwijabara" [Brahmin] and cordially invited him for the cultivation of their learning. Only through atonement and education can man eradicate illiberality in the mind and become virtuous. In any case, regardless of the inconvenience of the "frog in the well" attitude of society at the time, he began to do his work regularly at an appropriate place. Those who appreciated virtue would come to the fellowship and joyfully discuss the subjects. After a while, the sabha continued on at his house with no obstructions.

With the help of the scriptural discussions, Kriyayoga sadhana also began to spreads lowly and gradually . Fascinated by its merits, Brahmins and non-Brahmins—seekers from all levels of society were now receiving initiation from him. Eventually, with the increasing membership of executive and ordinary members, he began to feel that there was a need to form a non-sectarian spiritual institution. At this time, nearby in Chatra was an enthusiastic Brahmin-born seeker named Sri Motilal Mukhopadhyay, who was overcome with spiritual longing and whose search for a guru, upon hearing his words, ulti-mately brought him to Swamiji Maharaj. The Truth-seeking Brahmin youth was captivated by the scientific discussion and analysis of scrip-tures. He surmised that the Satchitananda filled Brahman-substance for which he had desperately yearned could be found in this realized being. Respect, determination and aspiration filled his heart. He forgot about the divisions of caste, as well as the narrow-mindedness and boundaries of society, and having directly experienced the touch of the Guru's divinity within this mahapurush, he took Shelter in the master. Sri Motilal was initiated in Kriya yoga. From an ordinary viewpoint, this deed of Motilal's was considered courageous. How much degra-dation he had to withstand from society, country and relatives because of this. Disciplined in Truth and steadfast in consciousness, the sad-haka Motilal boldly said up until the last days of his life, "Knowledge of the Brahman-substance is priceless. Where is caste in this? I received Knowledge of Brahman from one who was established in Brahman and in doing so maintained the honor of the virtue of magnanimous sages; I received God's blessings; after the touch of the divine Light of Brahman Consciousness, I understood the eternal relationship of guru and disciple."

The appearance of Sri Motilal assumed a significant place in the life of the propagator and great Acharya Swamiji Maharaj. Through the intermediary role of the disciple Motilal, many enquiring people received initiation from him. At this time, the establishment of a pow-erful spiritual group by some passionate youth and middle aged peo-ple from Calcutta and Khidirpur who were acquaintances and followers of the sadhaka Motilal greatly enhanced Swamiji Maharaj's desired propagation work. Enthralled by the sadhana-discipline and the dutifulness of the groups of sadhakas—Amulya—Charu—Shyam etc.—from Khidirpur, he would say from time to time, "Khidirpur is my right hand." The people of Khidirpur are forever fortunate in having received Guru's grace.

Srirampur's Gita Sabha took on a special appearance upon the arrival of Sri Motilal. Due to the influence of the enthusiastic Motilal's organizational capabilities, all areas became orderly. Appropriate workers were found. A press was obtained for the propagation of philosophical and astrological explanations of scriptures, the methodology of the almanac and the mission, work and ideology of the fellowship. Swamiji transformed his large, two-story building in Srirampur into an ashram, naming it "Priyadham." Work management, propagation, gathering people etc.—the responsibility of all matters were put upon Motilal. Through the skilled Motilal's care, Priyadham matured into a vital work and spiritual center. We heard Swamiji Maharaj say, "At the root of these fellowships and congregations is Motibabu. If it weren't for him, none of these organizations would happen." With the intention of having a non-sectarian designation, the sabha was named "Satsanga Samaj." It was written in the mission statement: "The Universe-Brahmanda-pervading Source of All, the Brahman-substance Reality has been named by luminary sages as Truth. The goal of attaining the company of that Universal Truth-substance along with providing an environment for sadhana matters comprises the mission of this institution, etc. Those who are involved in the sadhana functions are executive members and those involved in the discussions of holy books, gathering in discussions of Truth, and helping in the many different works of this fellowship are normal members."

A while after the sabha was up and running, invitations on paper were sent out to call everyday people for a great conference on behalf of the Satsanga Samaj. The leading members of society had consulted and agreed in meetings of the fellowship that they would participate at the conference, but upon receiving the letter, many of them refused to come. The executive members of the sabha were unprepared for this sudden change of mind. Later, investigating the cause brought out the reason that they did not accept the invitations because of the usage of the word "Samaj," believing that this would be another segregating organization along the lines of "Brahmo Samaj" or "Arya Samaj." Immediately after this was known, the word "Samaj" was removed and replaced with "Sabha." Now, the name of the fellowship became "Satsanga Sabha"; therefore no one had any objections any longer about joining it. Using the name "Priyanath Kararswami," he began to preside over the fellowship in the form of Acharya.

Even after his Gurudev's departure from the body, Swamiji regularly visited Benares. Why should devotees renounce opportunities to have the divine experience of the ever-alive Presence and Grace of Guru-Shakti in Guru's house in the spiritual arena of Benares, the land of knowledge? Swamiji stayed at his aged mother's house, who had been living there. For scriptural study, especially detailed discussions on astrological treatises, he would go back and forth to certain significant scholars of Benares.

One day, he was sitting with the principal mahasaya of Benares' Sanskrit College when two German scholars arrived there. They introduced themselves to the principal mahasaya and said that even while in Germany, they became attracted to India's immense culture and civilization and proceeded to study philosophical books written in Sanskrit, the root Aryan language. Finding out about the holy sages' conclusive discoveries on essential matters, they came as seekers of Truth with the utmost respect and humility in their hearts to the guru of the world, India, and particularly to the principal of the highest educational institution in Benares, India's greatest center of knowledge, in the hope of receiving some illuminating knowledge. The principal mahasaya cordially received the German gentlemen and informed them of a time when they could meet for discussions. For the further benefit of the foreign scholars, the principal mahasaya also invited Swamiji to be present at that time.

At the appointed time, the German gentlemen arrived at the Sanskrit College for the meeting with the principal mahasaya. As previously arranged, Swamiji Maharaj was also present to greet them, after which everyone sat down and the scriptural discussion commenced. The German scholars presented numerous questions and the principal mahasaya, knowledgeable in many shastras, recited examples with quotes from all kinds of scriptures with all sorts of footnotes, commentaries, statements etc., and kept trying to solve their enquiries in this way. Listening with deep attention to the principal mahasaya's deliberation, the German students from time to time would say, "We have studied these words and footnotes but we have come here especially seeking the experience of the heart, or the essence, of these things. Please help us to understand the true, inner meaning of these priceless sayings and realizations of these great beings." No matter how much the respected and scholarly principal lectured on the many scriptures, the foreign student-scholars, questioning and energetically enthusiastic, could not be satisfied in their hearts and again said, "We are fascinated by the illustrious scriptural statements but the deep significance of the shastras that we seek to absorb in our hearts—we don't seem to be achieving that." After the lengthy discussion that day, the principal mahasaya set an appointment for another day. The curious Swamiji Maharaj this time came to the appointed place on his own volition on this second day and greeted the foreign truth-seeking gentlemen. After appropriate salutations to the principal mahasaya, the discussions began. On this day, it seemed that the scope of scriptural talk from the principal took on oceanic breadth and depth. He stupefied the listeners by his explanations using the statements and deductions of indigenous and foreign sages. The discourse was filled with gravity. The German scholar-students were also stunned. But the entire shastra-ocean ultimately did not satisfy them. They wanted the hidden nectar flowing in the ocean, the ambrosia from the ocean's churning, the arising of direct experience of the Light of Knowledge—or at least the shedding of some light with scientific analysis, with the aid of which they could possibly taste a little of the immortal elixir of Brahman-experience that the Truth-seeing sages had. Reverent of India—the guru of the world— her sages and her luminescence, the foreign scientist-students brokenheartedly gave their salutations and quietly prepared to leave. Swamiji, quietly observing and saddened by all of this, followed to help them board their vehicle. Upon their departure, the sullen German scholars asked him, "Is there no sadhaka or scholar in this sacred land of sages that can grant us a little illumination through direct experience, and have us comprehend the essence of these incredible treatises?" Regardless of being embarrassed at witnessing the tarnished pride of his country in the present day, India's child Swamiji Maharaj remembered India's eternal and luminous glory and succinctly answered, "Of course there are, but they somewhat live in secrecy." There was no more opportunity to speak. After saying their farewells, everyone returned to their own places.

This event left a significant mark in Swamiji Maharaj. Envisioning the rescue of India's lost glory, he began to think of ways to that the organization might be of use. How the shastras, particularly the spiritual and philosophical treatises could be a part of discussions in life through education, how the essential matters could manifest in usual intellectual talk, and how the knowledge of the scriptures could cause the sadhaka to proceed toward direct experience—he began to conceptualize processes relating to these issues. He determined in his mind that the logical, experiential and scientific perspective must be established at the root of the Satsanga Sabha's education programs, sadhana, discussions, propagation etc. in order to bring to life the knowledge of the shastras for the sanctity of the Soul and the benevolence of the world.

While cultivating the science of astrology, Swamiji saw that it was in a decrepit state. He was fascinated by the astrological calculations and consequences thereof as concluded upon by the shastras, but could not find an existing treatise that helped to realize the application of those conclusions in an easy or vital manner. Whether philosophical, astrological, or some other kind of significant shastra, all of these only spoke of the amazing resolutions of the sages attained by sadhana, investigation and cultivation, but a simple way or method of practicing the techniques, the processes of sadhana, or scientific analysis were lost somewhere. Because of this, the deliberations on shastras and the understanding of them—not having any living application in the present day—were being expressed only through memory and recitation. Swamiji believed and agreed with the opinions of historical scholars that because of political changes, abuse and pillaging, many priceless and essential books of knowledge had disappeared. It is necessary for Indians to do intense sadhana so that those fragmented memories may be restored.

Examining the calculations and the consequential results from them, he saw that changes had taken place in the lunar days and constellations since the time the ancient astrologers had written down their conclusions thousands of years ago, but the present-day astrological books continued on without accounting for these changes, and it seemed to indicate that reference books like almanacs etc. were written with formulations riddled with these errors. He used to say, "How can the astrologically based rites in the scriptures to be performed during certain lunar days and certain positions of constellations bear fruit in relation to the progress of time? To form an iron into shape one must strike it while it looks like blood, but if the appropriate time passes, then even thousands of strikes will not yield that result. That is the state of our rituals. The occasions are set according to the almanac, but the root of the almanac is wrong." He felt that a working knowledge of astrology was a necessary part of human life. Thus, he decided on having discussions on the practical applications of astrology as part of the work of the Satsanga Sabha. Because of the perspective and desire of the learned, and following scriptural injunctions to do benevolent work at auspicious times, he calculated with the corrected formulae: two equinoxes (approximately the 9th of Ashwin and the 9th of Chaitra at present)* and two solstices (approximately the 9th of Ashar and the 9th of Poush at present)** during which times he would inaugurate prescripts of the Satsanga Sabha. Therefore, with pure calculation, with the accepted beginning of the year [Bengali] on the 1st of Baishakh after the great equinox—at present 9/10 of Chaitra is possible.*** He said, "In a little while, through free thinking and logic, the learned will find the significance of this correction in the astrological culture, but then my earthly body will not be here. We also saw that employed under the government of free India, the astrological scholars adopted Swamiji Maharaj's ascertainment of equinoxes and solstices along with the year's beginning.

* The parentheses and the text are in the original.
**The parentheses and the text are in the original.
***The sentence could not be stated differently without it becoming interpretive.

He returned from Benares and continued to direct the affairs of the Satsanga Sabha. He became especially involved in the cultivation of the studies of the almanac and the ephemeris. Even after the consultations on astrological culture with scholars in Benares and successfully proving his own understanding, because of the prevalent blind beliefs and lack of first hand experience among people, he could not find any significant opportunities to correct the errors in the astrological calculations in practice. At this time, upon hearing about the great renown of the astrologer from Orissa, the late Pandit Chandrakanta Shiromani Mahasaya, he left for Puri. Because the scholar was not in Puri at that time, Swamiji presented his findings to the group of scholars that were present there. Even though they found his conclusions flawless, the learned group still said, "Without the approval of our country's greatest pundit, Sriyukta Shiromani Mahasaya, we cannot accept any conclusions fully." A few months later, it was decided that a fellowship of study would be founded under the direction of Shiromani Mahasaya. Swamiji Maharaj arrived in Puri at the appointed time and found, to his grave sorrow, that suddenly the great Pandit Shiromani Mahasaya, the jewel of Orissa, had left his body. All of Orissa's almanacs were composed under the calculations established by Shiromani Mahasaya. Swamiji used to say, "Although there are many more changes and corrections that need to be made, it seems that the calculations of the almanacs in use in Orissa are more accurate than the present calculations from other lands. About the distant villager Shiromani Mahasaya's eminence, he once said, as the subject came up, that while practicing common astrology, the astrologer Pandit Mahasaya came to feel that deep research was necessary for the discovery of many things at the present time. Following through, he took some ordinary pieces of glass and some pieces of wood with which he created an unremarkable instrument, which helped him to calculate and establish the locations of the zodiac and constellations in the cosmos and left us amazed. At the eve of his life, upon hearing about his accomplishments, the eminent professor and astrologer in the Katak College, Yogeshchandra Vidyanidhi Mahasaya, had him explore the cosmos, looking through the college's telescope. The astonished and captivated Brahmin scholar of little financial means was taken aback for a moment at the revelation of this glory so far hidden from him, and then like a child, he ecstatically said, "Oh my! If I had such close access to an instrument as this at the morning or midday of my life, then how many mysteries I could have solved! But now it's the day's end." The progenitress of gems—how many of Mother India's jewel-like children, unknown and unrecognized, soiled by the dust of life, are disappearing in the bowels of time.

Although Swamiji Maharaj did not find success with his desired goal in Puri, the form of the huge ocean in the land of Jagannath [Puri] enraptured his mind. He obtained a piece of land in the Swargadwar village by the sea from the local municipality's board, stating that he wished to establish an educational center specializing in astrology and philosophical-spiritual studies. In the month of Chaitra of the year 1310 at the time of the holy great equinox, a small ashram-house was founded at this place. Swamiji Maharaj named the ashram: "Kararashram," in keeping with the identity by which he was known amongst people. Keeping in mind that the meaning of "Karar" was "servant," and in memory of his lineage—the ashram's name would be referred to in both ways. After he adopted the life of sannyas, he used to instruct the usage of the "servant" definition.

While he was disseminating the Kriyayoga sadhana method as authorized by lineage and the wisdom of the scriptures, he met the president of the Sri Bharat Dharma Mahamandal, Srimat Swami Jnananandaji Maharaj. Surmising Swamiji Maharaj's sharp intellect and brilliance, Jnanananda Swamiji Maharaj gave him advice during a conversation that it was good to be initiated according to prescribed edicts as a sannyasi in order to propagate this kind of spiritual work properly. Doing this would bring the good wishes of everyone, beneficence would come to one's own life through one's own experience, as well as allowing the work of Acharya to be directed according to scriptures and in an orderly fashion. This advice seemed valuable to the traveling Acharya, Srimat Kararswami Mahodaya. He made haste and arrived at Buddha-Gaya to meet with its Mahanta, the Venerable Srimat Swami Krishnadayal Giri Maharaj. While describing his work, Swamiji mentioned that there was one special prescript in the fellowship which he founded: no one would be addressed as "Babu" or "Mister"; instead, whether the name was Bengali or English or any language, the prename "Sriyukta" would be used. Hearing this, the Mahanta Maharaj happily said, "This is a novel thing today, because when a gentleman's name is written, especially in English, it doesn't even arise in anyone's mind to use the Indian "Sri" or "Sriyukta." For this reason, I am now declaring this sacred statement as a sadhu: Let it be that your name in the Shelter of Sannyas is 'Sriyukteshvar Giri'." Receiving the Knowledge of Non-dualism from his sannyas-guru and experiencing the blessings of the supreme renunciate Jagadguru Sri Shankaracharyadeva, the vessel of knowledge Swamiji was now firmly established in Knowledge by this blessed societal ritual.

Acharya of the Era, Swamiji Maharaj gave salutations to Sriguru and returned to his ordained place of work. We have seen that many follow the usual procedure [for writing or saying someone's name informally] and drop the "Sri" and say only "Yukteshvar," but this is not correct. If one wants to put a "Sri" at the beginning as in the prevalent fashion, then his name would look as: "Sri Sriyukteshvar Giri."

To rise above the small-mindedness of sectarianism and unify spirituality was his life's resolve. Dedicated to this cause, he personally met acharyas from different sects and for the same stated purpose, he formed a fellowship of sadhus from all of India and appointed the head of Puri's Gobardhan Peeth, Jagadguru Srimat Madhusudan Tirthaswami Shankaracharya Maharaj, to govern over the fellowship. As directed by the sadhus, in order to spread the universal religion [Sanatan Dharma] free of sectarianism and narrow-thinking, a fellowship that would carry out this work was created named "Sadhu Sabha." Swamiji Maharaj began to be known as "Sadhusabhapati", having taken the position as president of the fellowship. The main place of work was established in Srirampur's Priyadham. The work was to be carried out by the president, assistant-president, Sadhu Sabha's executives, consultant, editor of the paper etc.; with all this, the Sadhu Sabha was formed. Arrangements were made to publish "Sadhu Samvad," a periodical that would carry articles in Bengali and English on astrology, almanac study and numerous spiritual matters. With the goal of propagation work, the Calcutta Satsanga Sabha was established on Calcutta's Jeletola Street in the house of the publisher of the "Indian Mirror" periodical, the disciple Narendranath Basu Mahasaya, along with Rai Bahadur Radhacharan Pal and other such distinguished devotees and disciples. Thereafter, according to the new rules, the Satsanga Sabhas in Srirampur, Khidirpur, Calcutta, Benares, Jamalpur, Kanpur, Puri etc., in Bengal and other provinces, adopted the format of the Sadhu Sabha and went on to function well.

It was proposed that in order to excel in the ordained work of sadhus, three ashrams should be established to accommodate the different ages and levels of the sadhakas from Sadhu Sabha. Those who were in the first stages of sadhana, meaning beginners who would live as celibates [Brahmacharis], they were to be in Puri's Kararashram. The students would stay there up to about the age of twenty-five. For those that wanted to continue after finishing here onto the second level, or would accept the ways of a sadhaka, a house was rented in Benares and founded as "Pranabashram." It was decided that here there would be a proper printing press, as well as an environment for interactive gatherings and facilitation of advanced instruction, education and practice of the spiritual path. At this time, meaning the second stage of the sadhaka's life, the sadhakas, living as sadhakas, would serve the public according to the fellowship's rules, for the benefit of body, mind and soul. For this work in Benares, he received the company and help of his Guru-brother-disciple, the disciple of Sri Sri His Holiness Yogiraj and author of the "Pranab Gita", the eminent Swami Pranabananda Giri Maharaj. For those who were advanced on the path of sadhana and attained some permanence in it, meaning the initial stages of being a siddha, and when usually one would have passed the age of fifty, a "siddha" ashram was proposed to be founded in Hrishikesh by the seven rivers in the Himalayan foothills, the land of meditation, for living the ideal of a self-surrendered spiritual life filled with the Paramatman-substance. But it was also instructed that the sadhakas of all stages would be attentive to education and service with the ideal of purity of consciousness. The aim of work for the fellowships carrying the identity, or the branches of and with the Satsanga Sabha, became: to provide proper education for boys and girls, avail satsanga for youth to discuss high matters and read sacred books, and give older people an opportunity for spiritual cultivation. That the propagation of Kriyayoga sadhana was a primary issue, need not be said.

Usually, just sitting in asana and doing japa with mantra or practicing yoga alone does not build a proper life of righteousness and it is also not possible. He frequently said that if the entire human being, body and mind, is not dedicated and directed towards elevation, then the ascension of the soul cannot happen. For this, it is necessary to discard the rubbish in all areas of human life and to adopt a new and transformed perspective founded upon scientific principles. In ordinary, simple words, he used to say from time to time, "Living life easily, playing and laughing is success of course. But underneath all of it, one must remember to not cheat oneself—above all be true to thyself—* meaning, always remain authentic."

*The phrase within the dashes is written in English in the original.

Without the aid of political power, even making excellent and proper arrangements of every kind for sadhana is not enough to do work successfully for the benefit of society . Understanding this, he used to speak of the wretchedness of subservience. We heard him say many times that it was not possible to attain humaneness unless the glory of nation and people were maintained. He saw the servants of the nation with eyes of respect. But if talk would come up about political stirrings, even though he would admit to necessity of such things, he would not think himself to be expert enough to come to any conclusions on those matters. He used to say that correct education in order to build man's character properly was the actual and ennobling work of societal, political and religious institutions. A wholehearted, nation-loving attitude—meaning, being interested in the work of constructing was a direction that attracted him. India's depth, culture, civilization, organized intellectual capacity, distribution of work, relationship with neighbors and abiding the lawful edict of the four stages of life (not only by birth)*—building a people through facilitating appropriate education based on these things are what he advised teachers over and over. While understanding the significance of lineage and the usage of rules, he would never accept proofs of ideas based on birthright and caste. His philosophy was that it was through the company of appropriate acharyas in an ashram-like educational environment that the beneficent societal work could happen, by which the divisions of caste could be brought into harmony.** He wanted to structure the ashram in Puri in this manner. He gave this very same advice when the Brahmacharya Vidyalay, led by Swamiji Maharaj's eminent disciple Swami Yoganandaji, and patronized by the late lord of Kashimbazar, Maharaja Manindra Chandra Nandi Bahadur, was founded. When the subject of sadhakas and others spreading righteous philosophy would arise, we would hear him laud the Yugacharya Swami Vivekananda's attitude towards nationality and service. With this kind of respect, he used to mingle with his contemporaneous friends Swami Vivekananda, Swami Brahmananda and Swami Shivananda Maharajjis. Before forming the Sadhu Sabha, he approached Swami Brahmananda for the possibility of making the Satsanga Sabha a part of the Ramakrishna Mission, but with his mission and methodology. Of course, this work did not find a means to go forward.

*The parentheses and the text within are in the original.

**The sentence had to be more loosely translated than the rest of the book in order to make sense. The translator apologizes for this, but maintains that the original intention in Bengali is preserved.

For educational institutions, he established a syllabus for scientific knowledge, particularly: physics, physiology, physical geography, astronomy and astrology.* He was very attracted to the many things we need to learn from western residential educational facilities and their psychologically based ideas and structure. Keeping in mind the educationally related issues of civility, truthfulness, servitude and self-sufficiency, he taught us that vocations such as farming and cowherd-ing, knowledge of spinning wheels, looms, sewing etc. and simple arts and crafts, nursing, physical exercise and, according to age, martial arts were necessary and worthy of being a part of formal education. The dissemination of knowledge through the mother tongue [Bengali], the Indian national language Hindi and the prevalent ruler's language, as well as the language that would maintain the link with the knowl-edge and wisdom of other countries—English—programs to teach these languages were also a part of his written syllabus. Eventually added to the curriculum were programs to study Gita, philosophical treatises, high-level astrology etc. The reader must remember that these syllabuses were presented in the Christian year 1900. One has to be amazed when contemplating the farsighted vision and profound knowledge of the Acharya of the Era Swamiji Maharaj. According to age, capacity and ordinary knowledge, he organized the teaching of yogic asanas, mudras and pranayam, as well as recitation of hymns and salutary verses for the physical and mental improvement of stu-dents. He set up a procedure where the student, upon passing the test for completion of the first part of Swamiji's prescribed curriculum and completing research and experimental studies in general subjects, would be given the title "Vidyatirtha," and later, upon finishing the studies in specific subjects, would be given the title "Shastri" (such as: Vijnanshastri [scholar of science], Darshanshastri [scholar of philoso-phy], etc.).** He also expressed the wish that, at the end of institutional education, students would travel to many countries by water, land and sky, and having gained numerous experiences from such exploration would complete the educational goal of this organization. The general public could not even conceive of traveling by airplane at that time. But through astrological calculations and sensing the evolution of man after the change of Yugas in the development of subtle electrical and etheric sciences, he envisioned and firmly believed that, because of the power of the progressive new age, very soon airplane travel would become a regular affair.

*The educational subjects are written in the original in English and Bengali, except "astronomy," which is written only in Bengali.
**The parentheses and the text within are in the original, except for the brackets and bracketed text which are the translator's.

He used to say that for the collective and individual prosperity of human beings, it was necessary to have the self-sufficiency of the Vaishyas [commerce caste], the valor of the Kshatriyas [military and administration caste] and, in that same type of environment, the Brahmin [priest and scholar caste] establishment of religion. Without having personal experience of the company of high and virtuous beings, it was not possible in life to have the elevated injunction of the service oriented mind of the Sudras [service caste]. Having lost the root meaning of the practice of the four stages of life, the superficial, vanity-filled children of this sacred land have become unworthy of even being Sudras. Instead of being prosperous servants, the culture has become one of boot-licking, incompetent and vile slaves.

There could not be the proper practice of education, nation building, or even the Knowledge of Brahman, he said over and over, without the realization of the Kshatriya-power. Of course, his statement about Kshatriya-power did not infer only to training for war. He would say that without having a feeling of self-respect, humanness could not take birth, and in order to maintain self-worth and to strengthen and better the national spine, it was very necessary to have regular martial educa-tion. How can a spine-broken, weak and shy, slave-minded "good per-son" conceive the immense revelations of the sages? In relating to this subject, we remember the great Acharya Swami Vivekananda's renown statement: "In trying to follow the Sattvic [pure] way, Indians have become drowsy with Tamasic [inertia] stupor." Is it not so that the invaluable and appropriate unified insights for the age, by the great Acharyas of the Age were not, by themselves, able to make us properly aware? It is for this reason that he used to instruct that before initiation into the pranayam-based yoga of Kriya, the student should test himself to ascertain whether his physical and mental conditioning was in an optimum state; and he was usually not a proponent of initiation into Kriyayoga sadhana before the age of 16/17 years and if there was a lack of physical fitness. Before that, he would advise that one should pay attention to the study and respectful practice of yogic asanas and mudras. Relating to this subject, the illuminated words of insight from the world-conquering Acharya Vivekananda come to mind: "If you want to understand the Gita, first go and play football."

When teaching social servants and counselors about education, he would ask them to arrange for the general cultivation of medicine, herbology, astrology and philosophy. Meditation, study and the treasure-house of Brahman—these three things are at the root of all teaching and education. In all educational programs, he would prescribe that the study of music should have a special place. He used to say from time to time that among all that captured the senses, the melody of music was that which could help us realize the Brahman-melody in the inner world.

Day after day, many men and women continued to receive initiation from him. Through their invitations, he traveled to many different villages of India, especially in Bengal, and established Satsanga Sabhas. The Sabhas' work was carried out with the ideals and intentions described previously. At least once a week, he would regularly have a meeting with the members and, after having discussed the sacred scriptures, sadhana, worship and such subjects, he would advise that each person be a helper or servant to each other. He also gave instructions for a program to be held at least once a year for extended discussion and analysis by a group of learned people about holy matters, involving the general people of each Sabha's township in a large yearly conference. He used to say that just discussing or practicing among ourselves could make us "frogs-in-the-well" also; we could each be a mad person in our own circle. This is why it is necessary to form holy groups among ourselves—for the health of our ideals and sadhana. For the correction of delusions arising from negligence in our own groups, for the expansion and magnanimity of mind, and to introduce everyday people to the path of Truth that we found, it was important to organize general conferences or large and inclusive gatherings.

A few years later, a certain change took place in the flow of work of Swamiji Maharaj's main disciple, Sriyukta Motilal Mukhopadhyay. One day, while on his way to his place of work in Khidirpur, at the time of boarding a train at the Srirampur station, suddenly in a bush he saw a person on the verge of death, and the inherently compassionate-servant mind in him cried out. Forgetting about the office and taking the person in his lap, he began to nurse him. It was as if he received an incredible command from within: "This service of God-in-man is a special duty for you." Motilal forgot his job, his household, his small desires. With this understanding, it was as if he became a new person, and he prepared himself for the service of the downtrodden. He remained as a householder with wife, son and daughter, but it seemed that he surrendered the responsibility of managing the family to Sriguru-God. He established an institution of service that was set up for the aid of the distressed by the banks of the Ganges near Srirampur in the village of Chatra, called "Bhaktashram." The servant of God-in-man, Motilal's household needs were also being met regularly and properly. The flow of his sadhana became intense along with this work. The Light of Brahman from the advanced stages of Kriyayoga sadhana made him luminous. Although the work of Motilal's newly established ashram was not very connected to him, His Holiness Guru Swamiji Maharaj took Motilal near him and seeing the blossoming of the bliss of Divine Knowledge in his disciple, joyfully and proudly bestowed upon this advanced and deserving disciple the power of Acharya and the responsibility of giving Kriya yoga initiation. Eventually, many men and women would be attracted to Motilal Thakur's eminence and take discipleship under him. His renown was especially widespread around Ghatal Mahakuma in the district of Medinipur. Due to the zeal of the sadhakas and having received blessings of the lineage of Sriguru, he founded an ashram named "Gurudham" for sadhana and worship right next to his own house. He used to represent himself as a servant of Satchitananda at this time. Devotees would address him reverently as "Satchitananda Swami."

Through Acharya Motilal Thakur, the reputation of Gurudev Sadhusabhapati Swamiji Maharaj was growing, and upon the desperate call of the men and women seekers from the Medinipur district, His Holiness Swamiji Maharaj established different Satsanga Sabhas and continued the propagation of teaching in a simple way the easier aspects of the manifestation of the new age and the practice of sad-hana. Formerly disregarded, distant villagers became freed of their dogma by having received initiation and education from him, and with the attainment of spiritual light, they found the opportunity to have a proper, humane life and prosper. Fellowships, book presses, medical clinics and schools were established in village after village. Even His Holiness Guru Maharaj would attend their yearly festival-conferences, enlightening the eager seekers on the meanings of the scriptures and resolving many issues, as well as giving them initiation and inspiration.

Swamiji Maharaj had remembered His Holiness Sri Sri Babaji Maharaj's indication for propagation of spiritual matters in the Western world. He believed that Babaji Maharaj's directive would actualize in working form at the appropriate time. In 1910 of the Christian Era, Swami Yoganandaji (then Mukundalal),* after having advanced in Kriyayoga sadhana which he received from his father, a disciple of the Lord Lahiri Mahasaya, and later from his tutor who was also the Lord's disciple, Yogacharya Shastri Mahasaya (Hansaswami Kebalanandaji),** the dormant renunciate in him awoke and following this longing to take the path of a renunciate monk, he left his college studies and became a resident of Benares. One day in the holy pilgrim-age of Benares, in a strange way Mukundalal met a sannyasi unknown to him. Immediately at the meeting of their eyes, the stranger sannyasi touched his heart. Mukundalal felt that he had found the company of the lord of his life in the momentary touch of divine sight. Even at the sadhuji's first call, he surrendered himself at the sannyasi's feet, feeling him to be his own. In the throne of the kingdom of profound love, Swami Sriyukteshvar Giri Maharaj became established as the helms-man in the form of Guru in Mukundalal's life. His consciousness was illuminated like lightning; divine initiation was complete. The formal initiation into sannyas took place at a later time.

*The parentheses and the text within are in the original.
**The parentheses and the text within are in the original.

Mukundalal forgot about his desires, forgot about his responsibilities at his Benares residence Sri Bharat Dharma Mahamandal, forgot about his petty self-interest. He poured himself in the directed path at the eternally longed-for Feet of Sriguru. Immediately after receiving Gurudev's suggestion, he returned to Calcutta and reenlisted in college. The Acharya of the Age Swamiji Maharaj saw the possibility of the desired fulfillment of Mahamuni Babaji Maharaj's previous directive in Mukundalal. Through Gurudev's direction, Mukundalal became as if being operated like a machine and continued to experience supernatural evidence in many ways of Guru-power in sadhana, study and everyday life, and thereafter received his B.A. degree with Gurudev's full blessings. Although he had done the "fire-witnessing" on his own and initiated himself and some of his companion-friends who followed him in the past into the vows of sannyas, in 1915 of the Christian Era at the pilgrimage of Sriguru in Srirampur, he was formally initiated in the Shelter of Sannyas by Sadhusabhapati Swamiji Maharaj and became known as Swami Yogananda Giri. At Yoganandaji's leadership a group of spiritually minded youth had formed. Swamiji Maharaj thought these youth to be able to appropriately carry out the service of the Satsanga Sabha and bestowed upon Yoganandaji's hands the responsibility of the Calcutta Satsanga Sabha. Following Gurudev's wishes, Yoganandaji studied in the M.A. program for philosophical studies at Calcutta University for a while. There were a couple of professors who were also attracted to his Guru-graced dissertations on philosophical matters.

In 1916, Swami Yoganandaji found a sudden opportunity and traveled to Japan, but not staying there for very long, he quickly returned home. On the ocean liner, the sadhana-immersed Yoganandaji felt Sriguru's blessings and met a fellow traveler from a certain Western land, and upon discussions on some subjects, Yoganandaji presented to him the first, abbreviated manuscript of his well-known book, "Science of Religion." Returning home, he established the "Brahmacharya Vidyalay" with complete patronization by the lord of Kashimbazar, Rajarsikalpa Maharaja Manindrachandra Nandi Bahadur, and under the direction of Gurudev on the holy great equinox in Chaitra of 1313 (22 March, 1917).*

*The parentheses and the text within are in the original.

Shortly thereafter, Mahamuni Babaji Maharaj's instructions began to be realized under the direction of Guru Maharaj. Swami Yoganandaji attended a stellar gathering—a great conference of spirituality and religion—in 1920 in the American city of Boston. By the Grace of Guru, the powerful Swami Yogananda crossed all boundaries of narrowness and mounted the flag of India's glory in this international fellowship. Group after group of American residents received initiation in Kriya yoga from him. The Satsanga Sabha was founded in America. Mahamuni Babaji Maharaj's incredible indication, Yograj Sri Shyamacharan Lahiri Mahasaya's prediction and Sadhusabhapati Srimat Swamiji Maharaj's direction and work were now being manifested. Eventually, in the West, the Satsanga Sabha came to be known as "Yogoda Satsanga" and "Self-Realization Fellowship." In 1936, Swami Yoganandaji Maharaj returned to India and founded Yogoda Satsanga and "Sri Shyamacharan Mission." The establishment and management as well as organizational responsibilities for many regions were given to this servant-me. It should also be mentioned, when discussing propagation, the efforts at founding of sadhana-ashrams, schools and medical clinics etc. in different villages of the Medinipur district by Swamiji Maharaj's industrious disciples, Swami Bhavananda Giriji and Swami Paramananda Giriji.

Swamiji Maharaj used to usually refer to his sannyas life as the life of a servant and told his sannyasi disciples to adopt that same attitude. He would reprimand any negligence in the field of work, and at the same time give special warning to the disregarding of spiritual practice and deviating from the area of Self-Knowledge and becoming obsessed with work. He used to point out this perspective: "Serve for the purity of consciousness, but if you lose yourself then all is lost. All of the work of the world is secondary. Let the attainment of Satchitananda, the root of which is surrender to God through meditation, be the first priority. Only then can one walk on the right path."

He believed that the essential wisdom of the four stages of life as prescribed by the sages of India was the highest method for the process of ascension for human life and society. His opinion was that after the completion of learning at an ashram of brahmacharya, adopting the life of a responsible householder was the normal way to live. If anyone wanted to adopt the ideals of renunciation or became a disciplined brahmachari or sannyasi, he would advise the person to be completely committed, according to one's natural inclination, to the service of the general public until at least the age of fifty. When giving instructions for work to be done, he would say that one should be devote oneself to the service of the world beginning at sunrise—upon the completion of Soul-work at Brahmamuhurta, and that immediately at the time of sunset, one should return to one's own work, meaning that one should become immersed in spiritual sadhana and worship.

Following the directive of His Holiness the Lord [Sri Sri Shyamacharan Lahiri Mahasaya], he advised the householders to remain afar from the field of worldly duties for a few days at least once a year, and it is with this purpose that he arranged for a three-day festival in Puri's Kararashram.

It is true that if he saw skillfulness in the work of the ashram, propaga-tion and other organizational work, he would give encouragement, praise and express joy, but it seemed to us that, if we observed beyond the perspective of ordinary people, the disciples who advanced in sad-hana were able to make him much more joyful and honored. Supremely dear, his deep, affectionate blessings would naturally shower upon them. Who knows how many unknown and unrecog-nized sadhakas have received such blessings and become sanctified in Self-Knowledge and Bliss in the experience of the manifestation of the form of Self-Understanding in Sriguru's Grace.

I have mentioned before that the sadhakas and congregation of devo-tees from Khidirpur were especially able to attract him. That is why we were acquainted there with the secretive, great sadhaka (now gone to the after-world)* Sri Amulya Charan Santra Mahasaya's spiritual rise. He is not a so-called highly educated man and many times one cannot find evidence of ordinary skillfulness in speech or flowing linguistic orderliness, but, surrendering his life to Guru, this mystic sadhaka's wealth is in Guru-wisdom and sacred scriptural knowledge. We have seen vain authorities on scripture become amazed by listening to his explanation of the meanings of certain sections of the shastras from his realization through sadhana. We have understood through these events that even if we are to become knowledgeable in the wisdom of the scriptures through the usual intellectual means, it is necessary to connect that intellectual understanding with the illuminated experi-ence of yoga-united consciousness. When in the company of this soli-tary, ordinary householder and silent sadhaka Santra Mahasaya, it seems that we are receiving the holy touch of Guru's blessing in the presence of this yogi-purusha's sadhana-attained Light of Consciousness. That the supreme yogi His Holiness Sri Guru Maharaj has with great care placed the priceless gem in the body-vessel of a socially disregarded "Amulya" [priceless]—how many of our vain selves have found that? Perhaps we can excel a little in our work of fellowship, congregation, ashram and other organizational work if we, deserving of very little, can take care of Guru's spiritual touch that we receive from Santra Mahasaya's presence; and this does not cause any interruption or cause us to leave the field of Sriguru's instructed work.**

*The parentheses and the text within are in the original.
**The account of Sri Amulya Charan Santra Mahasaya, even though indicated has having passed on in the parenthetical in concordance with the previous footnote, is written in present tense in the original.

Who knows how many sadhakas from solitary villages have become realized through Sri Guru Maharajji's holy blessings. I do not think that we have truly come to know all of them. How nectarous has the flow of sadhana made the heart of the wholly dedicated sadhaka, Dr. Sri Bipin Bihari Bhuiyan (now gone to the after-world)* of Khukurdaha in the Medinipur district. And how many new sadhakas are progressing toward elevation because of having received his company. We do not know in which or how many places this precious stone of the Lord is being secretly preserved. Eager, enquiring, one-pointedly determined, the jewel-seeking sadhakas going round and round can find the universal flow of Light from the power of Sriguru and the lineage in this way. This, of course, is the root of the essential philosophical ideal of India's ancient and holy wisdom.

*The parentheses and the text within are in the original.

Dharmasyattvam nihitam guhayam

The truth of Dharma lies hidden in the heart.

ACHARYA'S PRESENCE AND THE TEACHING OF A MULTI-FACETED VISION

It seems that the timing of Acharya Swamiji Maharaj's appearance at this transitional period of a Great Era was truly appropriate. It is not an easy task to measure his immense storehouse of knowledge, but, in our understanding, we can find quite enough statement of the realized sages' subtle and farsighted visionary qualities in him. The scientific and open-hearted mentality of the newly manifested age was revealed in his words. The appropriate path of progress and the proper steps for advancement were the specialties of his skillful work and teaching. This is why he would become elated at seeing the enthusiasm and drive of the youth, and while advising to keep the young ones rightly disciplined, he would let them be as they are in their natural exuberance. He devised many types of teaching methods for children. To make the difficult Sanskrit grammar simple and easy, he composed and published a book of understandable grammar in simple poetic form. At the same time, he wrote an unprecedented book for learning primary English and Hindi called "First Book"* and created an easily understandable booklet of astrology. In his spare time, we have seen him teach the mysteries of science in story form to children in such a way that it was also beneficial to us. Some complex things in science that were not clear even after reading books were easy to understand upon hearing those stories of his. We found that in order to make education more applicable he designed a modern practice of basic education.** He was especially attentive to Indian civilization and culture (nationality)*** in education and in other affairs. One day in the midst of a conversation, I asked him, "What's the necessity in learning this cursory Sanskrit if you've taught everyone through the mother tongue [Bengali]?" He replied, "In current India, meaning the time that we are about to forget our depth and culture, from this time to at least fifty years from now it will be proper to have the facility to learn Sanskrit in even ordinary schools." Later, he became interested in education for women. He deeply felt that the realization of humanness of future human beings in this country was dependent on women, and for this reason, if he could find the right people, he wanted to make his ashram in Puri a center for women's education.

*The words "First Book" are written in English in the original.
**The words "basic education" are written in English in the original.
***The word "nationality" is written in English and is within parentheses in the original.

He would chastise any fault he would see of anyone who was somewhat close to him. Sometimes his reproof was deprecating. There is no point in not admitting that from time to time, even if his reprimand was not physically hard, the meaning of it would become unbearable to us. Because he used to grant us freedom as a matter of course, sometimes we would get agitated and—who knows how many times we argued with him. He did not ever have any contempt for us because of that. Although his wordss may have been harsh and incisive, most of the time I was able to withstand them and benefited from them. Regardless of how stern he sometimes might have been in the roles of Acharya and guardian, it is absolutely true that although he observed the respective hierarchal responsibilities of Acharya, teacher, worker etc., as far as the management of the ashram was concerned, he preferred the process where work was carried out according to the rule of the by-laws of the fellowship.

Everyone would become fascinated upon hearing instruction and advice on every subject related to organizations by this Acharya of the Age, the great being who was the Incarnation of Knowledge. Who knows how many missionaries, educators, ashrams of service, assemblies, congregations etc. have gained renown in their organizational endeavors after having received even a grain of his advice on these matters. But the strange thing is that he was not successful in actualizing the manifestation of his ideals by his own hand. Referring to his relation to householder life, forming ashrams and along with those things, his writing of books, he said, "My virtuosity in studies and education is quite known, yet I composed grammarian books! So many have become famous in organizational work from having received my counsel and I wasn't able to acquire even the tactics* of building an ashram.

I see that I am the beloved son of Mother Saraswati, but Mother Durga's disowned son." In any case, by God's will, the magnificent education and initiation that His Holiness Acharyadeva bestowed upon us, dispelling our inertia—for this we are blessed and fortunate. There is not a scintilla of doubt that if we try to respectfully make use of our understanding of even a speck of his essential wisdom on organizational work, that we would be blessed and that there would be an abundance of beneficence for the world.

*The word "tactics" is written in English in the original.

He was a Guru who knew Brahman. Feeling our insignificant situation, we were hesitant to come to speak to this great man about anything or even just go near him. But, he did not like to take undue advantage of the opportunity as was the usual practice of guru-business. Regardless of being disciples, he showed appropriate courtesy toward human beings and would elevate their stature by offering them his seat. I do not think that I have ever experienced even a spot of the vanity of guru-ism from him. He deplored the medireview practice of covering oneself with the filigree of guru-talk and expressing excessive superiority through the blind belief that was prevalent. This is why he would give advice and help to even so-called uneducated villagers, inciting their powers of discrimination on pertinent spiritual concerns in their pursuit of attaining success. "Prapte tu shodashe barshe putramitravadacharet"—it was as if he used to follow this statement from the Aphorisms of Chanakya in totality. In many matters, he would engagee himself in argumentative analysis with capable disciples even after having stated his own opinion. He would take pride in the excellence of a disciple. If he saw that some work instructed by him was being done well by a disciple, he would give him more encouragement. But, if it became necessary to reprimand mistakes, he would not hesitate to do that either. There is no way to not admit that weakminded disciples would sometimes become aggravated and try to hide from him. That one would again receive his affectionate invitation after one had moved far away—this was also a particular aspect of Acharyadev's behavior.

The proper guru is knowledgeable and a man of Truth. He taught the significance of this sacred saying. In order to make us understand practical methods, if the subject of guru was brought up, this immense, magnanimous and ego-less man would say in a simple and ordinary way, "What is the point in being taken aback by the word 'guru'? Guru means weighty, meaning one who is more weighty or knowledgeable than you, from whom you can learn. If it is necessary, then after completing your learning from him, you can take Shelter in an even higher guru—like going to a professor of an institution of higher learning after grade school. But one must remember to have proper reespect and humility towards everyone." He tried to make us clearly understand that even if one were firmly established in the spiritual knowledge of the Causeless, Infinite Brahman, a physically embodied man cannot attain Total Brahman-ness (Full Perfection).* Still, the Eternal Light of Brahman within Gurudev becomes illuminated in the life of the disciple and seeing Guru as Supreme Consciousness beyond the body, one receives the divine touch of Guru-Brahman-Shakti, and that realization establishes in one's mind the truth: "Sriguru Bhagavan Swayam" [Sriguru is God Itself]. Having steadfast reverence and belief towards Guru, through the method of sadhana given by him one gains a firm understanding that the one whose lord is mind is also the Lord God, the one whose guru is wine is also the Guru of the World, and the drunkard's soul is the Soul of All. "The Soul is the Soul's friend and the Soul is the Soul's enemy. It is by the Soul that the Soul will be saved and [the Soul] will not allow the Soul to tire." To understand this scriptural statement one needs the direct blessing and Grace of Guru. He used to say, "It is because of Swami Vivekananda's self-assurance and extraordinary reverential radiance that Sri Ramakrishnadev was known to the world as an incarnation of God." When talk of the Lord Sri Sri Lahiri Mahasaya would come up, even if he would sometimes speak of the Lord's truly amazing teaching and lilas [miraculous play], he would usually explain: "It is possible that profound reverence can come upon you about Him from what you have heard through people, but what can you understand about His true importance without having had the company of my Gurudev?" "Sraddhavan labhate jnanam"—it is in making this scriptural statement steadfast in one's life and progressing in Guru-given sadhana that one tastes Divine Bliss. It is in this way that Srigurudev's priceless gift of Divine Knowledge erodes away the sins of the initiated sadhaka. I have heard this scientific, great Acharya of the Age say at the time of giving initiation: "Look, there is no point in blindly believing that after I touch you, you will be saved, or that a chariot from heaven will be waiting for you. Because of the guru's attainment, the sanctifying touch becomes a helper in the blossoming of Knowledge, and being respectful towards having acquired this blessing, you must yourself become a sage and proceed on the path to elevate your Soul by applying the techniques of sadhana given by the guru. It is in the path of meditation, truthfulness and surrendering to God that the Guru-graced sadhaka becomes successful in gaining revelation and understanding of new methods of learning." It is with this perspective that Guru Maharaj used to say, "Real wisdom is one that beats the guru's—now that's a disciple."

*The parentheses and the text within are written in the original in English.

The feeling of self-confidence was present in Maharajji in a special way. It is wrong to think that feelings of self-respect or self-assurance are a kind of egoism and a right to the proud elevation of one's status. It is in the simple, fearless, responsible, guileless, open-hearted and high-minded person that this special characteristic of self-reverent awareness manifests. It is with the aid of this that human beings become capable and successful at gaining true humanness, and then, without hesitation, become immersed in the spiritual sadhana of attaining the Brahman-substance. Perhaps it was to explain the significance of self-respect on the ladder of spiritual ascension that he said, "Uddhavetatmanatmanam natmanamvasadayet." Fear (meaning the feeling of awe)* and feelings of deep respect would arise in us in the face of his profoundly serious and gigantic personality. Sometimes upon looking at him we could not find the courage to open our mouths. But from time to time, he chit-chatted, joked and kidded around with everyone in such a way—as if we friends of the same age—that we would forget about his extreme solemnity. Mixing openly with us as equals did not ever diminish his personality. This is evidence of true self-respect and its significance.

*The parentheses and the text within are in the original.

In matters of education in schools or in the household environment, he would say to be especially attentive to the feelings of self-respect in children. Even though it might be necessary to administer punishment or reprimand, he would tell us to be careful that the self-worth of the child is not harmed, because if man loses self-respect, then he has nothing. Using animalistic strength to mete out punishment can make the child's natural mentality and temperament base and lowly. This does not remove the root problem. He used to say that negative statements of warning, like "do not lie" or "do not steal," often had the effect of opening up the wicked side of the child's simple mind. Instead, it was better to make the child understand the ideals and inner meaning of the path of truth and honesty, and then the young mind could walk on righteous way with self-respect. From time to time, he said that man is omniscient in the fundamental state; therefore it was erroneous and wrong to try cheat anyone; and it was not really possible to cheat children either. Man's learning and his relationship to the world around him manifests unknowingly in his innate behavior. To help walk on the path that cultivated good habits and self-reliance, he would from time to time ask children about food and bathing, or discuss with them their general preferences and tastes. He said that if one were to be observant and attentive even towards life's very ordinary and small things, one could attain much excellence. Learning the scriptures at his feet, we have seen that instead of imposing his commentary on us right at the start, he would help us to awaken our own analytical intelligence and would encourage our freedom to acquire our own understanding and meaning. In this way, taking the thread of our insignificant efforts to look within and become free thinkers, most of the time he was able to make us internalize the core meanings of the shastras. The observation of the wisdom of the two injunctions "Sraddhavan labhate jnanam" and "yuktiyuktamupadeyam vachanam balakadapi" was a particular characteristic of his teaching.

Although he encouraged travel to foreign countries to acquire knowledge, from time to time he would say in sadness, "The youth of other progressive countries in the world travel to many lands and they fortify their own culture with the gathering of new experiences, which then enhances their own and their culture's glory. But it is shameful that, because of India's present educational systems which are full of faults, the children of this land of sages return from foreign countries having learned only to follow other people's ways by which they besmirch the cultural pride, even the reputation of their families." It is because of this that until the last moments of his life that he spoke about modern educational systems of sagacious wisdom for the benefit and improvement of India. He would clearly point out the need for political support on this matter and the necessity for cultures to come forward. He did not like hesitancy in any field. He used to say that there is no sin in work. Doubt and weakness are the real sins.

Even though he was proud of the glory of India's sages, India's civilization, India's spiritual knowledge, the Vedas, philosophy, astrology, science, literature, arts and crafts etc., and would in solemn tones declare the profound foundation of the culture of saints in our education, politics, society, religion etc. as demonstrated by truth-seeing sages, still he would become irritated if one only spoke vacuously about the grand events of the past without being attentive to one's own sadhana or one's competence in work. His philosophy was that by taking the seed mantra of the enlightened sages along with the beneficial elements of the modern and international communities' multifaceted knowledge, science, education and culture—one must know these things and move life forward. This is how the culture would be properly represented and how humanness could be exhibited. In every step was the word of caution: "Don't become a foreigner." He revered the multi-directional abilities of human beings. We understood from his sayings that the influence of the works of knowledge and science dispels the narrowness of mind and makes man open-minded and noble. I am remembering when he was shown the Acharya of Science, Jagadish Chandra Bose's house and laboratory, seeing which he said, "This of course is a place of pilgrimage." That sages and wise beings only existed in the past, or that saints and sages can only be from India and not take birth in other places—this sentiment had no place in his mind. Although he proudly believed in India's special contribution toward spirituality and its esteemed profundity, he could not perceive the different cultures of the world as some low-level human beings in regards to this.

"Sraddhavan labhate jnanam"—This root mantra for excellence in the path of life—he very much wanted to write this in our minds and instructed us to realize the truth "Tadbiddhi pranipaten pariprasnen sevaya." He did not understand the meaning of reverence to be only the usual bowing and prostration. Instead, he became very disturbed when he saw the performance at every step of pranam, prostration, glorification, head-bowing or a terribly cowering and milquetoast demeanor. At the demonstration of this type of overblown adulation he would say from time to time: "Be careful of too much devotion." But, using the excuse of passing out so-called judgment, he would ask us to be alert and not neglect the usual proprieties of greeting, bowing and other such courtesies. He used to teach us by following civil manners himself, as part of his own behavior. Even in the area of the Guru-given authority to bestow initiation—as long as Guru's son was present in Guru's house, Swamiji would not give initiation to any aspirant in Guru's land, Benarees. Once it happened that a certain devotee of his in Benares became extremely desperate to receive initiation from him and because of respect for the authority of initiation in Benares belonging to Guru's son who was present there at the time, he went outside of Benares for a while to give initiation to that aspirant. Intellectual understanding, sentiment,* or purifying reverence are ideals which are in agreement with each other. He used to say that the real form of reverence was the innate inclination of love in human beings towards the Infinite, towards Truth, towards the highest. The natural practice of that within one is what could allow man to walk on the path of his real being and remain true to the ideals. By the simple application of that, behavioral civility is compelled to manifest. Of course, it is important to tend particularly to the behavioral side of the unformed mind of a child also. This why he was a situational proponent of scriptural recitation, rituals of offering, worship, homage to elders, salutations and such formal procedures, but in all things, he disliked any excessive external showmanship. He would simply say, "That much good isn't good."

*The word "sentiment" is written in English in the original.

Many times, he became harshly critical if he saw the predominance of outer apparel in a religious sadhaka trying to show his sectarian spirituality. It is possible that some mala- and tilak- clad renunciates have become upset upon hearing his criticism. We also became intolerant of this, and trying to comprehend him according to our intelligence, from time to time ended up asking him, "Why do you make these types of baseless comments?" But after settling down, we understood from his explanations that he disliked excess and pomp, but if different sadhakas—during meetings with their sectarian congregations or at times of holy gatherings—put on the special clothing of their sects simply and respectfully, then he was very much a proponent of that. While living in his ashram, we have also experienced that when he saw a certain simple and dedicated devotee of the Vaishnava sect going to a gathering of their sect dressed beautifully in their typical sectarian clothing with mala, tilak etc., he praised the devotee's discipline. Many people have misunderstood him on this issue, but who is going to judge truthfully? How far can our miniscule intelligence take us?

His teaching was that the Eternal Truth-Brahman-substance is universally present equally everywhere. Because of place, time, prospective recipients and cultural differences, the internal and divine Guru-Shakti has flown through many different sadhakas and great beings, and, for the beneficence of human beings, has created various sects appropriate for the situation only; the root substance, meaning dharma, is one and universal [sanatan]. He accepted the appropriateness of the existence of different sects. But he did not at all support any sectarian illiberality. He used to say that realized acharyas have given and are giving teachings fitting to different circumstances. We, not being able to discern or comprehend the whole of it, judge and view them in contempt from our encircling dogma. On this subject, it is sad and shameful that in the present time, honorable, educated and intelligent personages versed in scriptures have not only settled at defiling the viewpoints of India's respectable and venerable acharyas, but they have continued to employ baseless and ignorant statements about the character of those universally hallowed realized beings. I do not believe that these extremely prejudiced people of renown will be able to rightly use their exceptional capabilities in proper service for the benefit of the world. With the blessings of the Lord of this world's destiny, the banishment of this smallness would make it possible to apply the teachings and wisdom of these sages for the abundant benefit of the country. The country whose truth-seeing and open-hearted sages, upon sensing the desire for realization of Truth from people of different nationalities who were seeking the guarded wisdom of spirituality with their various perspectives, said: "Vedah bibhinnah smatayah; bibhinnah nasou muniryasya matam na bhinnah"; the country whose divinely incarnated Great Sadhaka told us of the essence of the beautiful and experientially egalitarian statement, "As many views, that many paths"—to hear the character of divine teachers be ridiculed from the mouths of sadhakas of the same country is without doubt a saad affair. It is one thing to dissect the opinion of another by direct experience or logical analysis in the interests of truth, but it is quite another thing, after having destroyed the proposition, to attack the personal character of that person. This is what is called narrow-mindedness. The great yogi Swamiji Maharaj's experiential perspective was established in non-dualism [advaita], but whether it was advaita, bishishtadvaita, dvaitadvaita or dvaita—even though there may have been the desire to ridicule or destroy the perspectives of certain speakers and acharyas, I do not think that I have ever seen any feelings of disrespect from him towards these universally holy great beings. Instead, we would hear him say with his egalitarian perspective that everyone's destined path is one, and travelers from different lands need to adopt particular methods for their particular paths. For example: a stick for the hilly and mountainous roads (hill stick),* a boat for the waterways, etc. After arriving at the royal gate of God, there is no more need for the use of those things. If one wants to be inspired by ideals of one's own experiences, then one has to walk that spiritually appropriate path with one-pointed discipline, and once those ideals manifest, one has to endeavor to investigate the wisdom-jewel through numerous opinions, otherwise restlessness can arise and make one aggravated. He used to cryptically say, "Ram's Guru is Shiva and Shiva's Guru is Ram, but the conflict is in Shiva's ghosts and Ram's monkeys."

*The parentheses and the text are written in English in the original.

If the subjects of sense-enjoyment or renunciation was brought up then he would make us understand through the wisdom of the Gita about the demonstration of restraint from sensual coercions for a Karmayogi. He used to say that the embodying of a physical form itself naturally consumed sense-pleasures, and that the Soul-established sadhaka, with the help of the consummation of the culmination of sensual gratification from prarabdha [predestined events], could then complete the enjoyment of physical pleasures and subsequently turn inward to the service of the lord of the senses, Hrishikesh. That is when a human being became a real renunciate. But the scattered and restless human being, running after pleasure, loses his authority over the senses and becomes enslaved, and being immersed in the senses, is swept away in the ocean of sorrow.

It has previously been mentioned that he used to consider the Srimad Bhagavad Gita as the greatest spiritual book. During discussions of Sadguru Sri Sri Lahiri Mahasaya's beautiful and yogically experiential commentaries on every character's essential purpose and His yogic explanations in the Gita pertaining to the spiritual path of sadhana, Swamiji Maharaj made us understand that in the form of those such as Duryodhana, the hundred demonic pravritti [externally and inductively oriented] tendencies caused turmoil in the sadhaka's path of sadhana and were ready to draw him towards the path of pravritti oriented sense-pleasures. When unobstructed by and renouncing the pravritti-allied demonic forces of sensual enjoyment produced by the five elements (the five Pandavas),* one could walk the path of nivritti [internally and deductively oriented] in the spiritual life. It is for the presentation of this that the Gita begins in the Mahabharata. Besides this type of yogic commentary, he also taught us that the Gita's directives, advice and philosophical substance were necessary and applicable to every level of human life. It for this reason that the Gita is the all encompassing spiritual treatise. He believed the truth of the battle of Kurukshetra at the transitional period of the Yugas and in the historical truth of the Ultimate Man, Sri Krishna's ultra-incredible ideal, character and deeds, and agreed with the views of the philosopher and Emperor of Literature, Bankim Chandra's opinion that the character of Sri Krishna was the highest and ideal character ever written about in the world. But he did not think, according to the prevalent belief, that Sri Krishna Himself recited the Gita in that way, full of yogic substance, at the onset of war as the charioteer of Arjuna on the historic battlefield of Kurukshetra. We have understood from his words that the divine-sighted Maharshi Vyas experienced the manifestation of the Divine Guru in his life as a sadhaka, the One who descended into human consciousness and was the eternally incarnate God in the heart of all matter, and it is with that experience and employing the immaculate characters of Sri Krishna and Arjuna that he composed the Highest Upanishad, the nectarous Gita in the guise of a story-poem. This is why the substance spoken in the Gita is eternal and why the Srimad Bhagavad Gita is the universal spiritual scripture. The dutiful and righteous sadhaka, obtaining the Grace of Guru, from continuous spiritual study is able to receive the true meaning of the Gita, and applying the nectarous wisdom of the yoga-shastra Gita and becoming able to excel in every field of life, is gratified by it. When discussing the unique discourse on Purushottama in the Gita he pointed out: "In Hindu philosophy the manifested

Brahman is present in three forms: 1) One imperishable, eternal, unchanging, infinite and undivided Universal Consciousness; 2) the Presence of this infinite Consciousness which reflects all, being reflected in division after division of molecular, atomic, subatomic and the subtlest levels of the substance of the Universe, bringing into being this consciousness-filled physical world; 3) this visible physical world. Although there is no difference between Presence Consciousness and the Universal Consciousness, but it is with the aid of this that Nature creates bacteria to man to gods etc. and the search for the true Self and place of Bliss, gradually leads to the Land of Bliss. The indivisible and infinite Universal Consciousness is represented as Sri Krishna in the Gita. This Purushottama Sri Krishna is the goal and attainment of the sadhaka. In many slokas of many chapters of the Gita is this manifestation of Sri Krishna evident for us to read and understand. The Sri Krishna of the Gita is not an ordinary butter-thief and neither is He a diplomatic politician. He is the very Purushottama Ishwara.

*The parentheses and the text within are in the original.

Through His Holiness Sri Guru Maharaj's experiential exposition of spiritual matters we became acquainted with the proper and harmonious perspectives of Samkhya yoga and Vedanta Darshan. He said:

"Nityam purnamanadyanantam Brahmaparamam tadevaikamevadvaitam sat Tatra sarvajna premabijshchit sarvashaktibijamanandashcha."

"Eternal, perfect, beginningless and endless is the supreme Brahman; it is the Truth, one without a second. It is the seed of all-knowing Love, it is Consciousness, the seed of all Power, and It is Bliss."

Not understanding the natural and spiritual attraction[fn 1] to the Infinite, the Self-ignorant, embedded to the three gunas, multi-appareled, deluded individual soul goes toward the side of repulsion[fn 2] and turns round and round, caught in the spiral of Maya's measured divisions, believing in the intelligence of his ego-self, drowning in his self-dug, watery grave. The means to become free from such spiral or sorrow is the attainment of the True Self through Soul-Knowledge. The root of that sadhana or spirituality is Karma, or in the path of Kriya yoga, self-surrender to the endearment of Vishnu through the guileless, free of all attachments, blossoming of devotion by the great attraction of Love towards the Paramatman within. In the knowing of that Oneness—fear, the forms of fear and the other great obstacles are dispelled, and realization arises: "Swalpamapasye dharmasya trayate mahatobhayat." Being attached to the three gunas, we have moved from the Great Substance and come to take the form of a physical body. To go back to the True Self, we have to again take the path upward, meaning that we have to progress from the physical through the different levels of the subtle existence and arrive at the Brahman-Shakti or Guru-Shakti within, meaning, that with infinite Divine Grace, become settled in Brahman. In the discussions of the subject of Kriyayoga sadhana, he showed us the practical[fn 3] and experiential path for this theoretical[fn 4] quest. We understood from these discourses that by yama, niyama or following the prevalent prohibitive directives and taking up the practice of a still, comfortable posture, the restlessness of the body goes away. Practicing attention on the manifested path of Shakti, the sushumna—or its physical representation in the passage through the spinal column, the nervous system[fn 5] becomes peaceful, which results in the mind turning inward in this harmonious body and becoming stabilized in the path of the Brahmanadi, and subsequently the life-force is gradually concentrated and eventually pours into the expanse of the Great Truth. [fn 6] Slowly, in the state of inward bound pratyahara one begins to see the luminous presence of the All-Wisdom Eye in the subtle-body; the consciousness becomes stilled in the manifestation of that Light.[fn 7] And in the tranquil mind of the meditator, meaning when mind, intellect, consciousness and ego are at equilibrium, the Pranava Shabda or Nada or the Primordial Resonance spoken by the Great, All-pervading Divine can be experienced naturally and unscattered.[fn 8] When in the Guru-graced path of Pranava Shabda, the state of the inward bound, Brahma-Yonimudra manifested, illuminated by Divine Light[fn 9], Soham-filled sense is experienced, by concentration on which the self-surrendered and meditation-immersed sadhaka attains the profound wisdom of Samadhi, it is then that the veil is removed and the vast Consciousness-Bliss of the Truth of the True Form of the Soul is gained, meaning, the total dissolution of the threefold suffering, or the attainment of the eternally longed-for Satchitananda-ness. "Yam labdha chaparam labham manyate nadhikam tatah." Reverence, service and worship help to purify consciousness in the path of the sadhaka. The many types of worship and prayer were created to help in the practice of reverence for different levels of the human mind in the worldly field. "Apsu deva manushyanam divi devo manishinam kashthaloshtreshu murkhanam yuktasyatmani devata."

fn 1—5: The words [1]"attraction," [2]"repulsion," [3]"practical," [4]"theoretical" and [5]"nervous system" are written in English in the original.

fn 6—9 are Sanskrit slokas provided by Swami Satyananda to elucidate particular aspects of the text. They are as follows:

praano hi bhagavaan iishah praano vishnuh pitaamahah
praanena dhaaryate lokah sarvam praanamayam jagat

The Prana is indeed Lord Iisha (= Siva), the Praana is Vishnu and the Father (Brahma). By Prana the entire world is supported. The entire world is full of Prana.

fn 7—
Neehar dhumarkanilanlanam
khadyotvidyut sphatik shashinam
etani rupani purahsarani
Brahmanyabhivyaktikarani yoge

—from Svetasvatar

In Yoga, the forms which come first, which manifest the Brahman, are those of misty smoke, sun, fire, wind, fire-flies, lightnings, and a crystal moon.

taila-dhaaraam ivaacchinnam deergha-ghantaa-vinaadavat
yas tu veda…sa vedavit

One who knows That without any break like the flow of oil and like the long sound of a bell…he indeed is a knower of the Vedas.

fn 8—
sarve vedaa yat padam aamananti
tapaamsi sarvaani ca yad vadanti
yad icchanto brahmacaryam caranti
tat te padam sangrahena braviimi—om ity etat

—from Katha

That Word which all the Vedas proclaim,
Which all penances aim at,
Desiring which the wise practise Brahmacarya,
That Word I shall tell you in brief: It is Om.

fn 9—
mantraartham mantra-caitanyam yoni-mudraam vinaa tathaa
shatakoti-japenaapi naiva siddhih prajaayate

—from Tantra

Without knowing the meaning of the Mantra, without possessing the consciousness of the Mantra and without practising Yonimudra, Siddhi shall not occur even by a hundred million repetitions.

During the nineteenth century, and even after that, the usual belief was that there was no relationship between science and religion, and that the scientifically minded could not be religious. Swamiji Maharaj said that it was the scientist who could be the truly religious person. The unearthing of scientific knowledge and mysteries make it easy to understand the secrets of the Universe and Nature and help in the progress of life, mind, intellect etc., and it is by that that the human mind can naturally take up the true path of religion. Controlling the multi-directional, scattered energies, applying the Brahman-method, the Brahmachari sadhaka becomes inwardly attracted to the Great Satchitananda-Self and surrendering all in the natural way, gains salvation. "Dharanat [unreadable due to print]"

In discussing astrological knowledge, he believed in scientific reasons for the appearance of different conditions and situations in the solar system in the various ages of Satya, Treta, Dwapara and Kali, which affected the general movements, upward or downward, in the consciousness of human beings. Depending on whether the solar system is closer or farther from the Vishnunabhi (Grand Centre),* consciousness manifests in conditions according to that Age. In Satya the natural state is all four parts of Consciousness-Bliss; in Treta it is three parts out of four, meaning general magnetic attraction causing Consciousness-Knowledge; in Dwapara it is two parts Truth, meaning the attraction of subtle electrical power causing Consciousness-mind; and in Kali it is one part, meaning the stupor of the tamasic physical world manifest-ing the state of Consciousness-life-force. The natural movement of the normal solar-system and of all solar systems is to move toward and away from the Vishnunabhi and by scientific law, the positioning of the solar system through the various modes of attraction, causes the different and particular levels of physical, mental and spiritual atmos-phere to be prevalent to the specific eras. It is for this reason that in this created world, with the natural inclination to express different quali-ties, we see the appearance of the four yugas, Satya, Treta, Dwapara and Kali, fully and partially demonstrating Truth in their naturally changing eras. According to the process of evolution, these ages go in succession from Satya to Kali and again from Kali ascend, passing through Dwapara and Treta, arriving at Satya. Swamiji Maharaj's cal-culations show that at present, having passed two hundred years in the transition of Kali and Dwapara, we are almost a half-century into Dwapara yuga, and proving it is the evidence of the evolution of the perception of subtle things throughout the world. The presence of finer understanding is becoming apparent in historical events, society, poli-tics, culture, science and even in spiritual knowledge and insight. Electricity is a regular companion to daily life in the world today. The turmoil and violent revolutions we are seeing are transitional pains from the changing of the yugas. With these calculations, in the Christian year 1900, he predicted that soon there will be a cataclysmic event, like in Lanka or Kurukshetra, signifying the transformation into the new age, after which there will be a new vision into the subtler realms of politics, society and even in the field of spiritual sadhana, and peace will reign, appropriate for the age.

*The parentheses and the text within are written in English in the orig-inal.

The straightforward explanation of the duration of the yugas by Maharshi Manu, meaning, his instructions as to the calculations of the number of years pertaining to the specific yugas—instead of taking it in its simplicity, with the absence of the king of righteousness, Yudhisthira and other such enlightened beings at the end of the previ-ous Dwapara, other meanings were attributed to the daiva-years and erroneous calculations came to practice at the beginning of the Kali era. He used to say that just as days, lunar fortnights and months etc. were calculated with the help of constellations during a year, in that same way were they used for the aid in the measurement of yugas and time periods—as in: 7th Ashwin, 247 Dwapara Era. For pride in remembering kings of later years was the suffix "era of so and so" creatted. Calculating astrologically significant times in this way, he demonstrated with examples that the present times of solstices and equinoxes indicated in the prevalent almanacs were of a different date than should be, meaning, these dates were from a time in the solar system thousands of years ago. Thus, although the Great Equinox takes place in the modern 8/9th Chaitra, resulting in the equal division of day and night, one can still see the usage of the equinoctial dates in Chaitra for the Great Equinox from back in the Puranic times in the almanacs.

It is said, "That which is in the Brahmanda [macrocosm] is in the Bhanda [microcosm]." Which means that the structure and laws of the great Brahmanda and the small Brahmanda, meaning, the structure and laws of the body owned by the individual soul, are entirely the same. Modern science tells us that the construction, and the laws to which it abides, of an atom are exactly the same as the laws and construction of the solar world. It is amazing to think that the divinely sighted sages, through their research and experience, long ago expressed the same things that are being known throughout via the truth of science.

The Hindu visionaries agreed on certain essential things that caused the manifestation of this observable world. The evolution of these things is the evolution of Nature. The world moves according the present manifestation of these substances. The body of a human being is symbolic of this Universe. This human body is a tiny universe. This is why, the more a sadhaka progresses in the path of sadhana, the more— through the power of yoga—he experiences the elements of Universe-Nature in his body. The intention of the Universe-Nature is the evolution of the spiritual life following the line of the evolution theory* of the Universe. Nature itself has worked toward this goal age after age. Applying yogasadhana and progressing in spiritual life, a human being can help this great work of Nature along and can elevate itself much higher. We find the resounding shout of this wisdom in the deeply spiritual and experiential words from Rishi Aurobindo on the hope of the ideal of the superman, with which we can understand that, because of the exact law of evolution, the incomplete and partially realized human race of the present is absolutely destined to attain a level of divine consciousness. To attain the longed-for "liberation,"** studying the enlightened and Guru-revealed wisdom and adopting the practice of sadhana, a human being can move through the spiritual levels of Kali, Dwapara, Treta and Satya as they appear one by one, and ascending, leave behind the anxiety of concern for the afterworld, and in a short time, realize liberation within himself in this very life.*** Moving in the work of Brahman, or in Brahman, or walking in the laws of the Infinite Brahman, meaning, becoming aware of Supreme Nature, if one lives life according to this experience, meaning, being able to completely surrender oneself, it is possible to obtain the attraction of the Lord in the Form of Divine Grace and thereby become sanctified.

*The words "evolution theory" are written in English in the original.
**The word "mukti" [liberation] is enclosed by quotes in the original.
***Swami Satyanandaji's elucidation of the text by a footnoted Sanskrit sloka:

Ihaiva tairjitah sargo yemam samye sthitam manah
nirdosham hi samam Brahma tasmadbrahmani te sthitah

Here birth is conquered by those whose mind is established in equanimity. Guiltless and impartial is God; therefore they are established in God.

CONCLUSION

The work of the various Satsanga Sabhas continued on under the direction of Sadhusabhapati Sri Guru Maharajji. In foreign lands, the propagation work of his dear disciple, Swami Yoganandaji, was spreading more and more. The western devotees were enraptured, having been introduced to the Kriyayoga sadhana of the founder of the spiritual way of the Age, the Lord Sri Sri Lahiri Mahasaya, from the mouth of the one carrying Guru's Word, the Indian sannyasi Yoganandaji. Applying sadhana to the words of wisdom from the Acharya of the Ages, Sadhusabhapati Maharaj, they listened with reverence to the explanation of realizing humanness in this very realm, and bowed lovingly, paying homage to the spiritual power of the guru of the world, the Rishi India. Swamiji Maharaj was especially attentive to his spiritual son Yoganandaji's continuous work and if he sensed any mistakes in his son's method of work in the distant land of America, he would warn him even from so far away. He kept on giving situational instructions in order to properly organize the spreading out of work. He instructed that the Yogananda-introduced name "Yogoda" be adopted and the Sabhas' names be changed to "Yogoda Satsanga Sabha," and began to become quite eager to have his beloved disciple near him. From time to time, he expressed sadness at seeing the then-established Sadhu Sabha's ideals and methods of work for propagation not being done in the properly disciplined way for which he had hoped. He used to try to make us understand, "The mission of this body is coming to an end. Now you all get ready. You all must take the responsibility. No matter how much work Yogananda has, even if it is with a return ticket, he must come." Even though he was up in his years, when he would see us from time to time looking with captivated eyes at his powerful, upright and brilliant form and his royal and gloriously radiant face, understanding what we were thinking, he would say, "You are seeing it as beautiful from the outside, but all of the mechanisms on the inside are weakening." I clearly remember that in a conversation one day around the Christian year 1925/26, he said, "The hitch that will come in another ten years—it's not likely that this body will be saved from that." After those ten years had passed, not even in the early times of the now foretold period could we imagine, seeing always his yoga-attained excellent form, that he would leave his body. He continued to tell us, "The new insights that were revealed from the experiential truth of astrology, philosophy and other such sciences—these things may not be accepted while this body is still here. But whether you propagate this or not, because of the influence of the times, maybe immediately after this body goes, you will definitely hear this wisdom of truth resounding loudly from the sages of the world. At this beginning of betterment for the world, according to the maturing process as part of this transitional period of the ages, even though intense conflict and war goes on throughout the world, very soon—no, suddenly—India will become freed from her governmental subservience; freedom will come to the inhabitants of Asia; and after a huge upheaval, the turmoil of the world will come to an end, after which the environment for peace in the Universe will continue to grow." We listened dumbfoundedly to the farsighted words of the Acharya of the Ages, and, through the passage of time, became amazed at the gradual manifesting of his vision.

It was as if the very busy Yoganandaji felt the pull of Sriguru in the distant land of America. That his father, who had helped and blessed him in spiritual propagation and all types of works of benevolence, was now at old age—this also distressed his mind. The Yoganandaji who, even after fifteen long years of living outside his home country, did not take particular care even when he had free time to return to India, that Yoganandaji stunned his devotees at the end of the summer of the Christian year 1935, and although there were all kinds of problems, in a short time left for India. When someone tried to present to him the sensibility of staying in order to take care of the problems at hand, he said, "Even if the earth turns upside down, the eternal attraction of my aged father and my Guruji are calling me to absolutely go to India now; delay is impossible."

The victorious child of India, Swami Yoganandaji arrived at his motherland in August of the Christian year 1935 with his American disciples; the inhabitants of his homeland welcomed him resoundingly. Guru and disciple reunited at the Guru-pilgrimage-place of Srirampur. Seeing the pride of India manifested sagaciously in him, Swamiji

Maharaj joyfully and proudly embraced his spiritual son in affection, and introducing him and spreading the word to everyone as the deserving successor in his work and as the future Sadhusabhapati, Swamiji was then satisfied.

The great gathering of Kumbhamela was taking place in the month of Magh this year at the pilgrimage place of Prayag. Returning to the land of India after having been out of the country for so long, Yoganandaji wanted to see the congregation of sadhus in Kumbhamela. His friends, devotees and disciples also became engaged in wanting to take him to Prayag. Giving in to the eagerness of everyone, he did not delay any further and headed towards the gathering of pilgrims. Unfortunately, because of this one erroneous rush, he was not able to meet and see his Gurudev. Meanwhile, after waiting a few days in Srirampur for his beloved disciple, when His Holiness Swamiji Maharaj came to know one day that Yoganandaji had gone to Kumbhamela, he suddenly let out a deep sigh and lay down. The long-time companions of Swamiji Maharaj who were there at the time say, "In our whole lives we had never seen Maharajji become so suddenly despondent. When that steadfast, ensconced in wisdom, lion of a man and great sannyasi became so distressed at the flash of a moment, we became frightened at the possibility of some future trouble and were stupefied. Who knew that, in that strange and unusual state, the impossibility of another physical meeting of Guru and disciple in this world was now set. That the experience of the pain of farewell would manifest in this way in Guru Maharaj's mind—we could not in any way imagine this." Here was an incredible demonstration of the very human affection and love in the mind of a "superman,"* touching his innermost heart! After a few minutes passed, the Gurudev of Knowledge returned to his normal self and again began to converse open-heartedly with everyone.

*The word "atimanav"[superman] is in quotes in the original.

Taking up the ideal of "Atmano mokshartham jagaddhitayacha," the dutiful Swamiji Maharaj, upon receiving their invitation, headed for the yearly festival-gathering by the village fellowships of the Medinipur district. He arrived at the festival of the Yogoda Satsanga Sabhas of Ghatal, Mahakumar and Kukurdaha on the full moon of Magh. It was this Khukurdaha village that twenty years ago, because of the heartfelt call of the villagers, and the leadership of the late Dr. Parameshwar Maji Mahasaya as well as the efforts of other devotees, was blessed by the touch of his feet. Keeping that initial memory at heart, the Kriyavan devotees of Khukurdaha had been paying homage year after year to the Feet of the Holiest of Holies and Beloved Sriguru, the Lord of the Heart. Alas, little did they know that this was their last physical play with their heart-lover, and that this was the final time they would have his affectionate company! He seemed this time to overwhelmingly bestow his love on Vipin, Vinod, Neerad and other such disciplined Kriyavans. A photo was also taken with everyone. In the midst of chit-chatting and fun-filled festivities, Guru Maharaj said, "This is the last time that I will join you in this fellowship." The children were suddenly taken aback for a moment by their father saying such a thing, but, not paying much attention to this, nevertheless remained absorbed in the company of Guru and in the joy of the festival. Finishing the work of the Sabha, Guruji went then to Puri as usual.

Swami Yoganandaji was around Kumbhamela at that time with his group, and I was in ill health in Calcutta. The trip for everyone to Puri for the yearly Satsanga-festival on the Great Equinox in the month of Chaitra was set, but Maharajji unexpectedly wrote me a letter a few days before the Holi festival and insisted that we, along with Yoganandaji, come to Puri before the Holi festival. My health was ill, this is true, and therefore I, the unfortunate one, did not make the effort to arrive at his Holy Feet immediately after that call of his. I thought that the yearly festival will happen soon anyway, and that it would be better to go after I was a little bit healthier. Who knew at that time that this was the last pull and call of his loving embrace and blessing in this world! Swami Yoganandaji arrived in Calcutta just before Holi. Finding him again in their own house after his long stay in America, his friends in Calcutta, disciples and devotees took him and lost themselves in the enjoyment of the Holi festivities. That very day, Yoganandaji received sudden news that Sri Guru Maharaj was very in very ill health in Puri. He became very upset by this news, but because of circumstances, he could not leave that day. The anxious and distressed disciple journeyed to his Guru-pilgrimage the next day.

The horrific prophecy that he had made ten years ago, the heart-rendering indication that he had given us at the Khukurdaha festival, the

hint that he had given to us of the coming of the final days via that letter from Puri, calling our unaware selves to come before the Holi festival, all had now come together to meet each other. The earthly work
now ended. The beautiful, strong, tranquil and majestic body suddenly became somehow unable to function. Within a couple of days,
the two or three devotees and close friends from Puri that were present
became anxious to send word to the disciples in Calcutta. Hearing this,
Maharajji explained, "Let God's will operate as it is doing. There is no
need to interrupt anyone's work or duty to bring them here." As some
more time elapsed and Guru Maharajji's physical condition became
further desperate, those present became alarmed and restless, and
when they were ready to immediately send news by telegram to
Calcutta, he asked them add this little bit to what was being written:
"This is a malady that never happened before." Several of his beloved
disciples from Khidirpur along with Atulbabu arrived at his side.
Sheltered at Guru's Feet, the tireless servants such as Sri Narayan Giri
and others were giving all of their energies to help and all were especially waiting in suspense for the arrival of Yoganandaji. But what God
had willed is what happened. At the prescribed time of the Falguni
Krishnadvitiya Tithi, the greatest of men, Yogibara Jnanagurudev, in
profound peace and stillness, united in yoga, drew all Shakti up and
became immersed in Mahasamadhi. Struck by lightning, the helpless
devotees cried out in overwhelming grief. The world became dark.
Who else will now show the way of Light on this road filled with the
stupor of ignorance? Where did the helmsman to the shore go? On the
road, Swami Yoganandaji's sight suddenly became stilled at seeing a
light in the sky. In the silence of his heart he realized that it was all over.
The Life-Lover had left. Eventually, after arriving at the ashram, filled
with sorrow, this sannyasi and main disciple performed Sri Guru
Maharaj's last rites. Befitting the proper custom for yogis, the ever-
dear and the eternally worshippable form of Sriguru was buried in the
courtyard of the ashram.

The news of grief spread like lightning through the thousands of devotees and disciples nationwide. Even though they tried to remember the
injunction that one should mourn over a sannyasi's attainment of
Mahasamadhi, everyone's distressed minds became stricken and overcome with emotion. The stunned and saddened men and women's
steersman-less boat of life began to lose control. The Guru-surren-

dered, forlorn devotees attended to meditating on the form of Sriguru for consolation. Gradually, the Guru-Shakti seemed to manifest in the devotees' hearts and resolved this intricate quandary on the path of sadhana. Aggrieved sadhakas became gratified in seeing the ever-beautiful and regal dream-form. Travelers on the difficult and long road dedicated their souls and, receiving the company of the loving and Luminous Form of Guru came to recognize the ever-known path. It was as if the worshipful, ever-humble servant, who was the object of love, was suddenly being lovingly fanned in front of everyone. The Consciousness-attained, aware and able sadhaka, remembering the Eternal-Truth-bearing Jnanagurudev's manifested steadfast tranquility, experienced in amazement the perpetual flow of power in Guru's lineage, and in the commanding presence of that man, realized the exquisite revelation of character, as it flowed from the mouth of God and stated in the Sanatan Shastra:

"Eva brahmisthitih partha nainam prapya vimuhajhyati Sthitvasyamantakalehapi brahmanirvanamricchati"

Yogananda Sanga: Paramahansa Yoganandaji
As I Have Seen and Understood Him

by Swami Satyananda Giri

English Translation by Yoga Niketan

This translated book maintains that an almost literal translation of the Bengali words of the original author best serves both seekers and Kriyavans. No attempt has been made for the translations to be poetic or interpretive for the above-mentioned reason. If the reader notices irregular English grammar (including non-traditional sentence structure, punctuation, etc.), please understand that it is intentional. The translator has tried as best as he could to keep the work as close to the Bengali phrasing in the original without it being unreadable or incomprehensible.

Pranam, The Translator: Yoga Niketan

নমস্কার স্বামী যোগানন্দ গিরি মহারাজ

Paramhansa Yogananda Giri Maharaj

PREFACE TO ENGLISH EDITION

We had wanted a small explanatory note about "Yogananda Sanga" as some contemporary people are not understanding the vital role certain figures in the story had occupied. People should be made aware that the author, Swami Satyananda Giriji Maharaj was a supremely illumined Kriya Master and one of the most revered of all Sriyukteshvarji's disciples. We must continually take the dust of his feet. In fact when speaking of him we always prefer to say "Satyananda MAHARAJ". He was Swami Sriyukteshvarji's appointed "Ashram Swami", appointed to that post by the Swami Maharaj [Sriyukteshvarji] himself and also appointed as a Kriya Yoga Guru in his own right by Sriyukteshvarji.

Some vital and important figures mentioned in this biography such as Swami Satyananda Giriji Maharaj, Swami Shuddhananda Giriji Maharaj, Sri Sailendra Bejoy Dasgupta Mahasay ("Dadu"), and some others mentioned in the book were lofty Kriya Yoga Saints. They were Initiates of Sriyukteshvar Giriji Maharaj or Shastri Mahasay (Kebalanandaji) and were appointed Kriya Gurus in their own right. Be aware that they were Yoganandaji's brothers and contemporaries, not his initiates. They were selflessly laboring to help the work of their brother disciple whom they loved as only spiritual brothers can love each other. Contemporary people do not always understand that in those early days many devotees of Sriyukteshvarji and Kebalanandaji (Shastri Mahasay) were selflessly helping Yoganandaji in this work. Even Shastri Mahasay (Kebalanandaji) himself was helping! It has come to our attention that some readers are confused by the role these lofty beings played in the story and are assuming these people were all initiates of Yoganandaji Maharaj and this is not correct. Some were his initiates such as the beloved disciple Swami Premananda Giriji Maharaj. But other lofty beings such as the book's author, Swami Satyananda Giriji Maharaj, or Sri Sailendra Bejoy Dasgupta Mahasay were dearly loved disciples of Sriyukteshvarji, therefore occupying the position of being Yoganandaji's brother disciples and contemporaries.

When speaking of these lofty saints we must always show our respect to them all. To not give them respect is to insult Swami Sriyukteshvarji and Shastri Mahasay who appointed these great beings as their disciples and successors in Kriya tradition.

Divine Love,

kashi for Yoga Niketan
August 2004

CHAPTER 1

The memories of the past are full of happiness. For me, the remembrance of being in the company of Swami Yogananda is one of inspiration which stirs the deepest part of my heart. In 1906 of the Christian year, by the side of Upper Circular Road (now Acharya Prafulla Chandra Road)* and near the gate of the Calcutta Deaf and Dumb School situated there, my friend Kalinath Sarkar from Parshi Bagan came up to me along with a group of kids, with a football in his hand, and asked me to give him the instrument [pump] to fill the ball with air. After asking, I found out that a young boy of 12/13 years of age in that group named Mukunda Lal was the owner of that ball. Mukunda was very happy to have my help and he asked me to come and join in the daily games in the field nearby (Greer Park—now Ladies Park). Although Mukunda was a little older than me, we met and carried on as playmates and friends as if of the same age, as is natural during childhood. To make me happy, he used to say, "He is the manager of our club."

My father, Mohini Mohan Majumdar Mahasaya, was the primary founder and a singularly significant person involved with the work of the above-mentioned school. We lived in that school itself. A short while before, Mukunda father, Bhagabati Charan Ghosh, had begun renting the house addressed No. 4 Garpar Road, right by the north side of the school.

The most revered Ghosh Mahasaya was slight in physical stature, and his age at that time was close to 53. He was a high-level employee of the B.N. Railways; his monthly income was nearly one thousand rupees. Principled behavior, self-reliance, being reserved in speech and clear in his statements, rational, punctual, non-extravagant, simplicity and unostentatiousness in life, purity in intellect, adherence to responsibility, non-attachment, and all things such as these characterized his nature. I had noticed a deep reverence in him regarding scriptures, sadhana and Guru Lahiri Mahasaya, but never any overemotional feelings. Even at the death of his children, he held himself with as much emotional stability as there can be. From the time he lost his wife [to an untimely death] in the Christian year of 1904 to the time of his departure from the body at almost the age of 90 in 1942, he carried out all of the duties of a householder in both strict and gentle ways, being both father and mother to his sons and daughters. Some people used to think of his worldly approach as miserly, but we have known that for things that were necessary, he never hesitated to take care of any expenditures. In particular, he freely spent a great deal of money for the education of his children. My life was blessed at having received his closeness of affection, goodwill and blessings.

Ghosh Mahasaya was in Uttar Pradesh up to the year 1904. Yoganandaji's mother came to Calcutta for the occasion of the eldest son Ananta Lal's wedding, but she suddenly left her body, to everyone's shock and grief. This event especially struck Mukunda in his heart. I have heard from many people that his mother was of a gentle nature, devoted and dedicated to service. She used to freely spend money to take care of guests and visitors, which would sometimes upset Ghosh Mahasaya. These types of qualities of his mother were also seen to manifest Mukunda's life as well. The divine essence of his earthly mother's affection awakened his love for the Divine Mother, and was a great source of strength in his life. We will address this subject further when we come to the sadhak aspect of his life. Yoganandaji's countenance was like that of his mother.

৺ভগবতী চরণ ঘোষ মহাশয়
(পরমহংস স্বামী যোগানন্দ গিরি মহারাজের পিতা)

The Late Bhagavati Charan Ghosh Mahasaya
Paramhansa Swami Yogananda Giri Maharaj's Father

Swami Sriyukteshvar Giri Maharaj used to say, "Those who look like their mother are fortunate. Yogananda's face is like that of his mother."

If for some reason there was some harshness in the mind, the word "ma" seemed to completely soften Yogananda's heart. Once I was in Calcutta, engaged in following some regulations and duties set by Yoganandaji. When I brought up the subject of going to East Bengal, he refused to let me go, and told me to comply with the rules and stay in Calcutta. The discussion progressed, and when I said, "My mother is there. I am going to go and see her," his heart softened at once and he let me go with no hesitation. We have seen that if there was reverence for any woman, the essence of the Divine Mother would immediately awaken in his heart.

On the 5th of January of the Christian year of 1893—22nd Poush of the Bengali year of 1299, in the city of Gorakhpur in Uttar Pradesh, the physical form of Yogananda embraced the earth from his mother's womb at 8:57 at night, Gorakhpur time. Born as a Leo* and in the Kshatriya caste, the character and behavior of this being throughout his life made me feel that he was a "kshanajanma purush" [one who is born for the needs of the time]. His father had to transfer to many different places because of his work. Mukunda's education up to the higher 4th grade (meaning the 7th grade of today)** was actually through the Hindi medium. When he was in Berili in Uttar Pradesh, he became close friends with the son of the head of the town, Dwaraka Prasad, who was of the same age. This friendship left a deep and permanent impression in Yogananda's life. It can be said that he used to even judge the friendship and affection of other close persons of the same age by the measuring-stick of Dwaraka Prasad's friendship.

[*Translator's note: Although the zodiac used in India is the same as in the West, under Bengali astrological practices, a person is NOT identified by the sun sign of his/her birth, which is different from the usual practice in the West.]

[**Translator's note: The parentheses and the text within them are in the original.]

At this time (1906),* Mukunda was studying in Class 3 (now 8th grade)** of the Calcutta Hindu School. All of sudden, we heard one day that he is not at home and cannot be found. But 4/5 days later, he was found again. We learned that Mukunda, his classmate Amarendra Nath Mitra from Badurbagan, and his cousin Jotin-da had secretly left home to become sannyasis. The clever elder brother Ananta Lal Ghosh brought them back from Hardwar after making great efforts to do so. However, Jotin-da had actually returned before them from Burdwan without telling his friends anything.

[*and**Translator's note: The parentheses and the text within them are in the original.]

Right from childhood, a leaning towards spirituality and spiritual practice was seen to be impressed within Mukunda. He would become overcome with the attraction of the Himalayas from time to time. If he expressed this desire to his elders when he was a child, they called him mad and told him to let go of such thoughts. I have heard the elder Roma-didi [elder sister Roma] say, "That boy would become so aloof whenever he heard about the Lord and divinity…"* etc. Even before he came to Garpar, Mukunda once determined within himself that he would leave home within one or two days and take up the life of a renunciate practitioner. But on the other side, he had a great deal of affection and love in him for his brothers and sisters. On this particular subject, he told me, "I was completely set within that I would leave and become a sadhu. I wanted to properly see my brothers and sisters one last time. When I saw my baby brother Bishnu by the stairs on the way to the second floor, I just could not hold back my tears at all."

[*Translator's note: The ellipses […] are in the original.]

In any case, this time, he saved up money for food, and with some effort, collected almost 150 rupees right from his house, gathered things such as blankets, koupin [ascetic underclothing], khadam [wooden slippers], Gita etc., and at a certain time, he tied all of those things up in a bundle, and dropped the bundle from the roof of the Garpar house onto the alley by the east side of the house. It was rain-ing. He came down from the roof and quickly got past everyone pres-ent in the house, making a bunch of excuses—particularly to his youngest uncle, and was finally outside. The three friends rented a horse-drawn carriage and arrived at the Howrah train station. Wearing European clothes, they got up on the train, taking a compartment reserved for someone else. Because Amar Mitra was speaking English from time to time, many in the station thought that these must be children of Eurasians. Mukunda had to hold back his laughter with great effort. One companion—Jotin-da—went back [to Calcutta] from Burdwan without saying anything. The other two friends put on the garb of sadhus, but one of them still had the tie and collar were still fastened to his neck. On this side, people from home had begun to search for them. Many telegrams were sent out to many places and police circulars were sent out. One person who had one of these telegrams suspected them and held them in detention. Because of carelessness with their outfits, those suspicions became conclusive. In due time, [Yoganandaji's] elder brother went there and brought them back.

We again began to go to school, play sports and such things. We were also making many kinds of friends. We became close friends [Yoganandaji and Satyanandaji], and from then on, we played in the grounds of the Calcutta Deaf and Dumb School itself. One evening, after having played, we were all chatting, standing by the rail line nearby the gate. One by one, almost everyone went home. Mukunda, my brother Mukul—now departed—and I were the only ones left. In the atmosphere of the twilight, pieces of clouds were floating by in the beautiful sky; in some places they stayed still. Seeing this, Mukunda's appearance and feelings changed, and the direction of the conversation took a another turn. Mukunda began to say, "Oh my! I have seen so many mountains such as these! Oh how beautiful the Himalayas are there! How many sadhus are there..."* We two brothers were captivated as we listened to this. Later, Mukul also went back home. It was as if destiny came and brought the two of us—Mukunda and myself—together to begin on the path of a new life-journey. In the sliver of streetlight in the lonely darkness of the night, it seemed that an internal joy that was hidden inside radiated from Mukunda's face. He said, "Brother, I will show you the method of sadhana that I know. It is in this way that our friendship will grow." The next day, he showed me something about what he had learned only a short while ago about meditating on [Inner] Sound and [Inner] Light. My brother Mukul also learned a little bit. Although this was not [a] formal [initiation] in the customary way, from that time on, Mukunda became a friend-teacher and the charioteer of life's chariot in my heart. However, I have always related with him as a friend. We did practically everything together— eat, play, and all such things. Even when I addressed him, I called him "Mukunda" or "Yogananda." I do not remember ever addressing him by the formal "Swamiji" or "Paramhansaji." Later on, I sometimes addressed him in letters as "Swamiji." It is needless to say that because this servant [Satyanandaji] has had the company of Swami Sriyukteshvar Giri Maharaj, it is he [Sriyukteshvarji] who holds the place as "Guru Maharaj" for this servant.

[*Translator's note: The ellipses […] are in the original.]

Swami Satyananda Giri Maharaj

CHAPTER 2

After returning from Hardwar, the environment became quite favorable for Mukunda to live his ideals of life. Some [still] sarcastically called him "sadhu-baba," and some also had a bit of respect for him. But basically, when it became very well known—in school, playgrounds, sporting fields, the neighborhood, at home and among his relatives—that the boy just wanted to stay with what saintly matters, then there was no more hindrance in Mukunda's japa, meditation, devotionals, music and such things. He was openly known to everyone as a child with "special distinctions."* Classmates, playmates, relatives—whether older or younger in age—all held him as "Sadhu Mukunda."** For this reason, although he lived in the environment of the world, things such as frivolous behavior, unnecessary talk—otherwise known as "adda" [special chit-chat in Bengali culture], being stupidly boisterous, and other such things were not able to influence him very much at all. When friendly sarcasm towards his saintly behavior crossed a certain line, he would suddenly stop laughing along with that and become very somber. He felt this in his heart: spiritual things should not be treated lightly; that brings inauspiciousness.

[*and**Translator's note: The quotation marks and the text within them are in the original.]

Roy Bahadur Mitra—head teacher and significant educator devoted to the pursuit of knowledge—had a personality which was peaceful yet full of inner drive, and this had a deep effect in Mukunda's life. It is possible that the influence of the educator Aurobindo Prakash Ghosh awakened the sense of independence for the homeland and revolutionary feelings in him for a short while as well. Several of his classmate friends began to follow [Mukunda] around. Among them, Justice Sri Kamal Chandra Chandra, Sri Rajendra Nath Mitra—Advocate, and Sri Ramendra Nath Sinha (worked in the Ranchi Brahmacharya Vidyalaya at one time)* are those—meaning my elder "brothers"

154

[dada]**—who come to mind. Rajen-da and Ramen-da*** also received initiation into Kriya Yoga from Shastri Mahasaya.

[*Translator's note: The parentheses and the text within them are in the original.]

[** and ***Translator's note: In Bengali culture, boys or men who are elders—up to a certain age and respective to the closeness of relation or friendship—are addressed as "dada," meaning elder brother, and girls or women who are elders are addressed as "didi," meaning elder sister. This is regardless of blood relations. In this paragraph, the names "Rajen-da" and "Ramen-da" are short for "Rajen dada," and "Ramen dada." This colloquialism is used as a term of respect regarding many people throughout this book.]

Longing to see God and attraction towards spiritual sadhana were essential aspects of Mukunda's nature. At this time, those inclinations continued to become more and more strong, and wherever a sadhu, sadhak or devotee's name would be heard, he would run there to possibly get something [of spiritual value]. Close to home, he was able to have the company of his elder brother-in-law Satish Chandra Basu's brother Charu Chandra Basu. Charu-babu was an initiate sadhak of the well-known Radhaswami spiritual path. Charu-babu revealed the mysteries and techniques of [that] meditation to Mukunda. With intense effort, the child sadhak Mukunda engaged himself in that sadhana with his whole being and, within a short time, became absorbed in experience of listening in ecstasy to Divine Sound and seeing beatific revelations in Divine Light. For the sadhak Mukunda—the spiritually triumphant Swami Yogananda—the sacred dais that would seat guru-Paramhansa Yogananda's divine life was founded in hallowedness in his heart. That Light remained ever-undimmed throughout his entire life, and the profundity of that experience kept him always spiritually aware in many complex situations.

On this matter, it should be remembered that Mukunda never forgot his life-Lord, Yogiraj Lahiri Mahasaya. With reverence and discipline, he was engaged in the practicing the beginning stages of Kriya Yoga that he received from his father. In later life, he held this experience of Sound and Light as complimentary to Kriya Yoga. Even though in the beginning he was not able to experience all that much in Lahiri Mahasaya's method of sadhana, he had a natural and profound reverence for the Yogiraj. From childhood, the small picture of the Yogiraj that [Mukunda's] father had awakened reverence, devotion and an unearthly experience of refuge in the Divine. No matter which sadhak he would see, no matter where, no matter how much reverence he had for them from childhood throughout his life, this Great Being [Sri Sri Shyamacharan Lahiri Mahasaya] was ever-established as his life-Lord at all times. Whenever he thought about that event of his blessed life when he was able to have a place in the lap of the Yogiraj for a short while, he would go into a kind of ecstatically mad state. When he began to practice the small preliminary practice of Kriya Yoga but did not attain much, he still had the firm belief in his heart that it was through this Kriya Yoga as taught by Lahiri Mahasaya that would attain that for which he longed. This is the most excellent and most direct path to God-realization. His conviction to this standpoint was impressed firmly within him from the very beginning. In later times, this faith was thoroughly realized in the testimony of his spiritual life.

Though he was reverential towards the teachings and sadhana of Sri Ramakrishna-deva and such other realized beings, and although he especially experienced the devotional beauty of Sri Ramakrishna's teaching and reflections in his own life, [Yoganandaji's] natural attraction was towards the path of yoga. For this reason, he used to gaze at the picture of Mahatma Tailanga Swami [Trailanga Swami] with tremendous respect and become absorbed in it. Yoganandaji's] physical stature was naturally of a slight nature, and he had an unseen wish that in the future of his yogic life, he would have a weighty body like that of Lahiri Mahasaya or Tailanga Swami Maharaj. When he was older, that wish was fulfilled—he came to weigh almost 2 1/2 mon [1 mon = 82 pounds].   206#

Although he was not especially drawn to the worship of idols/images, it was seen that he had devotional inclinations towards Sri Krishna, somewhat towards Lord Shiva, and especially towards Mother Kali. On some days, when we were going to school, we both used to do pranam at the door of the Radha-Krishna temple situated opposite an ironworks plant on Harrison Road in Benetola. During childhood, he had traveled all the way down to Srirameshvaram in South India with his elder brother Ananta Lal. The temple of Chidambaram, the glorious image of Shiva, the statues, and the atmosphere had made a strong impression upon him. The statue of Ma Kali especially put his heart in ecstasy. For this reason, he used to go to Dakshineswar and Kalighat. But it was the statue of Devi in Dakshineswar—imbued with the essence of Thakur [Sri Sri Ramakrishna Paramhansa]—that greatly attracted him. He also did sadhana to Divine Mother there to witness Her manifestation. The words of Sri Ramakrishna-deva: "Whoever calls Ma here in Dakshineswar filled with true longing in the heart—that is the person who will have her darshan"—this was embedded firmly in [Yoganandaji's] heart, and with this faith, he had had the darshan of Divine Mother in the Dakshineswar temple, and was blessed to have experienced the Immaculate Radiance of Divine Light from Mother's Body fill his own body, mind and soul. As far as the subject of worshipping Divine Mother, he used to feel great joy in discussing and reflecting upon the teachings of Sri Ramakrishna as well as the stories of the great sadhak Sri Ramprasad. Although he was not all that skilled in music in those days, he would sing the songs of those great beings with deep love and longing. Present next to him, I would also sing with him. He sang "Majal Amar Man Bhramara," "Dosh Karu Noi Go Ma—Ami Svakhat Salile Dube Mori Shyama," "Doob De Ma Kali Bole," "Amon Din Ki Hobe Tara," "Jaag Jaag Jaag Ma Jaago Kula Kundalini," "Tanaye Tar Tarini" and such other songs, and even though they were not sung precisely, he sang them with great feeling. Later on, he also loved to listen to "Aar Kobe Dekha Dibi Ma," complete with rhythm and accompaniment, especially sung by the sweet voice of brother-disciple Sri Krishna Chandra Addhya Mahasaya.

When he was 14/15 years of age, the fiery and intense aspect of Ma Kali grew in Mukunda's heart for a time. Going to the cremation grounds and the desire for sadhana on corpses also arose intensely in him, and he even endeavored to inspire me towards this type of sadhana. He even tried to employ some methods to get rid of the fear in my mind. Although we frequented the cremation grounds, we did not exactly carry out sadhana on corpses; only some japa and contemplation were done. At this time, he used to elatedly sing songs like, "The Overflowing Flood of Mother has come in the Deep Night." From to time to time at that time, the feeling that if the heroic presence were established, then it would destroy the demonic presence—this obsession took a hold of him—of course only for a short while. "Come, I'll show you an astonishing and fantastic picture of Mother"—saying this, he very excitedly took me to the temple-house veranda that was there at that time at the Belur Math, where there was a picture of Mother in Her terrifying Form, three-eyed and blazingly Radiant. He liked to construct the statue of Ma Kali by his own hands during the time of Kali Puja. There was not always a setup to have formal worship of that statue. I also had the practice of constructing a little statue of Ma Kali just for my own heart's sake. Because of this secret or latent element within ourselves, we had a special encounter with each other in a more or less insignificant celebratory occasion. That event was played out in the very courtyard of our Deaf and Dumb School—opposite Mukunda Lal's house. Seeing our animated state, the late Jamini Nath Bandopadhyay Mahasaya, the head teacher at that time, came to us to be in our company in this joyous celebration—particularly to check on the preparations for prasad and its distribution. Within a short time, Mukunda became very taken by this distinguished founder of the Calcutta Deaf and Dumb School who was a close friend of my father, who was our guardian and like a close relative, and one to whom aspiring students were so dear; and [Yoganandaji] held this joyful memory with him for a long time. It was somewhat because of the influence of this [event], as well as with Mukunda Lal's enthusiastic instigation, that we endeavored to create a sadhana-cave in a secluded corner of the southeast side of the garden in the school.

Although he had taken up the practice of reverence to idols for a while, he was not seen to be much attracted to that area for too long a period. "Bhava" [divine feeling] was what was essentially established within him, and his heart leaned toward the bhava of "Nirakar Brahman" [Formless Absolute]. For a while, he took me to the peaceful atmosphere of the Naba Bidhan Samaj of Mechuabazar—a branch of the Brahmo Samaj. We used to sit on secluded asanas in the samaj-house and be absorbed in meditation. We became friends with one of the members of the movement, the eminent—now departed—Jnananjan Niyogi Mahasaya. Niyogi Mahasaya held Yoganandaji in reverence as well. While in America, [Yoganandaji] was greatly benefited by knowing about the work of this friend, and by consulting with him in many ways about his methods of work for success. During the time of taking part in this samaj, [Yoganandaji] came to know another special friend, follower and companion, Sri Jitendra Nath Majumdar Mahasaya. We will have to speak about him again later. As was customary for these occasions, [Yoganandaji] became drawn to Brahmasangeet [mystic songs of the Divine] and Rabindra Sangeet [songs of Tagore]. Even though he could not sing very well at that time, he loved to hear all those songs from others. He used to be entranced by listening to songs such as "Amari E Ghare Apnar Kare," "Amal Dhabal Pale." "Mandire Momo Ke," "Esheche Brahma Namer Tarani," and "E Hari Sundar." Before going to America, he used to sing the songs of dream-breaking waterfall—particularly "Ami Jagat Plabia Berabo Ghuria," a phrase which he sang with total euphoria again and again. A while later, he came to greatly appreciate reading and experiencing the writings and teachings of the eminent Swami Rama Tirtha on Oneness, Non-Duality and Radiant Beingness. At that time, he always carried an English version of a condensed biography and/or book of sayings by Swami Rama Tirtha with him. The influence of that went with him to America as well. He used to set the short, English poems of deep spiritual experience by Swami Rama Tirtha to the usual Bengali-types of melodies and sing them with all his being. Sometimes, when he was so taken over by feeling, he would sing his own Bengali translations of the songs and go on singing in his spiritually immersed state. He would become invigorated and full of fervor upon reading Swami Rama Tirtha's heroically spiritual statements just once. In those times, [Yoganandaji's] bliss-graced face would dispel the darkness in ourselves. A resurgent elation would also awaken in our hearts. At those times, if he found near him a friend or companion who was of the right kind, he would recite one of Swami Rama Tirtha's sayings with loving adoration and intensity, and then elaborate on its significance himself. Many of the songs or poems in Yoganandaji's "Songs of the Soul" are influenced by the writings of Swami Rama Tirtha.

CHAPTER 3

I once again recall the time of 1908 of the Christian year. We [Yoganandaji and Satyanandaji] grew more and more close. It was as if the two of us could not stay apart. Our homes were next to each other. We used to try to stay together as much as possible. Even when we were separate, we were vigilant that both of us carried out our own responsibilities from one [set of principles]. He always kept me aware of this. To walk the righteous life, we created a situation where we both would eat in a disciplined way, behave [accordingly], exercise properly, regularly do japa and meditation and such other things. Two diaries were purchased for us to keep a daily journal. Although friendships were close on the football field, he decided at this time that if—on the path of sadhana—we wanted to protect ourselves from hindrances, distractions and the company of people who were outwardly oriented, we could not take part in these types of games in the usual kind of way. It is needless to say that my childlike heart was a little hurt by this act. Nevertheless, I bowed my head and accepted his words. It should be known that the usual restlessness associated with the age of childhood-adolescence was never able to overcome Mukunda. Yet in his younger days he was an athlete; he won prizes in races; he even used to train with weights. But at this time, the intense longing to attain God was fully awake in him, and as his companion, I also was becoming passionately filled with the same deep feelings.

Because of carrying myself differently from the usual lot of kids, because I was not at home very much, and because I—the "good and obedient boy"—was spending time with Mukunda concerned with spiritual things and somewhat neglecting studies and other things, my parents were saddened by this. One day, he [Satyanandaji's father] could not help but sarcastically blurt out, "Let's see how much of a Prahlad [child-saint of mythology] you have become." I admit that such a loving father would naturally be hurt upon seeing his eldest son suddenly begin to behave in this detached way, letting his studies slip and such things as these. Without stating this in a superficially fervent way, I can say from the depths of myself that the principles such as: adherence to duty, treating everyone with care, service and work of organized teaching continue to have the greatest influence throughout my life because of my epitome of a father. He gave me so much respect and support for my ideals and the duties that I had to perform in the working field, and gave my fellow-workers and fellow-servants such encouragement. He prepared so many things by his own hands and collected things to help me or our institution. Taking my students into the lap of his own affection, he gave them advice and practical counseling in unaccountable ways, for which he drew their heartfelt gratitude. And how many times did his teachings help me in sannyas life and in the area of work. And so many times did he encourage me to be dutiful. He was greatly distraught with the worsening of my studies as a child, and at that time, he wished that I should not be around Mukunda. But in his heart, there was affection for Mukunda. This is why when in later years Yoganandaji returned from America and came to see him, [father] welcomed him with a profound embrace.

We prepared our daily practice. As much as possible, we planned to follow the principles of being vegetarian, being self-reliant, maintaining restraint in speech and such other vows of the life of a brahmachari. In our own homes, we arose at dawn, practiced japa, meditation and Kriya regularly, studied, went to school and carried out all such work. After school, we returned home, washed ourselves, had a little repast, went up to the [flat] roof of the house, practiced a little japa and meditation there, and then went for a walk together. At this time, we decided upon a large count on the rosary beads and practiced pranava japa, meditation on [Inner] Sound and [Inner] Light and some simple performance of the pranayam of Kriya Yoga. Sometimes on the days off [or holidays], we went away to sit in seclusion. We would go one mile from the house and sit at the veranda of the Pareshnath temple or by the bushes of its garden at times, and sometimes we would even go three miles away to the Eden Gardens sporting field and practice japa by the bushes there. We decided on a certain number of japa, sat separately to practice by the bushes and then meet each other afterwards. It is needless to say that even though we sat at the same time, [Yoganandaji's] discipline and concentration was much stronger and deeper than mine. Spiritual inclination and sadhana were a part of him. I was trying to keep up with him. My respect for his spiritual nature made me reverent to the path of sad-hana. Although I felt him to be strict at times, his high ideals and his personal direction paid for the expenses of the road on my path. Some profound experiences also came about when I did my sadhana in his company.

[Yoganandaji] proposed that we must do japa and meditation at night as well, and that we must try to sadhana all night from time to time. It was decided that when everyone went to sleep at night after dinner, we would meet at his family's house (No.4 Garpar Road).* Because he slept in the living room of the house, we felt that we would be able to pass the night unnoticed. So that we would not fall asleep, we made arrange-ments to have tea from time to time. A little stove and kettle were pro-cured. If not for the whole night, we sat almost until the end of the night. But we did not continue like this for long. It seemed that there was not as much tiredness in the body when we sat [for sadhana] at night.

I used to get past the closed gate of the Calcutta Deaf and Dumb School. Mukunda would quietly and slowly open the door [of his fam-ily's house]. But we were not able to keep this secret for long. We were caught. My father and other guardians became angry with me. On the other side, Mukunda Lal's father also figured everything out. Sometimes, he would come downstairs very quietly and knock on the locked door. We would hurriedly get up. The hurricane lantern used to be lit at a low level. Mukunda used to brighten the lamp and sit with a book like a good boy studying while staying up all night, and just before that, I used to silently escape through a door to the outside out onto the street. We thought that we were fooling the master of the house. But we children could not understand that our respected and experienced elders knew and understood this deception. [Yoganandaji's father] would say nothing, and laugh and walk away. Then on some days, he would come downstairs and knock on the door so hard that we would become flabbergasted at not knowing what to do right away. Setting the lamp to the right level and opening the door to the outside—all became very confused, and we thought that we would definitely be caught because of the sounds being made. It went on like this for a short while. After that, we were not able to carry on like this for many more days. Sometimes, for some occasions, we stayed up all night. In this way, the need for sleep became lessened in natural way for Yoganandaji and me for the rest of our lives.

In writings about realized beings, a attribute called "nityasiddha" [ever-perfected] is [sometimes] mentioned. I do not actually have a clear idea about exactly what kind of a condition nityasiddha is. In my association with Yoganandaji—being in his company during childhood, adolescence, youth and more advanced years, I have seen him actually as a human being. When I saw the usual weaknesses natural to human beings in the working world, I perceived them just as weaknesses. (In the eyes of devotees, those things have also been known as "lilas" [divine play].)* But I have seen his exceptionally one-pointed discipline in spiritual life as well. Many times, he and I began the practice of sadhana at the same time. I have seen him naturally and easily become immersed in the sadhana-practice. I sat as if to perform an order—to perform a task.** Perhaps both of us would get up from the asana after not feeling like doing it longer. I would be tired and sort of let out a sigh of relief. But he seemed to just be relaxing the body a bit, as a natural thing. Sometimes the behavior at that time could look the same as ordinary pleasure-oriented people, when the tamasic pull of the body would seem to make the mind weak; but the spiritual attention within him would never be completely gone; the divine melody of his heart was ever tuned to the music of the Infinite. Thus, when sadhana-practice would begin after relaxing, other work or casual chatting and such, he would sit already with the music continuously flowing within him. For us, it seemed that it was more like trying to re-tie a broken string. On the outside, we both carried ourselves the same way. It is probably for this reason that when certain faults and errors with him would be evident in the usual ways, and even if I argued with him back and forth from time to time, he always kept me in his respect because of the natural spiritual beauty deep within him. In every human being, there is True Consciousness—Kutasthachaitanya. Because of behavior and latent impressions, it is as if that Essence is unmanifest in us. And although a kshanajanma purush is also subject to latent impressions and thus faces difficulties at times, that Supreme Consciousness is only momentarily dormant in him but flows like an inner river within. For an ordinary person, the awakening to Supreme Consciousness happens by taking up hard practice and non-attachment; for a kshanajanma purush, the brilliant Light of Supreme

Consciousness is revealed by the slightest touch of the beckoning within.

[*Translator's note: The parentheses –()– and the text within them are in the original. The bracketed –[ ]– phrase within the parenthetical is the translator's, used for the purposes of clarification.]

[**Translator's note: The work "task" is in English in the original.]

In 1906, right before going to Hardwar, Pandit Sriyukta Rakhal Chandra Sen Kavyatirtha Mahasaya was Mukunda Lal's home tutor. We also studied with him at the Mitra Institution. A youthful young man, this calm, student-loving scholar mahasaya was respected by all of us. When teaching at [Mukunda's] home, he gave a great deal of encouragement to Mukunda to cultivate his spiritual inclinations. A short while later, he gave up teaching. Saying, "I will take up the vocation of my family," he began a naturopathic healing practice. His clinic can still be seen in Maniktala. Whenever we would run into him on the streets in his later years, he would praise our ideals of sannyas life and affectionately say, "So, sirs. I am the one who is your adi guru [first guru], no?"

Though we were not participating regularly in organized sports, we were not totally divorced from fun and games either; and it can be said that we did not carry ourselves with all that much solemnity. So, around late afternoon, we would run around the neighborhood, play "chor-chor" [similar to "tag"] and such games. A toy air gun came into our possession. Mukunda used to take that and demonstrate his heroism as the head, or captain, of the group. The inclination towards leadership was forming in him from the beginning. He also enjoyed eating together with his friends since childhood. Sometimes, some money would be saved up and the two of us would even go to a shop to eat. Once, our saved and collected monies totaled almost five rupees. I did not really contribute all that much to it. Suddenly, Mukunda set upon a whim that a musical instrument should be purchased. Yet he did not know very much about singing or playing music at all. He had no training or practice either. Actually, I was the one—having inherited such from my parents—who could sing a little bit of everyday music. In any case, no one had the capacity to stop his intense wish. One evening, we went to Chitpur. For about 4/5 rupees, a small behala [folk violin] was purchased. Until then, Mukunda had not even touched a musical instrument at any time. Getting a little instruction from the storeowner about the technique of using the bow and string, he started playing the behala right on the street. He played that behala day and night for a few days, particularly at the times when we would have been playing with the air gun; he would just play whatever came to him on that behala, and walk around the neighborhood while playing it. He was completely caught up in the intoxication of that music.

Another reason to save money was thought up. A box was obtained and named "Daridra Bhandar" [savings for the poor]. That box was completely sealed. There was no way of taking the money out without breaking the box. There was only a slit-opening through which the money could be deposited. It was decided that when enough money would fill the box and there would be no more room, the box could then be opened. A few days afterwards, the auspicious day of Ardhoday Yog was upon us. Many beggars come to Kalighat by the Ganges during that occasion. Remembering this, we decided to open the box before it was filled up and we took the money to Kalighat and gave it to the needy. After distributing most of the money and only keeping what we needed to pay for the tram, we were coming back, when we saw a few infirm beggars desperately pleading for help. Mukunda's heart was taken aback. He said, "Oh my! These are the people who need this money." But then what money will be left? [He said,] "Come, we will just walk home. Let us give them the money." We were not used to walking 5 long miles of road from Kalighat to Garpar. Kids who were from a more or less well-to-do family, like Mukunda, certainly were not used to it. I was also a young boy. Perhaps I was just a little unhappy, but I still agreed to follow this ideal principle. I think that there was still a very little bit of money left over, and after having walked most of the way, we rode the tram for a short distance. In those days, the abundance of mass transportation that is there today did not exist. Even to take the tram, one had walk a good distance. Mukunda Lal had a desire in his childhood days to become and serve as a physician. He even fancied going to England to become an I.M.S. once.

It was in [Yoganandaji's] nature to be welcoming and caring to guests and visitors. Even if just any person came to meet him, [Yoganandaji] treated him with respect. However, his attention seemed to wane from time to time for those who grew close to him. It actually seemed to be disregard, and this caused us to feel hurt at times as well. Certainly, it is by behavior and intent in different circumstances that we assess people. Guru Maharaj [Swami Sriyukteshvar Giriji] used to say, "Righteous living and correct behavior is the garment of human character."

One day, while I was standing on the side of Garpar road, I suddenly saw Mukunda Lal gleefully running towards me. Immediately upon coming up to me, he said, "Hey, something great has happened. My elder brother was very happy that Rakhal Pandit Mahasaya, who used to teach me at home, had left. [Ananta Lal] thought that it was good, because now there wouldn't be anyone to speak about all this spirituality and make me all restless at this young age. So they [Mukunda's guardians] very carefully looked and checked and finally settled on an elderly scholar mahasaya to teach me Sanskrit. I immediately became respectful upon seeing his dignified being. Right after he began to teach me with loving care, I asked him, 'Pandit Mahasaya, have you read the Vedas, Puranas, all the philosophies?' He calmly said, 'Yes.' Seeing his tranquil state, I got up the courage to ask again. 'Well, Pandit Mahasaya, do you know that we do a little meditation on [Inner] Sound and [Inner] Light and such things?' With the same calm manner, he said, 'Yes.' We were talking about all of this, and my heart was filling up with joy, and my curiosity was growing greatly too. I asked him, 'Have you heard of Lahiri Mahasaya?' He laughed a little and said, 'Yes. I am his disciple.'" While he was saying all of these things, Mukunda's joy began to overflow, like currents breaking over the banks. No one at his home—not even his Yogiraj-disciple father knew that this scholar—Ashutosh Chattopadhyay—or Shastri Mahasaya—was [Mukunda's father's] gurubhai [brother-disciple]. It was so blissful to just practice the preliminaries of Kriya Yoga showed by [Mukunda's] father. [Mukunda] blessed me too by making me his companion in practicing that sadhana. Mukunda Lal told the scholar mahasaya whatever we had known. Shastri Mahasaya extensively explained to us about the parts of Kriya Yoga, such as: Mahamudra, Pranayam, contemplation of the chakras in the spine, Yonimudra and other such things. Mukunda Lal became immersed in sadhana with new zeal. I became his blessed companion in following him in the practice of sadhana.

I have said before that although Mukunda Lal pursued different practices of japa and sadhana in his young days, he felt a natural pull towards Yogiraj Lahiri Mahasaya. The carefully kept picture of Lahiri Mahasaya that his mother had was like an alive Divine Being to him. He had experienced the fulfillment of his heartfelt prayers to that picture when he was ill. Sometimes, he even experienced the Divine Touch of Living Light from it, upon mediating on that picture. Being in the company of the profoundly deep and great sage Acharya Shastri Mahasaya, the presence of [Yoganandaji's] life-Lord Lahiri Mahasaya became luminously awakened. It seemed that he finally surrendered himself completely to the sadhana of Kriya Yoga. I do not remember any practitioner practice sadhana with the kind of intensity that he did while he was with Shastri Mahasaya. It is another thing to talk about attaining the spiritual Nectar of the Stillness within, whether without practice or through regular and hard practice.

There were separate home tutors for Sanskrit and mathematics. But Mukunda Lal did not have much interest in studying. Sitting down to study, going to school and such other work went on because of having to obey rules. He liked to listen to Shastri Mahasaya speak about Yogiraj, about sadhana, and such other things. He even received permission from his father to regularly read the Gita with [Shastri Mahasaya] for short periods of time. Sometimes, when Shastri Mahasaya would come to teach, I would go there and sit quietly by the side.

From this time on, Mukunda became recognized everywhere as a person with special distinction—in his home, with neighbors in the neighborhood, school, and all such places. Classmates, those of the same age, and many others came to him as friends and began searching spiritually because of his influence. Many of them came and received initiation into Kriya Yoga from Shastri Mahasaya. At this time in 1908 of the Christian year, [Mukunda] was a student of the entrance class at the Hindu School. A special friend came into his life, the great Sri Jitendra Nath Majumdar, student of the entrance class at the Herr school, and resident of Badurbagan by Amherst Street. Jitendra Nath was initiated by Shastri Mahasaya. Mukunda Lal received this new friend in a very close way, and made him a companion for the practicing of sadhana and spirituality. In my childlike mind, it seemed that maybe we were growing apart a little bit. Coming into the company of Mukunda, the new sadhak Jitendra Nath's studies and housework suffered somewhat, and that naturally upset his father. At his father's orders, elder brother (now departed)* Upendra Nath Majumdar came to Mukunda with the purpose of reigning in the situation, and met with Shastri Mahasaya as well. Instead of being able to impose himself, Upen-da heart melted at the spiritual touch of his younger brother's friend, and he received initiation from Shastri Mahasaya. [Upendra Nath] was always dearly and favorably regarded by his father because he responsibly managed the duties of their household. In the future, Upen-da would become a sadhak of special distinction, friend, helper, and a singularly disciplined devotee of Shastri Mahasaya, and would live his entire life as an unparalleled servant of humanity, filled with guru-given spiritual energy.

[*Translator's note: The parentheses and the text within them are in the original.]

The younger grandmother of Upen-da's household was very happy about the dawning of spiritual nature in her grandchildren, and she used to call Mukunda to the side and quietly and affectionately give him encouragement. In later years, due to his father's loving nature, Jitendra Nath's friend Mukunda and we as his companions received the affection and care of [Jitendra Nath's] father (the late, eminent paper businessman Bholanath Majumdar Mahasaya)* as well. There are sweet memories of the celebration of Sri Sri Jagaddhvatri puja held at their village-home in Triveni in 1916 of the Christian year. Later, more will be spoken about this matter.

[*Translator's note: The parentheses and the text within them are in the original.]

CHAPTER 4

So that he would take good care to study in the entrance class, [Yoganandaji's] father made special arrangements for his son. But it was right at this time that Mukunda became much more interested in sadhana and its associated practices. He somehow just managed his studies. In the company of Shastri Mahasaya, Mukunda Lal had found new life in sadhana, in which he continued to progress. In a few days, he crossed the first stage of Kriya, and he pierced the tongue-knot. The enthusiasm and overflowing joy of that day brings a thrill to the heart even now. Because of the pull of his sadhana-meditation and its associated activities, the studies of his companions Jitendra Nath and myself also went on to suffer some indiscipline as well.

Inspired by Mukunda, we tried to leave ourselves out of the usual way of living that was followed by ordinary people and tried to keep ourselves absorbed in subtle and spiritual ideals. It is needless to say that we were also the recipients of our guardians' anger, because of neglect in studies and leaving the house at indiscriminate times. But we were attentive to make sure that we did not behave disrespectfully in any way towards them. Actually, we used to silently pray for their blessings within ourselves. It was because of these prayers for blessings that our education was basically completed successfully in the end, and why we were able to maintain the position of being able to take care of them.

[Yoganandaji] was very much attracted to the effects of yogic powers, fruition through willpower, and what could be learned from supernatural accounts and other such things. And at this time, he was also seized by the desire to follow practices that would bring about those powers within himself. He was always firmly convinced in the depths of his being that the instrument of the intense power of will in a human being's mind empowered by union with the Infinite Divine Power, or the Divine Power using the instrument of the power of human will, could make the impossible possible. Even during childhood, he used to try to awe the members of the household by concentrating for a couple of days and making physical signs appear on his body after that time, gaining victory in sports by simply taking up Ma Kali's name and demonstrating such other extraordinary occurrences in ordinary situations. One day, Mukunda Lal went to his middle-sister's house in Bhavanipur (the mother of the eminent devotional singer and master of physical culture—Sri Bijoy Mullick),* and came to know that for the improvement of roads in the town, a part of their house would end up on the street; and everyone was unnerved by this terrible possibility. Mukunda Lal sat silently and received an inspired message within himself and said, "No, sister. No harm will come to this house." Just a few days after this, his middle-brother-in-law came to Garpar and elatedly exclaimed, "Brother Mukunda, the house has been saved. It has been decided that the road will go by the side of the house." It has been seen sometimes—while trying to scold someone because of wrongdoing—that he ended up saying things in such a way from the hurt within him—that those things came to fruition almost like a curse. He also was very saddened by seeing the destruction that the power of his own words could cause as well. I cannot say that everything he said came to fruition in this way every time either. However, because of the confirmation of the power of his will, I always believed in it deeply.

Around this time, he was also very interested in the practice of hypnotism and its applications. He did not actually learn this from any specific person. Through his own desire, the power of his observational abilities and practicing the touching of different parts of the body and physical manipulation in different ways, he was able to apply these techniques on young people. It was also seen that he was unsuccessful in applying these techniques with people who were somewhat older or even some younger than him.

Whenever he would hear about any supernatural event or about some person with miraculous powers, he would go there to learn about that wisdom. One evening, Mukunda Lal, my neighbor Atulya Mitra—who was like a younger brother to him, and I were sitting on the sporting field. We were all quiet for a while and then [Mukunda] said to us, "Look, look—how bright that star is in the sky, and see how beautiful the face of Sri Krishna is in that star, wearing His crown." I looked with great intent in that direction but there was nothing that I could see. Atulya went on to say, "Yes. It is so beautiful. How beautiful that crown is! Isn't it so?" Atulya was not a sadhak. Instead, I was actually the one who was known as a better boy than him in everyday circles. And it is also not entirely so that I did not have some pride about this within me. But I felt that I was completely unworthy because of failing this test of "Krishna-darshan" and I was deflated with sorrow within; and I went on to say, "Mukunda, all of my sadhana and meditation is wasted. I am no longer fit to be a companion on your spiritual path. Teach Atulya all of the knowledge of sadhana." But he did not pay much attention to what I said. My place with him remained unshaken.

Mukunda Lal told me that he had just learned how to perform divination through paan leaves from someone and he would show me the applications of this knowledge. One morning, we went to a secluded field and sat down. One paan leaf was oiled. He told me to stare at that paan leaf with one-pointed focus. I had heard that whoever is thought about, especially if it is a dead person—that person's form will appear on the "mirror" of the paan leaf. Brother Mukunda sat with deep calmness next to me. As I went on concentrating on the mirror, a radiant-eyed and blue-hued beautiful form bloomed. I was instructed, "Mentally ask whether there will be betterment for you and such things." I silently prayed and asked from the depths of my being. I do not seem to remember getting any answers. Right at that time, brother Jiten came up to us. Our concentration was also broken.

One day, he came and said that he had learned—from a tantic sadhak, I think—a method through which, if performed strictly for a few days, one could attain some supernatural powers. Some part of a lizard's body was necessary for this. My brother Mukul, some kids from the Calcutta Deaf and Dumb School and I busied ourselves in trying to catch some lizards from the trees in the garden. For a couple of days, a few lizards were also kept tied to strings. But because the feelings of non-violence awoke in us, every one of us abandoned all activities associated with that endeavor. That method was never carried out.

Due to the influence of the practice of hypnotism, he became more seriously interested in the hidden power of will within oneself. In later years, he would go on to say with profound faith rooted in his own experience that it was the play of the Lord's Infinite Power that manifested itself through the life of the sadhak. The world can be benefited through the controlled use of this Power. During the time of application, one should remember that the Operator is God Himself and is working through the instrument of the person. We should also remember this when we speak about yogic miracles. The wise ones say that if one is not especially disciplined in regards to applying yogic capacities or yogic powers, one should beware, because one can easily fall. Through the application of will, he healed many people with health problems until the end of his days. On this matter, he laughingly said one day, "When I was a child, I used to imagine that I would grow up to be a big doctor and serve the infirm. By the Grace of God, my imagined wish manifested itself in this way."

Direct encounters with ascended beings, the radiant and divine appearances of supernatural power-endowed realized beings, the arrival of the spirit of a dead person in the midst of mesmerized people and speaking with that spirit, and ordinary sightings of ghosts and such were things that he believed in, and pursued with concentrated means in situations and occasions. Once, after crossing the pool in Rajbazar and after traveling for a good while on the road to Narkeldanga, we entered a quiet, large factory where he said, "It's very possible that there is a holy disembodied soul present here. Come, let's pranam." We did pranam. One day, because of some situation, he said to me, "Oh! Of course, you don't believe all this?" I told him, "I cannot say something so big and certain like 'I don't believe.' My knowledge is limited. But I don't have much interest in these things—meaning these kinds of supernatural workings, and I have managed my own explanations for these things as well." In any case, his belief in these remained firm and unshakable throughout his whole life.

One day, he showed me a bright amulet made out of some metal, given to him by his mother. This amulet was carefully kept in a container. Some written things were carved into the amulet as well. We could not make any sense out of the writing. He said that his mother had received this amulet in a supernatural way after receiving some instructions from a sadhu. Supposedly, the sadhu told his mother that her second son—meaning Mukunda—would become a sadhu, and that he should be given that amulet for his beneficence. When his mother came to Calcutta to be at the wedding of her eldest son Ananta Lal, Mukunda was in Uttar Pradesh with his father. His mother left for the afterworld right before the wedding and at her deathbed, gave instructions to give that amulet to Mukunda. She also said that that amulet would protect Mukunda from dangers and problems for a while, and that it would also keep the highest ideals in tact in him. [Yoganandaji] used say with deep belief that he had divine revelation and found his ideal life—meaning the sannyas life—through the touch of that amulet. Once when I had to take a test [in school], he very carefully put the amulet in my pocket and gave me assurance that the difficult questions on the test would become easy because of the touch of the amulet. With faith, I took that amulet with me, but other than the first excitement from it, I do not remember that I received any benefit from having that amulet. Regardless of results, I did return the amulet to him with deep respect.

Ordinarily, he seemed to be somewhat of a shy nature, as if he wanted to be in the protection of being behind the scenes. But I witnessed the power of his inner strength when it was necessary. Let me recount a more or less ordinary incident: I was on the field one day when I suddenly ran into a group of boys. Seeing me, they started to make all kinds of derisive and sarcastic comments about Mukunda. The leader of this group was a slightly older person called "Jate Pagla" [Mad Jate], who was known to be of a bad sort. For no reason whatsoever, he all of a sudden spoke out, "If I find Mukunda, I'll break his bones..." and such other things. I was scared when I heard this. Without any delay, I came to Mukunda and told him of all of this. He also was astonished, and began to consider why there should be this kind of meanness. A little while later, he said, "Come, I will go to them myself." I was completely beside myself with fear. I forbade him, "No! Don't go now! Don't go alone. They are very bad people. They will beat you up!" He disregarded what I had to say and ran towards the field. After arriving there, he stood with great somberness in front of them and asked them what reason they had for their hatred. Mukunda's age, body and strength were far diminutive to them, but they became completely silent. Jate Pagla's proudly upheld head bowed to him. He silently came along with brother Mukunda. Having touched the touchstone, Jate Pagla completely became transformed. Instantly, he became a follower-friend and devotee. From that moment until now, that Jate Pagla—Sri Jatish Chandra Sen—has been a dear, benevolent and helpful friend of Yoganandaji and us. I recall that one day [Sri Jatish] had bought a pair of glasses out of fancy for his own use. Mukunda spoke out, "Hey! One shouldn't wear glasses like these. It'll make the eyes get worse." Immediately upon hearing this, brother Jatish crushed, twisted and smashed the new glasses, case and all. Mukunda jumped up and said, "Hey, hey, Pagla [crazy]! What are you doing? What are you doing? It's a costly new pair of glasses!" Brother Pagla said to us, "You said that this would be harmful. I don't want to keep this any more!" Praise you, brother Jatish!

Although it was imminently necessary to prepare for the entrance exams, it was right at this time that the feelings of vairagya [non-attachment] began to grow in Mukunda. He also was helping his friend Jitendra Nath cultivate those feelings. Some austere sadhana was taken up as well. I too became involved in this practice. We practiced sleeping on benches, sometimes lying on the bare floor, walking barefoot, being spartan in clothing and eating, restricting speech, traveling far distances on foot and such other things. He told me, "We must remember our vow. After our entrance or matriculation studies, we must leave home. I am going to go the Himalayas and settle on a place. When your last exams finish, I will come immediately. And I will just remind you once of the vow. Please don't forget it." He used to travel far distances to have darshan of sadhus and sannyasis. At that time, if he noticed something even slightly wrong in the appearance or behavior of some famous sannyasi, he would become very disappointed. He did not have any hesitation in offering his reverence to any great being in any place regardless of the rules of caste. It was during this time that—because of him—neighbors, relatives, classmate-friends and others came and received initiation into Kriya Yoga from Shastri Mahasaya. Also at this time, Sri Tulsi Narayan Basu of Pitambar Bhattacharya Lane in Garpar, a student of the entrance class at the Metropolitan Institution, became drawn to Mukunda. Tulsi Narayan's father, Hari Narayan Basu Mahasaya, was the principal of the of the Government Art School. Among many artworks created by his own hand, the beautiful picture of the flute-playing Sri Krishna remains widely known and famous. The practical dutifulness, unostentatious life and loving outlook of Basu Mahasaya awakened the deepest reverence in us.

The entrance exams were taken. Even though there was not much preparation and study, after being helped by some classmates during the last days and having had some idea about a scattering of some of the possible questions, he attended to his studies and somehow passed the test. He was convinced that he was successful only by the Grace of God. In due time, at the orders of his father, he enrolled in the Metropolitan (now Vidyasagar)* College. Books were bought; classes began; but there seemed to be no peace in the heart. The plan that was there to leave home right after the exams made him restless. He used to remind his friend Jitendra Nath about this goal as well.

[*Translator's note: The parentheses and the text within them are in the original.]

At this time, Mataji Tapasvini from Uttar Pradesh arrived at the Mahakali School near Garpar on Sukia Street (now Kailas Basu Street).* I believe that it was with her that Swami Dayananda—disciple of Swami Jnanananda Maharaj, the founder of Bharat Dharma Mahamandal—and some other sadhus and brahmacharis came and stayed in that building. Mukunda was very drawn to the ever-youthful, vairagya-radiant, tranquil-countenanced, young Swami Dayananda. It seemed that this he was the model of the renunciate life. Within a short time, both became endeared to each other. The intellectual brahmin-progeny Dayananda ignored his B.A. exams, wrote some spiritual tenets on the test paper, left home and began to live as a disciple-sadhak at the feet of Guru Swami Jnananandaji.

[*Translator's note: The parentheses and the text within them are in the original.]

With the financial help of the Indian government, Swami Jnanananda Maharaj had founded a brahmavidyalaya (College of Divinity)* in Benares, its philosophy based on the fact that all religions were reflected in the model of Sanatan Dharma [universal religion]; and to run the operations of that school, he had been training Swami Dayananda. Unbeknownst to the masses, the visionary and dedicated teacher Dayanandaji attained an exalted level in the world of education. His deeply knowledgeable Bengali and Hindi talks and scriptural lectures were listened to by captivated audiences.

[*Translator's note: The parentheses and the text—in English—within them are in the original.]

The being and character of Dayananda seized Mukunda with fervor. He spoke about his feelings of vairagya—particularly with Jitendra Nath, and both of them decided that for the time being, they would leave home and go to live in the Bharat Dharma Mahamandal in Benares. Mukunda gave away his books here and there, sold some of them, and prepared to get ready to go to Benares. At his instructions, Jitendra Nath went to Benares before him. Now there was no running away in secret, and [Mukunda] spoke about his plan to his father. His father tried in many ways to get him to let go of this idea, but all efforts were fruitless. Even Shastri Mahasaya tried to prevent him from leaving home at that time by presenting him with many kinds of reasons and wisdom. But Mukunda was unmovable in his focus on vairagya. When this was happening, he all of a sudden sang out [a Bengali spiritual song] right in front of his father, "Why the delay? Make preparations for the far journey that has to be made," and so on. In due time, he set off for Benares. When he left, he gave me his address, words of caution, encouragement and good wishes.

CHAPTER 5

In October of 1909 of the Christian year, Mukunda had arrived in Benares with his friend Jitendra Nath. Swami Dayanandaji had made arrangements for both of them to have residence at the Bharat Dharma Mahamandal. Mukunda was very happy to have received a room for himself where he could carry on with his meditation practice. The Mahamandal was a center to help propagate, and aid in the flourishing of, Sanantan Dharma [universal religion] in an organized way throughout India. All of the residents of the ashram had to carry out their assigned duties. Doing so much work and interrupting sadhana did not agree with Mukunda. Some of the other working residents of the ashram even began to deride him upon seeing his indifference to ordinary tasks. The vairagya-oriented Mukunda had left home with the intense longing to realize God, or attain Atman, hoping to be deeply absorbed in spiritual sadhana, but he was disappointed at not being able to find enough opportunity here to do so. Just as Mukunda had been drawn to Swami Dayanandaji with great respect from the very beginning, a spontaneous feeling of affection towards Mukunda had also arisen in Swamiji. We had seen that it was not just affection towards a younger brother, but a feeling of reverence for Mukunda's spirituality that had awakened in Swamiji's heart. Even though the residents of the ashram stopped the insults after Dayanandaji spoke with them, Mukunda was not very happy in that activity-oriented environment. It was gnawing at him from time to time to go to some other appropriate environment and place, where he could dedicate himself into being absorbed in meditation.

On this side in Calcutta, Mukunda's father and relatives became worried. At this time, Mukunda's uncle, the eminently established attorney of Serampore [Srirampur] of the Hoogly District, Sarada Prasad Ghosh Mahasaya (now departed)*—the father of the co-president of Yogoda, Sri Prabhas Chandra Ghosh Mahasaya—said, "Our Priya-babu [Swami Sriyukteshvar Giriji Maharaj] from Serampore is a disciple of Guru Lahiri Mahasaya. He has now become a sannyasi, and has recently gone to Benares for a while. Why don't we write to him saying that perhaps he can make Mukunda understand and then bring him back home?" Following up on this proposition, a letter was sent to him, and Mukunda was written to as well, saying, "Go and see such and such sadhu—etc."

[*Translator's note: The parentheses and the text within them are in the original.]

In due time, Swami Sriyukteshvar Giri Maharaj (Priya-babu)* sent someone to find out about Mukunda at the Bharat Dharma Mahamandal. Mukunda, at the same time, felt an unseen, benevolent attraction to find Swamiji and set out for him. When [Mukunda] was near the Bangalitola section of Benares, he all of a sudden caught sight of a long-armed, beautifully countenanced, sweetly smiling sannyasi with a walking stick in hand moving along on his late-afternoon walk. Suddenly their eyes met, and as if unknowingly, Divine Grace brought them into feeling that they had a close relationship with each other. For a short while, they both stood still. Mukunda came up to him. Sadhuji tenderly asked, "Are you Sarada-babu's nephew? Come with me."

[*Translator's note: The parentheses and the text within them are in the original.]

By the banks of the Ganges in Benares, below the huge northern ramparts of Ranamahal, yet quite a bit above the shores of the Ganges, in some residential quarters, Swamiji had founded Pranavashram for the internally oriented sadhaks of his Sadhu Sabha to cultivate their wisdom. His elderly and venerable mother also lived here. Swami Sriyukteshvar Giri Maharaj usually came to Benares during Durga Puja, and traveled to different parts of western India at the invitation of devotees, making Benares the center at the time. On Mahashtami, he held a special event in honor of the memory of Yogiraj Lahiri Baba's Mahasamadhi occasion, and that event went on until the Kojagari Purnima. On the night of the full moon, the event was concluded with spiritual talk, celebratory meal, and other such things. It still fills me with joyous inspiration to remember the profoundly peaceful form of Guru Maharaj in the beautiful, peaceful and sacred moonlit night in the northern banks of the Ganges in Benares, his wellspring of wisdom, and his straightforward, nectarous and heart-touching wisdom. We would be filled with delight when he sometimes would tenderly laugh and joke with little children. And how much wisdom was given to us through that laughter! And we sometimes received disciplinary instructions in that way too.

He had no introduction, did not know him, did not have any acquaintance with him, but somehow, as if entranced by some incantation, Mukunda walked forward at this being's beckoning. He arrived at the secluded place in Ranamahal and was now in the company of a mahapurush. It seems that what comes to mind from sadhuji's words are his affectionate and melodious voice—somehow very familiar, the visionary teaching of an acharya, and the pacifying words for a restless heart. This realized being claimed Mukunda's heart-throne as his Divine Guru of Spiritual Wisdom. Time passed while speaking about many things, and then suddenly Swamiji Maharaj [Swami Sriyukteshvar Giriji] spoke out, "Oh, but you won't listen to what I have to say." The heart-surrendered youth [Mukunda] said, "Yes. I will listen to everything. You are going to tell me to go and study, right?" Swamiji said, "Yes. That's what I have to say." Without any hesitation in his voice, Mukunda said, "Your will is my command. I will return to Calcutta to study." The one who abandoned college, ignored everyone's advice, who was vairagya-bound and had the firm resolve to be immersed in sadhana, who had expressed just moments ago that he would keep unmoved in that resolve even with this Swamiji Maharaj—how he just bowed and surrendered himself by the spell of some magical mantra just like that! The Jnana-Guru-Swami lovingly gave him his blessings. Mukunda went back to the Mahamandal, told his friend Jitendra about everything and then returned to Calcutta. He asked Jitendra to convey his farewell pranams to the absent Swami Dayanandaji. Jitendra also came back to his home in Calcutta.

His father, elder brother and relatives were overjoyed by his return home. His friends were elated at having their companion and leader back again. Although he stayed in Calcutta at this time, he used to constantly go to Serampore to be in the presence of Swamiji. Already initiated in Kriya Yoga, it was as if sadhak Mukunda's entire being was given new life by the touch of Divinity. He completely smothered himself at the feet of Swami Sriyukteshvar Giri Maharaj, his much-longed-for charioteer for his life's chariot and the spiritual guide of his life. It was as if two great souls, related for many lifetimes, became united again in Divine Love. Our ordinary reasoning does not understand the magnetism of Divine Love, the soul-offerings of a devotee and Divine Embrace. It is must be in this way that the experience of the Guru—the dear one to the Self—and his spiritual touch truly takes one over with the feelings of discipleship.

Mukunda used to reverently remember his father teaching him the preliminaries of Kriya Yoga, receiving initiation from Shastri Mahasaya (Hansaswami Kebalanandaji)* on to the path of sadhana, and the rapid growth in spiritual experiences while at his feet [under his tutelage]. And he continued to hold satsang with Shastri Mahasaya from time to time as well. Normally, he would arrange it so that his interested friends would be initiated into Kriya Yoga by Shastri Mahasaya. Mukunda had to hear a lot of criticism at this so-called time of "guru-change." The heart-surrendered disciple Mukunda was not affected by any of these argumentations or gossip. His basic daily behavior itself expressed that he had completely surrendered to Swamiji Maharaj, and that Swamiji had also completely taken him up in his lap. The holy Shastri Mahasaya was always known as "gurudev." Even at this time, Mukunda called him gurudev. In usual conversation, he used to speak of Swamiji as "Jnanagurudev." The devoted disciple asked from the deepest part of his being to disciplined, directly to Jnanagurudev. We remember, "shishyastehham shadhi mam tvam prapannam." It seemed that to become thoroughly formed as the fit servant and teacher for the realization of the spreading and flourishing of Kriya Yoga that the Yogiraj-blessed Mukunda— a sadhak destined by the Lord—prostrated himself to the Acharya of the Yuga Swamiji Maharaj, presenting himself as a true representation of a human being willing to accept discipline as a student and disciple.

[*Translator's note: The parentheses and the text within them are in the original.]

At this time, Mukunda became acquainted with some youths of the same age as him and brought them to Shastri Mahasaya, from whom they were initiated. It was in this way that he went on making his environment more and more sadhana-oriented. During this period, I was apart from his company for a good while. It was now, in Garpar itself, that friends Tulsi Narayan Basu and Upendra Nath Mitra Mahasayas and he became close. Jitendra Nath and his elder brother Upen-da also used to go around with Mukunda as sadhana-companions. A regular satsang session was set up in Upendra Mitra Mahasaya's house.

Taking Sanskrit, logic and chemistry as his main subjects for the I.A., he enrolled in the Scottish Church College in July of 1910 of the Christian year. He continued to make more friends bit by bit in college as well. The routine of student-life began again. He used to also attend Bible study class in college with deep respect. He was amazed by the many messages about the mysteries of sadhana in the Bible. The Gita was a book that was always with him. There were times when he constantly kept the booklet of Sri Ramakrishna's teachings collected by Swami Brahmananda in his pocket. Whenever the whim caught him, he would sit wherever he was and begin to read it. If anyone was near him, he happily recited it to them as well.

Holding [spiritual] celebrations, cooking outdoors in the woods with friends, and sometimes sitting together and relishing the tastes of spiced crisped rice, fritters, alur dom [special Bengali potato dish], where everyone ate from one plate—it was in his nature to regularly do such things. Whenever those big, plump potols [zucchini/okra type of squash] were brought and fried for a meal, his childlike heart would jump up with joy. He was also very expert at cooking many kinds of dishes by his own hand.

At this time, he arranged for a [spiritual] celebration for the occasion of Sri Sri Shyamapuja [worship of Kali Ma] at Upendra Mitra's house. When the occasion began, there were only a few rupees for expenditures. Yet almost one hundred people were invited. It was believed that by Mother's Grace, the expenses would be met. That is actually what happened. Other than the expected gathering in the celebration and distribution of prasad, another 60 people were welcomed to the celebratory meal. Mukunda did not pay much attention to the regular puja and spent a lot more time singing devotional songs, chanting and meditation along with his friends.

He paid great attention to properly adorn the ceremonial areas. He himself worked to beautify the place. He set up the room in a way that was pleasing to him in this Kali Puja as well, especially displaying the picture of Sri Ramakrishna-deva with supreme dignity. Instead of casting off the image of the Divine Mother into the Ganges river on the usual day appointed for that, he stayed in that room and went on meditating daily there. One day, he even brought the venerable disciple of Sri Ramakrishna—"Sri M" (Mahendra Nath Gupta Mahasaya),* the compiler of the Sri Ramakrishna Kathamrita [The Gospel of Sri Ramakrishna], to the worshipping area; and filled with the feelings of Sri Ramakrishna's devotion to the Divine Mother, Mukunda was blessed at having the company of this great devotee "Master Mahasaya" (Sri M).**

[*and**Translator's note: The parentheses and the text within them are in the original.]

He had actually been keeping the company of Master Mahasaya a little while before this. Almost every day, Mukunda used to go to meet with him at a higher educational establishment founded and directed by Gupta Mahasaya [Sri M] known as the Morton Institution, which was located on Amherst Street. It was this building that was rented for the wedding of Mukunda's elder brother Ananta Lal, and it was in this house that he lost his mother with great misfortune right before the wedding celebration. So naturally, the presence of this building itself used to reawaken the pathos and pain of the loss of his mother. In the company of Master Mahasaya, who was intoxicated in the empowered Name of Divine Mother bestowed by Guru, Mukunda's heart was filled with the beauty of Mother's Divine Love. From the touch of this great sage and realized being, Mukunda received priceless spiritual capital and treasure for the path of life. Up until the end of his physical life, [Yoganandaji] would be taken over and become absorbed in the contemplation of Divine Mother (Devi Ma).* In the Western world, thousands and thousands of men and women who were in his presence were blessed by singing the Name of Divine Mother. They still sing ecstatically sing the Name of Divine Mother.

[*Translator's name: The parentheses and the text within them are in the original.]

Mukunda would become filled with the nectar of devotion whenever he would meditate on Sri Ramakrishna Paramhansa-deva, the divine worshipper of the Mother of the Universe. And so from time to time, he would suffer the pains of going by foot to Dakshineswar, and he would sit immersed in meditation there. Sometimes, I was also lucky to have been his companion [during these visits]. He used to also find out ways of meeting with and being in the company of the sannyasi-maharaj disciples of Sri Ramakrishna. I heard directly from [Yoganandaji] about a special spiritual experience he had had when—for just a short while—he was in the close presence of Swami Turiyananda Maharaj (Hari Maharaj).*

[*Translator's note: The parentheses and the text within them are in the original.]

Since he was young, the God-facing heart of Mukunda was not particularly drawn towards the service oriented activities of the Sri Ramakrishna Mission. His life's motto was, "I will attain God, and remain absorbed in His Essence." After having the taste of pure devotion in the presence of Master Mahasaya, Mukunda became devotedly drawn to him. From time to time, even the inclination to take him as guru would arise in his heart. Because of Mukunda, I was also blessed by the company of this great being. [Master Mahasaya's] humble nature, profoundly peaceful carriage, Guru-empowered radiance, effulgence from meditation and melodious-voiced singing still awakens luminescence in the heart. Mukunda used to say, "Look at how his devotion is and how reliant on the Self he is. Always—in speech, behavior, spiritual matters—he speaks of the Lord. It is as if the Lord Himself is the One Who is actually doing everything he does at all times." Yoganandaji had been in the company of many other sadhus and saints, expressed his reverence to them, and been benefited by being with them as well, but—with the [obvious] exception of Gurudev [Swami Sriyukteshvar Giriji Maharaj]—I do not think that any other sadhu or sadhak was as dear to his heart.

The college studies went on. For the study of Sanskrit, Bihari Pandit Mahasaya—the head teacher of Sanskrit in the Scottish Church College—was hired for home tutoring. Mukunda had great respect for this scholar mahasaya. [Bihari Mahasaya] also used to regularly help us carry out our dharma-oriented activities.

Mukunda always tended to his wish of having those of his age as his friends and companions in his spiritual life. Just as he was able to make friends amongst his neighbors and in his neighborhood, this did not change in college either. The [spiritual] essence was beginning to manifest in his behavior and in his personality. Among classmates, Shishir Kumar Ganguly from Bhavanipur, Basu Kumar Bakchi from Shantipur, Sachindra Lal Dasvarma—who came from Gaya, and Govinda Chandra Ghatak from Faridpur were particularly the ones who became close to him. Other than Govinda-da, all of the other three were initiated into Kriya Yoga by Shastri Mahasaya. They often came and joined in on our satsang occasions in Garpar. At this time, we do not have any news of Govinda-da. Shishir Kumar fell ill at the time of the B.A. studies and left for the afterworld. Sachindra Lal was first in the First Class in English Literature for the B.A. and M.A. and later acquired further degrees from England, after which, in Bihar, he was appointed to many high positions in the field of education, and a few years ago, he also departed heavenward. Basu Kumar graduated M.A. and became a Ph.D., and is presently an eminent professor in the University of Michigan in America.

It was Shishir Kumar and Basu Kumar that grew especially close to Mukunda. Meditation and devotionals, eating together from time to time, spending the night together, traveling to many different places, keeping the company of sages and saints, and all such things went on. Fortunately, I also was close to them. Mukunda was our director. Our ways of life went on at his direction. It was as if the four of us became a special kind of family. Mukunda and I used to sing together back from time that we were kids. I feel a little hesitant to say this, but I was probably the one who had whatever little musical understanding. Mukunda just went on singing somehow. Later, the heart-intoxicating songs of Yogananda that arose from intense sadhana gave such peace and joy to so many sadhaks and spiritual seekers. The recordings of songs in his voice entrance devotees to this day. And so, as we are on this subject, the nectarous-voiced songs of Shishir come to mind, sung with overflowing devotion and full of life.

Jitendra Nath, his elder brother Upen-da, neighbor Tulsi Narayan Basu, and other friends also used to get together with us. Guru Shastri Mahasaya's dedicated attendant Upen-da is now in the afterworld.

Tulsi Narayan Basu displayed inclinations towards organizational work from the very beginning. Somewhat with his and Upendra Mitra's help, Mukunda set up a library with the name of Sarasvat Library in the quarters of the Nag family adjacent to Upendra's house. It was originally planned that this library would only carry spiritually based books and such, but later, because of the demands of the neighborhood, this became a regular library. After this, Mukunda and Tulsi Narayan did not feel that they had to keep a working association with this library any more. To continue with this goal, another library—named Shankar Library—was set up in Tulsi Narayan's home. Tulsi Narayan's ability to gather books was a wondrous thing to us. At this time, we used to regularly meet at Mukunda Lal's No. 4 Garpar Road residence.

In the month of December in 1911 of the Christian year, the great convention of the National Congress was arranged to be held at the Greer Park (Ladies' Park)* on Upper Circular Road (now Acharya Prafulla Chandra Road).** The boys and girls from Rabibasariya Vidyalaya—representing the newly rising society—were presented to do musical performances. With this group was the beautifully voiced young boy Prakash Chandra Das (Swami Atmananda Giri—now departed).*** Because of being a part of the Rabibasariya Vidyalaya, Prakash was acquainted with Tulsi Narayan Basu. Prakash Chandra was easily liked by Tulsi-babu. From time to time, Tulsi Narayan used to bring the child to his home. At that time, Prakash was a child who had just lost his father. He had one elder brother and one younger brother, but they were bewildered by the death of their father and at a loss for what to do. Because their family had a partnership with the famous Harry Brothers Organ Builders, they were not desperate. Still, [Prakash Chandra] became somewhat despondent at that time, even though his brothers were there. Tulsi-babu was overcome with compassion and enrolled Prakash Chandra into the Bahubazar [Bowbazar] school. This was when the venerable Shastri Mahasaya was the head teacher of Sanskrit at the Bahubazar branch of the Metropolitan School. Eventually, Prakash Chandra became a member of Tulsi-babu's household and became as close as a relative. Although he was not a Kriyavan, Prakash Chandra began to join in with the activities of our group. The songs from his young voice filled us with joy. And although Tulsi Narayan was a Kriyavan, he took initiation from the great sadhak

Yogin Thakur and, at his request, became a member of the Brahmananda Society. [Tulsi-babu] set up a worship room in one part of the house and began to hold Mahavir Puja with songs of the Rama [Ramanama songs] every week, and on every new moon, he held Sri Kali Puja. Prakash Chandra followed Tulsi Narayan and became initiated in that way as well. However, the relationship and association with us remained just the same.

CHAPTER 6

In the month of August of 1911 of the Christian year, Mukunda proposed that we must renew our dedication to renunciation and meditation; we would have to become completely ready for sannyas. It was settled that one week before Sri Janmashtami [birthday of Sri Krishna], we four—Mukunda, Basu Kumar, Shishir Kumar and I—would take up a special vow and way of living for the entire week. Being barefoot, eliminating any indulgence, practicing self-sufficiency, and practicing control and discipline in many different ways, we would spend the week and on the day of Janmashtami, we would accomplish the goal of our vow.

At the auspicious time of Janmashtami we fasted. Four "dhotis" [cloth worn by males as garment for the lower half of the body] were stained [with the renunciates' color of] ochre. In the attic room on the roof of No. 4 Garpar Road, we performed many sacred acts from the morning on. At noon, while performing the fire-ceremony and oblations, with Mukunda leading us, we took up the resolve and ideals of sannyas—we put on the ochre garments. In the afternoon, we went to the festivities of the Sri Ramakrishna celebration in the Kankura Gacchi garden-park, and after having taken upon our heads the blessings from sages and saints in this joyous environment, in the deep of the night, we went to a place somewhat far from the city—by a new canal on the eastern edge. In this beautiful, meditative, uninhabited, silent and peaceful place outside the city, with Mukunda (for that time his name was given as "Yogeshvar")* presiding as priest, we cast away the tuft of hair and the sacred thread [renunciation of caste etc.]. Witnessing this was our companion-friend Govinda Chandra Ghatak, and Panchudidi in Garpar, who had kept the sacrament of sunned boiled rice and ghee from the oblations prepared for us, for the time that we would break our fast in the middle of the night. At that time, we were studying in school and college; Swamiji Maharaj had also ordered us to at least study through the B.A., which we had to do; so we took those ochre garments and carefully put them away, so that we could take up those symbols of our vow at the appropriate time and renounce the householder life. We told ourselves that for the rest of our lives, no matter where each of us may be during the holy time of Janmashtami, we would deeply think of each other during that time.

[*Translator's note: The parentheses and the text within them are in the original.]

Basu Kumar and Shishir Kumar, and later Sachindra Das Varma also, lived in One Hostel of Karbala Tank Lane. Many times in the afternoons, this hostel, particularly Basu Kumar's room, would become our joyous gathering place. Other students staying in the hostel would also join in this; some would also sarcastically deride us by saying "babaji"* and such. Although the head of the hostel, Brajamadhav Basu Mahasaya, was a Christian, he liked us very much, particularly because of Basu Kumar's and Shishir's high character and behavior— even though from time to time we would somewhat stretch the rules of the hostel.

[*Translator's note: The word "babaji," in this case, does not have anything whatsoever to do with Mahamuni Babaji Maharaj, the Great Guru of Sri Sri Shyamacharan Lahiri Mahasaya. The term "babaji" [respected father] is usually used to refer to a holy man, but sometimes it is also used in irony, sarcasm and derision, particularly among skeptics, and also when referring to pretenders of saintliness.]

At this time in Garpar, we came to know another youth by the name of Pulin Bihari Das. He was a little older and also physically very strong. Having had the company of a certain sadhak, feelings of non-attachment arose in his heart. Leaving his own home and village, crossing the channel at Maniktala, he had begun to live in a small cottage in Bagmari. He would join us in our little celebrations and make us all very happy by taking care of all of the difficult tasks of cooking by himself.

Because we did not have an appropriate and peaceful place for our gatherings and satsang, with the help of Pulin Babu, we began to rent—for five "sikis" [Rs.1.25] a month—an adobe-walled and leaf-thatch-roofed cottage right next to his home. We decorated the temple-dais with the pictures of Gurus and the adorned the walls with the pictures of great saints. We would gather at this place, located about a mile from Garpar, practically every day. Sometimes we spent the nights here as well. We also made arrangements to hold satsang here once a week. Cooking, washing dishes, house-cleaning—we felt a special joy in doing these things ourselves. In the Christian year of 1951, Paramhansa Yoganandaji wrote to me from America, in remembrance of Guru's Glory, "Satyananda, do you remember that room for one rupee? That tiny seed today has become a huge tree."

Sri Guru Maharaj Swami Sriyukteshvar Giriji came every Saturday to have satsang meetings at his disciple Narendra Nath Basu Mahasaya's house in the Jeletola Lane of Simlapara. This was actually the first meeting-house for the Calcutta Satsanga Sabha. He [Sriyukteshvarji Maharaj] would regularly hold meetings of the Satsanga Sabha on Sundays in Serampore [Srirampur]. Every Thursday, Tulsi Narayan Basu would do puja and Sri Ramanama Sankirtan [devotional singing in praise of Lord Rama] in the prayer room at his house. To address the difficulty of attending at all of these different places, we made arrangements to have Satsanga Sabha meetings every Friday in our cottage by the canal. The agenda of the Sabha were: recitation of scriptural texts, devotional singing, chanting, discussion of spiritual subjects, performance of Kriya Yoga in a gentle way and meditation. At the end of the meeting, sacramental fruits and sweets were given to everyone. With those who stayed the night, or stayed most of the night—we usually ate a meal of "khichuri" [a mixture of rice, lentils and vegetables] together.

Even though it was a distance from the city, interested friends—and sometimes persons of note as well—would attend the meetings held at this cottage. At this time—when it comes to the matter of ashram service—special memories of Purna Chandra Sen (now departed),* our Kriyavan friend from Triveni, come particularly to mind. He worked in an ordinary office job, but during non-working hours and holidays, he completely gave himself to doing many kinds of work [sacred service] untiringly. How eager Mukunda was to make that small cottage beautiful! Whitewashing the room and staying up all night and digging up the dirt floor—particularly with brother Purna—when, while cementing the floor, Mukunda's hands were bleeding, cut and torn-up—this I remember even now. I had returned home right after the whitewashing. The next day, brother Purna came to me and said, "Come. Swamiji is calling." I looked at him mystified, and with a feeling of surprise, asked him, "Who is 'Swamiji'?" Purna laughed and signaled to let me know, "It is Mukunda who is 'Swamiji'." This was not a sarcastic statement by Purna Chandra. Spending day and night with Mukunda and learning of his desire for the sannyas life from Mukunda's own mouth, brother Purna assumed that Mukunda himself must be calling himself "Swamiji," and thus greeted Mukunda with full reverence and respect as "Swamiji" in front of me, the very first thing in that next morning. Immediately upon seeing him, when Mukunda showed us his scraped-up pair of hands, we were mortified and ashamed in our hearts, and we thoroughly understood that he did not only give directions to others, but he himself performed the laborious work with resolve.

Near this very same cottage was a garden-house called "Panchavati." The "Bengal Technical Institute," founded at that house by Tarak Nath Palit, the eminent legalist during that time of nationalist stirrings, was closed, because Palit Mahasaya, in order to establish it as a college of science, had donated that house to Calcutta University. "Bengal Technical" was in a poor state of affairs at that time, and so that garden-house was also quiet. Later of course, that institute established itself in Jadavpur, upon having received an enormous endowment from the renowned advocate Dr. Rashbihari Ghosh. At present, that place has been transformed into the Jadavpur University. From time to time, at the direction of Mukunda himself, we would do japa and meditation in the tranquil, contemplative environment under the trees in this garden [of the garden-house]; we would also occasionally spend time discussing spiritual matters.

Basu Kumar Bakchi's guardians did not approve of his associating with Mukunda. They thought that his studies would suffer and that the honor of his orthodox brahmin family would be tainted. For this reason, they enrolled Basu Kumar in Bankura College. [Our] classmate, upon group-leader and director Mukunda's advice, at the time had been initiated into Kriya Yoga by the venerable Shastri Mahasaya, was within a short time deeply satiated in the nectarous taste of sadhana, and as well, the steadfast, calm-natured Basu had then been attached to Mukunda as if in a surrendered way, and he [Basu] was loved by everyone of us [also]. Ever obedient to his family, and the "good boy" of the household, Basu could not go against the wishes of his guardians. With abject reluctance, he went to Bankura with a sorrowful and heavy heart. Often he would run from that place and come to spend time and have fun with us for a couple of days.

Eventually, the time of the I.A. test came around. Mukunda did not want to take the test this year. He had not been able to prepare properly, but everyone at home knew that he was getting ready for the test. Right at the onset of the test, he became seriously afflicted with a terrible illness. With medical treatment for just a short time, he became well. This servant [the author] stayed near him day and night. Even before he was completely well, Swami Sriyukteshvarji Maharaj came to see him at the house in Garpar. It was as if Mukunda was cured of the entire illness at his arrival. The test of course was not taken. Mukunda said, "Even before, I had felt intuitively that I would not have to sit for the test. See, God saved my face."

After the test, Basu Kumar went to his family home in Shantipur. It was difficult to come and go in secret from there. Yet over here, Mukunda was anxious to hear of his news. He sent a letter to Shantipur with his friend Hema Chandra (later known as Swami Sadbhavananda—the founder of the Sri Ramakrishna Mission Vidyapeeth [educational institute] in Deoghar).* Somewhat disguised, Hema Chandra arrived at the Bakchi house (as a kin of P.M. Bakchi)** in Kashyappara of Shantipur, finding an opportunity, gave Basu Kumar the letter, said a few words and quickly took his leave.

[* and ** Translator's note: The parentheses –()– and the text within them are in the original. The bracketed –[ ]– statements are the translator's, for the purposes of clarification.]

All of the people at Basu Kumar's house were disciples of the then renowned sagacious sadhu Nagendra Nath Bhaduri Mahasaya. Basu too used to come to Calcutta and go to him from time to time, attending the "Hari Sabha" [congregation of God] at sadhuji's ashram. When he became close to us, he had stopped going. At the order of his guardians, he again began to occasionally attend the Hari Sabha. Even though practically everyone at the Bakchi house had disdain for us, Basu Kumar's eldest paternal uncle "Kanuda," Bhaduri Mahasaya's dear disciple—had sympathetic and fellow-feelings towards us.

Bhaduri Mahasaya's home was in a rented three-story house on Upper Circular Road (at present, Acharya Prafulla Chandra Road),* very near

Mukunda Lal's house. Eager for the company of sages and sannyasis, Mukunda Lal was blessed by the company of this saint. As befitting a yogi, residing alone and in solitude, the ever-ascetic Bhaduri Mahasaya's dignified being, deep scholarship of Eastern and Western scriptures, and his profoundly tranquil presence from the practice of yoga captivated Mukunda. An observant of norms of the culture, Bhaduri Mahasaya would sometimes jokingly deride Mukunda about his transgressions of ordinary norms and rites. Even so, Mukunda experienced affection and blessings from him, and before going to America, he took Bhaduri Mahasaya's blessings upon his head. Later, in front of the Ram Mohan Library, Bhaduri Mahasaya's devotees founded a temple in holy memoriam to him. When Swami Yoganandaji returned from America, he offered sacred and humble reverence to him in this place.

[*Translator's note: The parentheses and the text within them are in the original.]

The results of the I.A. test were published. Sachindra Lal Dasvarma took first place. Basu Kumar placed highly in the first division and Shishir Kumar placed highly in the second division. At the time of enrollment in the B.A. level, Basu Kumar came secretly to Mukunda; that small cottage was his living space. It did not take very long for the people at his house to locate him. Everyone together ultimately enrolled in the Scottish Church College. Basu Kumar again took his residence in One Hostel. Our old meeting room continued to still be the same place.

Basu Kumar, Shishir Kumar and I, at the loving leadership of Mukunda Lal, would gather together many times right in Mukunda's family's house. Sometimes we would spend the night there together as well. Because of an ailment in Shishir's leg, his comings and goings became less and less, and then stopped. Shishir's studies also ended. He actually went on residing near his mother and father at the Bhavanipur house, under proper medical care. From time to time, we would accompany Mukunda and go and see him. We would listen to songs sung in his devotion-soaked, nectarous voice. At Shishir Kumar's absence, we three became strung on one thread; some people used to call us "trio" in English—we would often rise, sit, sleep and eat together. Gradually, Mukunda Lal, because of his spiritual presence, drew our endearment and reverence and had his place in our hearts as a friend-guru. We began, without even questioning, to accept all of his directions as those to be followed with reverence. It was as if guru Shastri Mahasaya and Jnana-guru Swamiji Maharaj [Swami Sriyukteshvarji Maharaj] took their places in the sacred royal thrones above our heads. Friend-guru Mukunda's seat was established in the dais of the heart. The two classmates, Mukunda Lal and Basu Kumar were friends of practically the same age, and as was said at that time, would be with each other inseparably; I was younger in age, and even though we were friends, I would accompany them in a younger sort of way. In the area of work, in Yoganandaji's words, one of us was the right hand and the other was the left hand. With our self-offered acceptance as followers, Mukunda became our director and disciplinarian. I can frankly say that at times we would become upset at our dear friend-guru's sometimes sudden disciplinary statements. Whatever the case may be, at the foundation, we were strung together on the same thread. Mukunda was its centerpiece jewel, operator, instructor, advisor and heart-friend.

The desire to be group-leader, the mentality to be wayshower to brother-disciples on the spiritual path, the aspiration to be head of an institution and such was in his nature; even from childhood, these feelings were clearly present in his character. On this matter, he has only received sincere support from friends and collaborators in all occasions and events. That there was too much of a feeling of authority at times, or that sometimes slightly unpleasant situations would come about—this cannot be denied. Even when, by mistake, some undesirable behavior would present itself, there was a sweetness and tenderness in his character; this admission was made even by critics who did not like him.

Friends and relatives noticed another puzzling thing in his nature. In many activities and events, he designed the event, created the program, and arranged for safety and security. And at many other times, it was as if he simply trusted the operations and outcome of many duties on the Lord and went on that way. Even when at times he would be upset at our scrutiny, he would openly and confidently try to show his complete reliance upon the Lord which was in his nature. He would speak about certain incidents relating to this matter. We, those who were close to him, also saw these types of incidents happen from time to time in his life. There used to be discussions and debates on these types of things with his elder brother, Ananta Lal Ghosh Mahasaya. Ananta Lal was quite an economical man. That there was no unnecessary expenditure in the household, that Mukunda did not spend too much of his father's money—he tried to look after such things. He used to also expressly tell his younger brother that one would suffer in the future if one did not take care in the management of money. Once, in a moment of headstrong expression, Mukunda told his elder brother, "Even if one falls into circumstances where there are no means, if one has faith in the Lord, all needs are completely fulfilled." Saying this, he, with a friend, really left his brother's house in Agra and went to Vrindavan without a single coin. His friend was a bit hesitant too at seeing this kind of headstrong behavior. Still, drawn by affection to him and at the direction of his leader, he went along with him. They arrived in Vrindavan, and upon receiving unsought welcome from strangers, care, sacramental food etc., [Mukunda] proved the truth of reliance upon the Lord. When he returned, he came to his brother with his friend, follower-devotees, as well as some money—with the joy of having received God's Grace. Of course, his elder brother's heart was certainly humbled and softened. We have seen that elder brother would at times advise younger brother about moving carefully in worldly life. He would even mildly scold him. And we have also seen elder brother take the counsel of younger brother in order to solve many problems of his life. It seemed that sometimes younger brother took the seat of guru-advisor. Later, the sisters would also respect their brother in a similar way.

CHAPTER 7

When we would meet, we would chat and share stories, sing and play music, eat together and such things; with leader Mukunda's special attention to scriptural discussions [and such], we would do spiritual activities and thus make proper and good use of the time we spent. All in all, he would always make effort to preserve a spiritual atmosphere. Besides the three of us, when we would meet other Kriyavan friends, he would sometimes check and test if everyone's practice was going along properly. Having had the presence of jnana-gurudev Swami Sriyukteshvar Giri Maharaj, Mukunda Lal began to become an especially adept sadhak. He went on directing us in the same way as well; we also became filled with more enthusiasm from the experience of traveling on a high road of spiritual paths. I was his neighbor—so from time to time I would be the one who would have the most opportunity. But it is difficult to say how much I was able to properly use the opportunities. In any case, at Mukunda's proposition and powerful influence, we two would sit at the Garpar house itself and practice Kriya Yoga for somewhat longer periods of time. Even when sometimes tiredness would come over me, he would not indulge that at all.

All of our classmate-companions passed the I.A. test. Mukunda had not taken the test. At the order of Sri Guru Maharaj, his father's loving discipline, and the insistence of friends, it was as if Mukunda began to study anew. But it seemed that his mind did not want to really take to this conventional education. Sadhana, meditation, devotional singing, saintly company, spiritual discussions—if he found these things, he would be completely beside himself. Taking and directing friends along the spiritual path, drawing new youth to this way of Truth, sometimes conceptualizing the establishment and planning the operations of a future ashram for sadhana—much of his time would be spent in thinking and discussing about these things.

In the month of July in the Christian year of 1912, having passed the matriculation exams and with a governmental scholarship from

Srirampur [Serampore], Prabhas Chandra [Ghosh], the son of Sarada Prasad Ghosh—Mukunda's "na-kaka" [uncle—fourth in seniority], enrolled in Presidency College, and at the order of his father, took his residence under his great-uncle's [Mukunda Lal's father's] guardianship at that very house at No. 8 Garpar Road. Intelligent, speaking little, and beyond that studious as well, calm and polite, Prabhas Chandra became the recipient of everyone's affection. It seems that without his own knowing he acquired himself a special place in the heart of elder brother Mukunda Lal in a short time. The elder brother Mukunda, sadhana path's expert, would mingle with Prabhas in a simple way and try to instill the seed of sadhana and spiritual feeling. He would speak about Prabhas with us as well. Prabhas used to remain engaged in his work. He mixed and mingled with friends who studied with him. There was not much time spent going around with us. Still, we used to be very happy to have the company of this good young man. Along with Prabhas, his college-mates who were honor students in the University—particularly Saroj Kumar and Sanat Kumar—would often come to Garpar. His singularly close college-mate and friend, who would later—meaning in the present day—become the eminent teacher of philosophy, Dr. Sri Saroj Kumar Das Mahasaya, became very drawn toward Swami Yoganandaji, and he feels joy and is proud to introduce himself as one of his [Yoganandaji's] devotees. I actually knew Dr. Das from before. He used to study one grade [year] ahead [of me] in the same school. Even though I am "Swamiji" [now], his affection for me remains unbroken; instead, in the flow of spiritual life, that affection has become even deeper and sweeter. This sweetness is actually the beneficent fruit from he and I being in the company of Yoganandaji. It goes without saying that brother Prabhas is his ambassador.

During the holidays of the puja-season, Mukunda proposed that we—meaning, he, Basu Kumar, Shishir and I—go to Deoghar and live in the tranquil surroundings there for one month. There, for that time, along with the change of atmosphere, studies would also go better in the quiet environment. He also said again and again that the ill Shishir Kumar's health would especially improve.

The days in Deoghar passed very nicely. Walking in the mountains and solitary places, just sitting quietly—we did this quite often. As far as the subject of seeing sadhus and ashrams, I particularly remember the 52 bigha [about 17.3 acres] garden and [with] Sri Sri Lahiri Mahasaya's memorial temple, founded by Yogiraj's disciple and Arya Mission founder Yogacharya Panchanon Bhattacharya. We saw the arrangements for holy puja services to Shiva and Guru Yogiraj. Acharya Bhattacharya Mahasaya was not there at that time. We also went several times to the ashram of the renowned Balananda Brahmachari Maharaj and spent time in the company of his sannyasi-disciples. In conversation, upon hearing us speak of the issue of taking up sannyas in our lives, one educated and disciplined sannyasi said, "The sannyas life is very difficult. A lot of times, people become sannyasis in a headstrong state of mind. Just a few days later, they become overwhelmed for many reasons. Even saintly people become encumbered with worries from time to time, and it is as if they unknowingly create self-made obstacles in sadhana and contemplation. That is why I am saying: you are college-educated, enterprising youth. Remain disciplined in sadhana, yet study well, and according to the situation, take up the unmarried life and remain in study and teaching. In that, the mind will be calm; you will also find plenty of time for sadhana and contemplation."

After taking leave from sadhuji, Mukunda—who was steadfast on the ideals of the life of sannyas—said to us with a gentle laugh, "This sadhu is very simple and true; [see] how he openly spoke about the condition of his own mind." By hinting thus, he did not forget to remind us of the ideals of sannyas life. We continued to have a look around Swami Sri Sri Balananda Brahmachari's ashram. We saw the beautiful arrangements of daily worship with sacred images, as well as service, devotional singing and chanting, recitation of scriptures and such. In later years, an ayurvedic clinic and a university would be established here, which now continues to serve the good of the people. We also surmised that Maharaj was attentive towards ashtanga yoga sadhana as well. We came to know later that Brahmachari Maharaj was also a reverent sadhak of Kriya Yoga as taught by Yogiraj Lahiri Baba. We were truly elated and enthused when we saw him offer veneration towards Lahiri Mahasaya whenever any subject regarding Him came up. We were inspired upon going and seeing the place where he practiced his intense penance and sadhana in a mountain-cave in the jungles of the Tapoban mountain in that region. One afternoon, we were

sitting at Brahmachari Maharaj's feet and listening to spiritual teaching. It seemed that we were able to easily draw his affectionate attention as well. In the evening, at the time of taking our leave, Mukunda
said with palms joined (in Hindi),* "Please Grace us, Baba." He
laughed and answered, "O son, Grace is always flowing. Where is
there anyone to take it?" Mother Ganges' River of Grace is of course
continuously flowing along. It is we who have to take it and fill our
vessels with it.

[*Translator's note: The parentheses and the text within them are in the
original.]

After the morning walk, we ourselves gathered the necessities for
cooking—it was especially Basu Kumar who cooked. We were assistants. Everything pretty much went along well, but Mukunda Lal's
inattentiveness to his studies was a regular thing. Basu Kumar sweet-
talked with him, stayed with him and would have him study through
story and conversation. If even at that he became obstinate at the time
of studying, it seemed that the dutiful and noble-hearted Basu Kumar
would take it as his own responsibility, and calm Mukunda and have
him sit for study.

After the holiday, we returned to Calcutta. All of the regular activities
began—studying, coming together in the afternoon, assembling for a
spiritually oriented meeting every week. No matter how much work
we had, whether there was a test in the university, or any duty that
might arise, Mukunda would never allow the flow of our spiritual
mindset to come to a standstill.

On the day before the I.A. test, Mukunda took us to Belur Math for Sri
Ramakrishna's birthday celebration. There, after doing pranam to Sri
Sri Divine Mother, and having the company of the venerable Master
Mahasaya (Sri M.),* he felt himself to be blessed. On that day, we witnessed very well the evidence of Master Mahasaya's Guru-given
[internal] life—ever-engaged in meditation, his non-attached way of
being, and absorption in the nectar of Satchitananda—even in the middle of the noise and activity of the innumerable people who gathered
at that celebration. It was our aware friend Mukunda who pointed out
that state of being to us. In the midst of that joyous and festive place,

suddenly a friend, upon seeing Mukunda, exclaimed, "Hey man, have you forgotten about tomorrow? Test, no?" Mukunda only gave a little thought to it silently.

Once during study time, father Ghosh Mahasaya asked Bihari Pandit Mahasaya [the tutor], "How do you feel Mukunda's studies are going?" Pandit Mahasaya laughed and said, "Hope against hope,* what else?" Meaning, even if things are contrary to any hope, one can still hope. A little later, Pandit Mahasaya looked at Mukunda and went on to laughingly say, "Nothing but spending time with friends—and only 'Bas-su'!" However, Pandit Mahasaya actually saw our friendship as a good thing. He favored Mukunda's closeness with a youth like Basu Kumar, who was dutiful, pure in character, and from a respected and good family. Even college classmates, although they would from time to time joke and deride it, would respect that friendship. After Pandit Mahasaya left, Mukunda said to us, "See how nicely Pandit Mahasaya spoke. How in such succinct words he described my studying."

[*Translator's note: The phrase "Hope against hope" is in English in original.]

The test came. Mukunda took the test. Other than in the examination quarters, it was as if Basu was like a shadow, accompanying him at all times. Managing to save that last bit of hope spoken about by Bihari Pandit Mahasaya, somehow Mukunda passed the test. He invited his friends for a feast and celebration. His father unhesitatingly and joyfully took care of the expenditures for that.

Meanwhile, Bihari Pandit Mahasaya let Mukunda know about a certain sadhak. Even though he always had a great attraction towards renunciate sannyasis and sadhus, Mukunda felt an exceptional pull within him for the darshan of this particular householder sadhak. This sadhak lived in a very ordinary way. He taught at the Arya Mission Institution founded by Yogiraj's disciple, Yogacharya Panchanon Bhattacharya. At the time of his youth, it was through Guru Bhattacharya Mahasaya that he [the sadhak] was able to have the company of Yogiraj Lahiri Mahasaya. He spent his days doing intense practice in his life. Day after day, he practiced Kriya Yoga without sleeping at night. Upon having his company, and experiencing his ceaseless and beautiful sadhana while being around him, Yoganandaji [later] named him the "sleepless sadhu."

This holy sadhak's home was in Ranabajpur village, near Tarakeshvar. Mukunda started his journey to have his darshan. It was an inclement day; the road was full of water and mud. He made for Ranabajpur straightaway from the Tarakeshvar train station. Almost at the end of being able to tolerate the terrible conditions, tired from the road, at times not knowing the road, Mukunda searched and searched for this ordinary man in a country-village, and, completely exhausted and weary, he arrived at Ramgopal Majumdar's tiny, thatched hut. Surprised, the holy sadhak affectionately welcomed this steadfast and determined youth. They spoke about sadhana. Both sat for meditation together. In his divine company and effulgent radiance, Mukunda was blessed. In the nectarous presence of the great yogi, all tiredness left Mukunda, and seeing that a certain pain in his body was also healed, he was awestruck, and felt deeply grateful [upon witnessing] the glory of the saint's supernatural power. The holy sadhak Majumdar Mahasaya described the story of his life of sadhana. How he would go and practice in unknown places out of the overbearing sight of every-day people—he spoke about this as well. Speaking about his own life of sadhana, when Mukunda made it known that he usually sits in a room and practices Kriya, japa, dhyan, this great yogi-sadhak then excitedly exclaimed, "Hey, you mean you can lock the door and sit? How fortunate you are! What a great opportunity you have received." In conversation, when he made it known that Mukunda came straight to Ranabajpur from the station and that he suffered on the road, he then slightly scolded Mukunda and advised him that Tarakeshvar was an area of spiritual power, a place of sacred pilgrimage for many devo-tees and sadhaks. He should have done pranam there at the feet of Sri Taraknath—otherwise, one would get his "ears pulled."* At Mukunda's advice, Basu Kumar received the holy company of this "extraordinary in the ordinary" being in that village-home. I also had the fortune of having his darshan at the Arya Mission Institution in Calcutta. He was an ordinary teacher there. Seeing us with Mukunda, he laughed and said, "Walking around? No studies?" On the sacred land of India, how many saints and sages are unostentatiously absorbed in holy dharma, out of the sight of the masses? Abruptly abandoning the idea of going to a mountain-cave, and being inspired at seeing that it was appropriate to be a silent practitioner of dhyan, japa, Kriya Yoga sadhana and such while remaining at the feet of Sriguru, Mukunda returned home. With the intense action of sadhana, he made his very room a mountain-cavern.

[*Translator's note: "Ears pulled" is a translation of "kaanmola", which refers to a kind of mild reprimand by pulling the ears for doing something disrespectful.]

One evening, we arrived with Mukunda at a house in Calcutta's Jhamapukur Lane, for the sake of having the darshan of a sadhu. Srimat Nripendra Nath Dey, guru of Mukunda Lal's elder sister's husband had come there. Dey Mahasaya was a high-level professional in Deradun. He became inspired by the spirituality of Lord Sri Ramakrishna's Motherly Love, left his work and lived like a sadhak. Many have [had] taken up discipleship with him. An ashram of his was founded in Rupnarayanpur. After spending some time in the saintly company, when we were coming back, Mukunda asked me right in the middle of the road, "So, what did you feel?" I answered, "What should I feel?" Meaning, talking about analyzing—one should not analyze sages—and so on. We saw sadhu Dey Mahasaya several other times as well. From his words and behavior, I understood that Mukunda was not quite taken with him, and thus did not particularly try any more to be in his company.

Mukunda passed the I.A. in which he had taken the subjects of Sanskrit, logic and chemistry. Now it was time to begin with the B.A. studies. He did not have much of a desire for it, but it was Guru's order—he must at least pass the B.A. He made a request to his father that he desired to have the opportunity of being in the company of Guru. Thus, he wanted to enroll in the Serampore [Srirampur] College. Taking Sanskrit and Darshan Shastra (philosophy),* he enrolled in the Serampore Christian College, run by missionaries, when the time arrived. Having been entrusted to the guardianship of Prabhas Chandra's father, Mukunda's fourth uncle Sarada Prasad Ghosh Mahasaya, it was settled that Mukunda's place of residence would be at his house. The highly respected Sarada Babu was an eminent legalist of Serampore. He was a disciple of Lahiri Mahasaya. In later years, he was also a member of the Theosophical Society. Mukunda's Kriyavan brother Lalitdada lived here. Even though he was a householder, he lived like a sadhu in character, behavior, dedication to service and discipline of sadhana. It was upon being inspired by brother Mukunda Lal that he took up discipleship with Acharya Shastri Mahasaya. We also found great joy in having Lalitdada's company.

[*Translator's note: The parentheses and the text within them are in the original.]

From time to time, we went and gathered at Mukunda Lal's home in Serampore. It was there that our friendly chit-chat, devotional singing, discussions and meditations continued. A couple of local companions began to join us as well. Mukunda's attention was especially drawn to Basu Kumar's nephew, Sucharu Bhusan Bhaduri and Pramathnath, a relative. Both of them were around 15/16 at that time. They became initiated in Kriya Yoga by Acharya Shastri Mahasaya. Sucharu was around quite a lot. Mukunda was exceedingly delighted and enthused by his discipline and one-pointedness in meditation and devotion. Gradually, it became such that the classmate students from Serampore College would also come to that house often. Besides the studies, Mukunda Lal would have his characteristic discussions about spiritual matters with them as well.

Even though uncle Sarada Prasad Ghosh Mahasaya was an open-hearted guardian, Mukunda began to feel a little uncomfortable in this crowded situation. Because it would both facilitate easier studying and because it was not right to bring a crowd to his uncle's house, Mukunda Lal made a request to his father and then rented a room in a college hostel by the Ganges (Panti House).* He spent his time quite happily here for a while. Of course, there were frequent trips nearby to Sri Guru Maharaj's house, or ashram, situated below Burabibi at Rai Ghat Lane. How many nights were also spent at the Feet of Sriguru!

[*Translator's note: The parentheses and the text within them are in the original.]

CHAPTER 8

When he lived in Serampore, not only did Mukunda benefit in the path of sadhana by being near Sriguru, but he was also able to learn many things about living in the everyday world. Through his teaching and nature, Guru Swami Sriyukteshvar Giri Maharaj used to particularly inspire and stimulate people to be of high character, and to conduct themselves with courtesy and dignity. He disliked any neglect of the duties of worldly or social life in the name of religion or spirituality. Without non-attachment arising within by being naturally drawn to higher feelings, the fear remains that a person can fall into a false way of being by becoming unmindful with dutiful work because of things said in scriptures or because of daily pressures. He used to also say from time to time that even with an unencumbered life situation, one can be still be thrown off in the areas of sadhana.

Mukunda had a good bit of the spiritual dreamer in him. Thus, Guru Maharaj would from time to time deridingly reprimand him, so that he would become more attentive to areas of practical work. When at Guru's house, if Mukunda would take up his natural and easily acquired leadership role and give us, or even young ones, excessive orders like a director, [Sriyukteshvarji] would signal with signs and gestures and have him control that. To make him expert at work, [Sriyukteshvarji] gave him the responsibility of the ashram, and to teach him about proper behavior with people in general, [Sriyukteshvarji] would sometimes give him directives for the work of seeing to the guests of the ashram. By speaking about Mukunda's unmindfulness at the time, it was as if Guru Maharaj was keeping all of us—along with Mukunda—awake to the necessity of being and behaving appropriately with people. In his life, Mukunda would have to take the responsibility of teaching people, and be a true servant, and we too would have to follow him—[Sriyukteshvarji] also said this from time to time. Privately, he spoke to me several times about future plans when Mukunda would take the seat as propagator. One who will guide with a certain discipline will himself have to build his life under that discipline; his view was drawn to this ideal as a thoroughly valuable and useful one. On this matter, Guru Maharaj told me, "Tell Mukunda that he should read Swami Vivekananda's books." He also cautioned that, while reading Swamiji's books, one should not lose one's own original qualities either, and one should not disrupt one's own experience and understanding of one's own Sriguru-graced sadhana. He [Sriyukteshvarji] used to tell me to particularly keep an eye on his [Mukunda's] manner of exposition in lectures, facility to draw the hearts of people, and beauty of presence. [Sriyukteshvarji] also used to hint that taking up Swamiji's [Vivekanandaji's] feelings towards his homeland and his exemplary faith in the teachings of Guru were high ideals.

There were always two or three children and youngsters around Guru Maharaj. Being in his company, they had many different opportunities of learning. At this time, there were three children named Kanai, Ramkanai and Kumar in the ashram. It seemed that Guru Maharaj used to teach Kumar as a specially marked brahmachari, and would keep him [Kumar] very close to him. Kumar's peaceful and beautiful countenance, sweet voice and sharp intellect truly attracted us as well. Now and then, we would enjoy mingling together in Guru's house. Mukunda seemed to have them [the children] always accompanying him. Many times, to illustrate an example, Mukunda would speak to us of Kumar's dedication towards Guru. A few days later, we unfortunately began to see that Kumar's behavior seemed to be changing. It was Mukunda who first noticed this. Guru Maharaj also became saddened at seeing this change. The ideals of sannyas life did not remain with Kumar. But I have heard that Kumar, with his sharpness and because of having received the company of saints, continues to be spiritual within, and is presently conducting his worldly life in that way.

In the company of Sriguru, the wisdom-sage-incarnation of Wisdom, through many duties and works, spiritual discussions, explanations of scriptures, spiritual sadhana and such, Mukunda's Inner Light grew more and more radiant. But Gurudev's words of reprimand, sarcasm, and derision from people—sometimes hidden with friends—his weakness towards relatives, or some abrupt criticism about his being unmindful would from time to time upset him. At this, close people and even those younger than him would underhandedly perturb him.

For this reason, Mukunda would be very sad in our presence as well. It became such that he became very hesitant to bring even his reverent friends, particularly youths, to Guru Maharaj, lest they lose their respect for him [Mukunda] in outward behavior. In conversation, while speaking about the matter of Gurudev's strict behavior, he [Mukunda] said, "Oof! I remember when I used to regularly go to Satsanga Sabha at Jeletola in Calcutta. Then the respected ____* Babu said, 'Mukunda, I see that you are very devoted. That's good. But look, in the end, at Guruji's words, you will probably have to escape with your tail.'" One day, with a sorrowful and heavy heart, Mukunda submitted a letter of hurt-filled grievance to Guru Maharaj. Later, when he went to him directly, in a manner sort of like a child expressing the need for his rights to his father, he spoke out about these difficult things and let Gurudev know about his displeasure with his [Sriyukteshvarji's] terse talk and disagreeable behavior, and let him know what he felt should be done about that. Gurudev quietly listened to everything. Perhaps he even felt a little humbled by his disciple's view. But he was never hesitant in disciplining. In fact, even when Yoganandaji had conquered the world, if [Sriyukteshvarji] saw any carelessness in his disciple or any unseemly way of being or behaving, he would slightly scold him as if [Yoganandaji] was his young son. I remember that one day Yogananda, with an extremely pained heart, let Gurudev know, "Guru, I have surrendered everything to you. Why are you causing me to be in such despair? There was Sri Ramakrishna for Vivekananda. Where are you in my life? With whom else shall I take refuge?" Peacefully and with few words, Guru let him know through me, "The way you see me as being to you, that is of course how I will be." Saying this, he was actually speaking about the matter of the disciple's spiritual sadhana—meaning that it is when the Guru-given blessing manifests in the heart that one can receive the true presence of Sriguru's Love, and upon thus experiencing the Glory of Sriguru, one can have his refuge—he tried to make us understand this truth in the path of sadhana.

[*Translator's note: The "____" is in the original.]

Even though we saw all such wrangling and problems of mindset, Mukunda's foundation at the root was immovable and unshakable. "Whatever Gurudev does, I will not leave him for any reason. I've heard that many left him, not being able to withstand his harsh criticism. Even if he put me in the guillotine of intense scrutiny, I would still hold onto his feet." I remember that it was in Serampore itself that we were talking and discussing things with the venerable Motilal Thakur. Then Yoganandaji and Motilal Thakur sadly spoke up, "Look at how the Lord works. If today this beautiful Incarnation of Wisdom were a little softer in behavior—if that happened, it's possible that the people of this country would humanly pull a car with him in it and take him all over the world."

Guru Maharaj presented visionary perspectives on organizational work. Disciples, as well as who knows how many knowledgeable people—known and unknown—were amazed upon listening to his multidimensional and enlightening advice and discussions. Many, having seen new light on things, would do great organizational work. He himself used to say, "See how so many people are taking my words and going ahead and doing so much work, yet if I personally put my hands into such work, that doesn't want to happen through me. I am the blessed son of Mother Saraswati (as a wisdom-giver),* but the abandoned son of Mother Durga (in relation to the world and organizations)."** In his later years, Yogananda said one day, "See how much I argued with Gurudev. I understand that it is because of these excessive arguments that I am so drawn to him. Today, it is he who is the Lord of my heart. See how out of my view, secretly, he took me into his love-drenched heart as so much his own; sometimes I knew—and I have seen him come out of that tough covering and be in a state with tear-filled eyes too."

[*and**Translator's note: The parentheses and the text within them are in the original.]

Benefiting from the company of Guru, the ideas of spiritual propagation, educational institutions, traveling the country and such began to gel in Mukunda's mind at this time. The light of the future field of work for sadhak Mukunda began to awaken in this way. One day, he was sitting there thinking about other things. Gurudev even cautioned him a little for this. During that time, picture after picture appeared in his [Mukunda's] mind; he was seeing himself as being sometimes in flat lands, sometimes on a mountain and sometimes on the banks of the sea. Of course, he did not feel this to have any particular significance at this time. Later, he used to say that it seemed that the locations of his future foundations were indicated in those pictures. In the flat land in Dihika, later in Ranchi, he founded the Brahmacharya Vidyalaya. In 1925 of the Christian year, his institution in the Western world—the main center of the Self-Realization Fellowship—was founded on the edge of the City of Los Angeles in America, on Mount Washington, and in 1936, he received the prize of the sadhana-ashram on the banks of the ocean on an expansive piece of land in Encinitas, California.

We too were blessed at having the company of Sriguru in Serampore. Almost every Sunday, we attended the weekly spiritual gathering there. On the 24th of December, at the time of the Auspicious Solstice, we used to join in on the yearly festivities of the Serampore Sabha, learning and enjoying during that time. At the now departed knowledgeable musician and guru-brother [brother-disciple] Dr. Bijoy Basanta Bandopadhyay's endeavoring, music gatherings [small festivals] were held during the celebrations in Serampore, with which Mukunda was very enthralled, and he used to love to listen to the unique guru-brother Sri Krishna Chandra Adhya Mahasaya's rendition of North Indian Classical Music. He used to be absorbed in listening particularly to his "When Will You Show Yourself Again Mother?" rendered in Raga Hambir [a particular melodic mode of North Indian Classical Music]. It was such that when he returned from America, he [Yoganandaji] searched for and found Krishna Dada in a country-village and brought him just so he could hear this song. That this sadhak's heart-lute—who appeared as an ideal of Devotion to Divine Mother—would ring out with this music—that goes without saying.

One day in Calcutta, one of Mukunda Lal's classmates suddenly appeared and said that he had taken a house in Belgharia. For the sacred housewarming event, he was making arrangements for Sri Kali Puja. [He requested that] his great friend and sadhak, brother-Mukunda had to go there and complete the festivities. When the time came, we arrived together at Belgharia. Tulsi Narayan Basu, Prakash Chandra Das and many others came and joined the occasion. The guru-brother [brother-disciple] from Bali, Ramkishore Bandopadhyay, who was older than us, joined us and we greatly enjoyed his day-and-night singing of devotional songs. The festivities continued for almost two days, day and night. Mukunda was taken by Mother Kali's earthen image; he became deeply absorbed and made us intoxicated as well. He sent for guru-brother Shashi Bhusan Basu to especially come to this celebration. Even though he worked in an office job, Shashi-da had taken up unmarried life, and any time he would get an opportunity, day or night, he practiced Kriya Yoga very intensely; he progressed quite well also. A few days before this time, Shashi-da was afflicted with a terrible illness. There was no hope at all of staying alive. Mukunda Lal offered his desperate prayers to Sriguru so that his great friend would be cured. At Sriguru's blessing and through the application of disciplined treatment as directed by him, Shashi-da became quite healthy. For these kinds of reasons, Mukunda Lal wanted to have Shashi Bhushan near him during times like these [the Kali Puja].

Not paying much attention to the priest's usual worship, and maddened by the Divine Mother's Essence, Mukunda spent several long hours in this state. After about two or three days, the festivities were ended. Instead of offering the earthen image of the Divine Mother into the Ganges [as is often done as a symbol of Mother going back to Mother], it was suggested that the statue of Sri Kali would remain established in that house and from time to time we would go and partake in the joy of worship. But because of difficulties in our travel, our great friend cast the image of Divine Mother into the Ganges.

Meanwhile, in the Christian year of 1913, upon the awakening of Mukunda Lal's natural desire for travel, Mukunda, Basu Kumar, Govinda Ghatak and I went and traveled the South. One cannot help but be filled with awe at the huge architecture that still remain there today as evidence of Hindu culture. Our travels took us as far as Sri Lanka. It was because of the "pass"* that we received from him [Mukunda] that we were able to travel without customs' duties. The experience and joy of the travel are still vivid in memory even today. Of course, four youths involved in traveling like that also once caught the attention of the police at that time. We met with the eminent wandering Buddhist, Dharmapal, at his own endeavoring in Sri Lanka at the newly established Mahabodhi College Bhavan. Even today, we remember with gratitude the affectionate welcome by the youths in the many different places in Sri Lanka, as well as their help and empathic feeling towards us. Upon seeing Lord Buddha's Danta Temple in Kandi, Maharaj Dharmashok's son Mahendra's place of pilgrimage in Anuradhapur, which remains as a great sign of his propagation work, and the behavior and nature of monk-beggars in many Buddhist temples in many places, the spread of the Buddhist religion left quite a mark in our minds. As far as visiting places of traditional lore, such as the capital during Ravana's reign, and Ashok Kanan etc., "pandas" and "purohits" [priests looking to raise funds] also came to show us the sites. When it came to the beauty of Nature, the [high] place that Sri Lanka holds today regarding that was true at that time as well, being a place of wonderful sights. Even in distant Sri Lanka, there was a disciple of Shastri Mahasaya; so we found it to be quite easy from the beginning.

[*Translator's note: The quotations and the word within them are in the original.]

Because of the re-opening of our schools and colleges, we did not delay much longer and returned to Calcutta on the 23rd of July, 1913. Again began the daily activities—sitting together in sadhana sometimes, sometimes discussing scriptures, having the darshan of Guru or some saints.

CHAPTER 9

One day, we received news that the renowned "Soham Swami" of the Himalayas had come to Bhavanipur in Calcutta. Swamiji's name in the previous stage of his life was Shyama Kanta Bandopadhyay. He was a physical culturist and was a man of extraordinary physical strength. With tigers—not only that—he would go into the cage of a violent and angry Royal Bengal tiger—freshly captured from the jungle, and in a hair-raising manner, he would wrestle that animal and defeat it, while showing absolutely no signs of excitement on his own face. This mighty being was from Faridpur in East Bengal [now Bangladesh], and his place of work was in the city of Dhaka. There, he formed a partnership with his close friend, the singularly eminent wrestler Parshvanath (Paresh Chandra Ghosh),* and they together founded a school of physical culture whose curriculum greatly benefited youths.

[*Translator's note: The parentheses and the text within them are in the original.]

Basu Kumar and I went with Mukunda to have darshan of Swamiji. There may have been someone else with us to show us the way there. Even though he was in his later days, we were very inspired at seeing his still strong and beautiful body, and his peaceful, dignified and energy-radiant form. Once a strongman filled with the spirit of fighting, today that same Shyama Kanta was sitting there as Soham Swami, creating an atmosphere of profound tranquility. Because of the effect of that environment, we also sat there silently for a while. Gradually, the question was put to him: How did he—with what kind of courage or ability—bring about the defeat of those extremely violent animals? He gently laughed, and spoke in a peaceful manner, "Oh that is nothing much. If one simply has some strength of body, determination of mind and faith in oneself, this can be accomplished. If you all try, you can also accomplish this task." In a succinct way, he also let us know how—in his previous time of life [before having become a Swami]—because of his father's discussions and a transformation in his own mind as well, he became a traveler on the path of spirituality. That youths should pay particular attention to the maintenance of health, and that if one did not take up proper nutrition and exercise and have sufficient physical vigor, it was difficult to attain spiritual power—he had spoken these words with deep certainty and made it known throughout his spread of influence. Even though, right at that time, his words did not sink in the heart, the effect of this clearly bore fruit in Yogananda's life and in the field of his teaching.

Another day, a friend let us know that Swami Vishuddhananda Paramhansaji—who was known as "Gandhibaba"—had come to the house of a disciple for a few days. Mukunda, eager for the company of saints, took me and that friend and arrived at "Baba's"* place. It felt quite good to see the bearded and smiling Paramhansaji. There was also curiosity within to see his supernatural acts. We saw him manifest scents, according to whatever we wanted, in a scent-less flower and in a handkerchief. Being eyewitnesses to this kind of act, we were amazed. We thought that this was evidence of his yogic powers, but that is not what he said. He said that in far away Tibet, this secret knowledge, even though learned by yogis, is the work of a special science. This was not any kind of yogic miracle. Yogic miracles work differently with the mind. Mukunda was not particularly attracted to the attainment of these kinds of physical miracles [acquired] after having done extensive practice, and not attaining God. So, not letting us put our minds to these kinds of matters any more, he took us and came back home. But the funny thing is that the witnessing [of this event] had an effect in later years in Yoganandaji's life, when he himself gathered powers to cure disease and applied many kinds of mental powers/techniques for use in the outside world. He used to give the reason that one could become the instrument of Divine Power and could actually have the opportunity to serve people through the performance of such things. Even though my mind was not drawn to those feelings, saying that for the sake of the good of the people I could also attain a certain amount of those "good"** powers/techniques, he had also tried to awaken my interest.

[* and **Translator's note: The quotations and the text within them are in the original.]

Even though I did not notice, in that very same journey, he [Mukunda] went to seek darshan at Kalighat and had the darshan of a transcendent sadhu, from whom he received much spiritual advice as well as being told that the sadhana-attainments of saints and sages was the very culture of India, and that India would raise the world onto the path of Truth. Although there was not much of a sign of excitement about this in him when this matter was presented to him, this seed was planted deeply within him, which in later life became an enormous tree.

Although much time was spent at Guru's ashram, Mukunda's established place of address was the somewhat lonely room of the students' quarters of the college. The solitude would break when friends gathered; from time to time there was even some studying. The studying intensity was not quite like someone about to take exams; thus, as the [time of] examinations approached, he became a little anxious. What to do! Guruji had ordered it—the test must be taken. Upon coming to know about this fear of examination and doubt, Guru Maharaj gave him encouragement and said, "Keep a cool head and go on studying. Walk with awareness of everything around you, and discuss the matters of study with your classmate Ramesh." Having received Guru's blessing, Mukunda felt some courage in his heart and continued to do his duty. One day, it seems that on the road, he found a couple of pieces of paper with some questions on it. Classmate Ramesh's help also felt quite good. Remembering Guru, he [Mukunda] sat for the test. On the paper with the test questions, he saw that there was much there related to the questions he found on the road, and that quite a bit of what brother Ramesh had foreseen [what might be on the test] matched as well. In the Christian year of 1915, he [Mukunda] passed the B.A. exams. Besot with amazement, he was firmly convinced that he had become a degree-holder because of Sriguru's supernatural help. His father, uncle, maternal uncle and other relatives gave their happy blessings. With his father's help, Mukunda invited us, along with relatives and friends, for a celebratory feast in the Garpar house. In relation to the passing of this test, it must also be mentioned that there was help from Basu Kumar—who was engaged in the study of M.A.—as well as encouragement given by Prabhas Chandra—the paternal-nephew younger than him who was passionate about learning.

In the meantime, after the test, Mukunda Lal talked with some friends and upon getting his father's permission, made arrangements to visit and see Kashmir. During that time of the summer break, I was with my mother at my maternal family's home which was far on the edge of the Padma. Word was sent to me [about the trip], but because of recurring problems with the date of travel, I was not able to be there at the right time.

With the company of Sriguru, Mukunda and his friends—enjoyed and delighted in the beauty of Kashmir. When he saw the temple of Sri Sri Shankaracharya on a mountain in Kashmir, an image of a similar environment where he would also have an ashram floated up in Mukunda's mind. He stated that that experience was what eventually manifested itself as the form of the beautiful ashram on America's Mount Washington.

Leaving brother-disciple Jotindra Adhya Mahasaya to be in service with Guruji, everyone else returned so that each could resume each one's personal work. The unfortunate thing was that later Sri Guru Maharaj became very ill while in Kashmir. He had actually said before that according to astrological calculations, a deadly illness would befall him at that time. Although they stayed out of the public eye, when they were in the Kashmiri city of Srinagar, the resident scholars and spiritually inquisitive persons of respect had become eager to have the company of this great being of wisdom, and he [Sriyukteshvarji] was even requested by the monarchy to stay a few days longer in Kashmir. Not extending the stay for too many more days, he returned—even with weak health—to Serampore with Jotin-da, and after staying in the ashram in Puri for a few days, regained his health.

Immediately upon finishing the B.A. exams, renunciation and dedication to spiritual practice awakened in Mukunda's heart. Studies were finished according to Sriguru's orders; now, it was time to consider leaving the enclosing home-life. It was at his [Mukunda's] leadership that we took the resolve of sannyas a few years ago. Deeply remembering that, he offered a prayer to Sriguru for permission to take up the way of sannyas in full form. In the month of July in the Christian year of 1915, in an unostentatious yet profound atmosphere in Serampore, Sri Guru Maharaj gave the initiation of taking the path of sannyas life into the heart, and by his own hands, dyed the silk dhoti and upper garment for Mukunda. Guru Maharaj had a special feeling for the beneficial properties of silk. He even advised householders to use pale-yellow-colored upper garments made of silk if possible. In regards to the clothing for Mukunda's sannyas initiation, he [Sriyukteshvarji] had said that because this was an event with special meaning, he himself had made this arrangement for the clothing. Yet at another time, he somewhat pointed out the faults of a certain sannyasi, who was dear to him, for wearing silk at the time of a particular event, and he expressed some trepidation about that sannyasi breaking from higher principles in the future of his life-journey. Quite some time later, his [Sriyukteshvarji's] warning to take care became pertinent when that highly-principled sadhak became associated with problematic ways. From whatever I could understand, I surmised that unknowingly, according to behavior and environment, those activities continue to go on in the mind. That is why we have to remember the words of the great ones: "Sadhu, be careful."

A traveler on the path of yoga, fixed in the dedicated practice of yoga—Mukunda wanted to receive a name [of sannyas] that would be with [the word] "yoga," so that the ideals of yoga would be constantly evident even in the name. On the subjects of dress and name, he used to say that it was good if even these would be according to the higher ideals, because if some weakness came upon us on the journey of our path, it was possible that even the derision of everyday people [because of the outer garment] could remind us of our life-work, in indirectly clever or harsh ways ["by hook or by crook"]. In keeping with the disciple's mentality, [Sriyukteshvarji] gave the name of "Yogananda" to the new sannyasi entering the lineage. Having now become a member of the "Giri" order of the "dashanami" [ten names of the renunciate orders], which were created by Sri Srimat Shankaracharyadeva—the savior of "Sanatan Dharma"—according to the Vedic principles of wise and knowledegeable sages, [Mukunda] now became known to the world of everyday people as "Swami Yogananda Giri." [He] became newly inspired in the practice of yoga and dhyan, and in the ideals of Self-realization—constantly contemplating the great truth "I Am that Brahman" in his heart.

In order to attain the Knowledge of Brahman, it is very necessary to be pure within. Swamiji Maharaj used to teach us that the chitta was purified by service, and he also had us draw our attention to service-based work and, following that, the work of propagation. Just as he had spoken about becoming acquainted with Western philosophy and [western] methods of education through the B.A. matriculation, he also used to speak about giving attention to Sanskrit matriculation. However, that did not end up happening because of the flow of events, even though, after taking sannyas, he [Yoganandaji] took up residence in his previously known Sri Bharata Dharmaha Mandal in Benares, the abode of knowledge. To prepare and initiate his dear disciple as a proper speaker and missionary, at that time, during the auspicious event of the Winter Solstice, at the gathering of the satsang celebration in Kidderpore [Khidirpur], he [Sriyukteshvarji] asked and encouraged Yoganandaji to discuss and analyze some spiritual subjects right in front of him [Sriyukteshvarji]. Although Mukunda Lal had previously had discussions on scriptures and sadhana matters in small presentations at home, and spoke some at a gathering organized by us [the group of friends], still, at Guru Maharaj's foresight, it seemed that this little speech was what would give him his real and highest inspiration for his huge missionary work in the future.

Soon after taking up residence in Benares, the time for the yearly celebration of the Calcutta Satsanga Sabha drew near. We requested Yoganandaji, the administrator of the Sabha and our leader, to come as soon as possible. He arrived around the middle of September. The Sabha would start on the predetermined date of the 25th of September—9th of Ashwin [Bengali calendar]—at the auspicious time of the Autmnal Equinox.

The celebration, Sabha etc., went very well. Yoganandaji began to make preparations to leave for Benares. At this time, certain close friends—especially Swamiji Maharaj's disciple Bipin Bihari Dey (now departed),* who was a highly lettered scholar of Western philosophy and an Ishan Scholar in the B.A. matriculation—tried greatly to coax Yoganandaji into taking up the M.A. studies. A special request was presented to Guru Maharaj to permit this matter. At everyone's unceasing appeal, in the dress of a sannyasi, Yoganandaji enrolled in the M.A. class of Darshan Shastra (Philosophy)** in the university.

Yoganandaji used to become entranced in the nectarous essence of the scriptures, listening to the teaching by the eminent philosopher-sage and professor, Brajendra Nath Sheel Mahasaya, on the cultivation of profound wisdom in Indian philosophy. A good deal of books and such were bought. But those were somewhat decorative. Later however, some of them became useful in our work. It wasn't that he studied in his room much. He listened to the lectures in class, and took down notes as well.

[*Translator's note: The parentheses and the text within them are in the original. **Translator's note: The parentheses and the text within them in English are in the original.]

Not only with his friends, Yoganandaji continued his habit of having spiritual discussions even with the respected professors. I remember that one day he had a discussion with the professor of "Manovijnana Shastra" (Psychology),* Ramdas Khan Mahasaya. Regarding that discussion, the professor mahasaya expressed delight upon hearing the student Yogananda's experiential talk on the matter, saying, "It's quite something—a new perspective."

[*Translator's note: The parentheses and the text within them in English are in the original.]

After entreating his father to understand all of the necessities—that he had to study, had to go to different places, and had to be near Guru, [Yoganandaji] received a motorcycle from him. Saying that he [Yoganandaji] would regularly take his father out for recreation, he bought an adjoining mobile extension (side car)* as well. The compassionate-hearted father laughed quite a bit upon hearing that pretext. Oh, he [father] would ride that vehicle so much, no?! In any case, he granted his child's request. Of course, we were overjoyed at having that vehicle; Guru Maharaj also rode it and went about on it somewhat. I remember that his father rode in the vehicle a couple of times in order to keep up the reasoning given before. Even though the renunciate's outfit was there, the vehicle was driven while dressed up quite a bit. Eventually, with bare upper body, that ochre-outfitted sannaysi youth's driving around with the motorcycle seemed to bring an elated excitement in the neighborhood. Many known and unknown persons became friends and had the opportunity to ride the vehicle.

[*Translator's note: The parentheses and the text in English are in the original.]

Our usual gatherings, satsang and such again resumed fully. But our guardians seemed to become a bit disturbed when they saw that we sort of detached ourselves a little from studies and such and were again engrossed somewhat in the works of gatherings, ashram etc. During all of this, we were able to organize a gathering in the Athenium Institution in Garpar. How Basu Kumar, Jitendra Nath, and all of our other friends were looking forward to it! Brahmachari Suddhanandaji Maharaj, a significant member of the Theosophical Society who had been in the company of Guru Maharaj, gave us his vital and enthusiastic help in order to make our endeavor successful. Roy Bahadur Radhacharan Pal, Guru Maharaj's disciple and the administrator of the Calcutta Satsanga Sabha at that time (the son of the eminent Krishna Das Pal),* was the principal of the gathering. Yoganandaji's classmate, one who had just recently graduated with first place honors in English, the Kriyavan Sachindra Lal Dasvarma (now departed),** recited a treatise on religion and spirituality at Yoganandaji's request, and received praise from everyone, and made us proud [of Mr. Dasvarma] as well. Later, after returning from the city of Puri, Guru Maharaj made Yoganandaji the joint administrator of the Satsanga Sabha upon seeing his capability for this work. The responsibility of the duties of the Calcutta Satsanga Sabha truly became Yoganandaji's after this time. We went on with carrying out the work as his faithful assistants. Before this, we used to join in the tasks of setting up the yearly celebrations of the Satsanga Sabha, distributing invitational leaflets, as well as other typical duties. At that time, at Swamiji Maharaj's directive, the respected scholars of Eastern knowledge—particularly professors of the Sanskrit College—were the ones who were requested to take the principal positions in the gatherings.

One day in Garpar, while we were busy with all kinds of work, a youthful Hindusthani [non-Bengali] sadhu arrived, dressed in white. He approached Yoganandaji directly. The two of them spoke. As the sadhuji took his leave, Yoganandaji smilingly came and told me a few basically unbelievable things that the sadhuji said about future events. Of course at that time, we laughed away and blew off those statements. But at later times, those events really did happen. I cannot say for sure, but when Yoganandaji would later speak about Mahamuni Babaji Maharaj—it seems that the depiction at that time had some similarities with this sadhu.

Our ashram work continued even at that time at that little leaf-covered room in Bagmari, across the canal in Maniktala. On some days, it would get very late before we could get back home. One night, I was the only one returning with Yoganandaji; it was very late at night. After walking for a while, we both sat down on the wet grass on the ground by the canal. There was not much noise at that time. Suddenly, Yoganandaji began to speak about Kriya Yoga sadhana—speaking of his personal experience. He spoke openly and extensively even of the level that he had been able to attain, and made it known that there was farther to go. There was no emotion in his words that day; there was no abrupt excitement. In the silence of the night, as he spoke about spiritual matters in a profoundly calm and peaceful manner, I too tasted the essence of a certain tranquility; I was also captivated by the descriptions of his illuminated experiences. How he had gone forward even more than that after that day!

In a few days, at Sri Tulsi Narayan Basu's efforts, a small space with some adobe-walled, open rooms in an open area of his family's house became available for our ashram. It required little expense from us. The owner of the house, Tulsi-da's father Harinarayan Basu Mahasaya (now departed)*—the eminent visual artist and principal teacher of the Art College—liked us very much. And how we entreated so much from Tulsi-da's mother! This very house is now the beautiful and officially entitled Yogoda Ashram—no. 17/1 Pitambar Bhattacharya Goli.

Having found a proper place, we began to organize the ashram. We set up the gathering-room, lodging rooms, kitchen, a small garden and all such. A separate room was dedicated to Tulsi-da's regular puja and ceremonials, particularly the puja of Mahavir along with the devotional chanting of Sri Ramanama, which were held on Thursdays. We all used to attend those events. Each Friday, everyone assembled together at our satsang gathering-room. After the distribution of prasad [sacramental fruits and sweets etc.] at the end of the gathering, the khichuri [mixture of rice, lentils and vegetables] meals at night went on unabated. In the beginning, at Yoganandaji's orders, rice pudding for the guests at the end of the khichuri meal was an absolute must. Regardless of how little milk there might be, we would nevertheless have to prepare that [pudding] even if we had to add water and sweeteners.

Because of being ill all this time, our other special great friend who took up the vows of sannyas with us—Shishir Kumar—had remained in his family's house in Bhavanipur. We visited him from time to time. There, we listened to his sweet voice sing songs, and we would even hold satsang in a small way. When we arrived there one evening, we saw that a boy of 12/13 was massaging Shishir Kumar's body with oil. In a short time, upon seeing the boy's natural inclination towards spiritual service and sweet nature, Yoganandaji took a liking to him and found out from Shishir Kumar that he was a very good child who was studying in the seventh grade, but because of terrible financial conditions, his father was making arrangements to employ him at a printing plant. Yoganandaji was deeply saddened when he heard these words. He said, "Oh! Why not give such a child to me? I will take care of his studies and his matriculation, raise him to be a man and then return him to his own house." When the child's father heard this from Shishir, he happily offered the guardianship of his son Sri Nirmal Chandra Basu at the feet of Yoganandaji.

Within few days by the grace of Yoganandaji, Nirmal and a brahmin child from Orissa—Sri Sushodhan—became residents of the ashram, by which, it seemed that our little place of learning had commenced. The two boys were enrolled in the Athenium Institution nearby. Now it was they who maintained the ashram, they themselves cooked, and from time to time we also sat and ate with them.

After having started with young schoolboys, college students also began to come to the ashram. We created a special daily schedule for the afternoons. Regular study, some physical culture [exercise etc.], a little bit of music practice, and a weekly spiritual gathering formed the body of our agenda. At the time of study, the students of higher grades helped their brothers studying in lower grades. One of our old professors who was employed by the national university of that time, the honorable Abani Bhushan Chattopadhyay Mahasaya, even taught French for a few days. Our new ashram began to resonate with the energy of service and the practice of building oneself. Our co-worker Yoganandaji's spiritual current kept us divinely inspired. During this time, we went to visit Kapilashram in Triveni. Its cleanliness, peacefulness, purity and spiritual atmosphere made a special mark in Yoganandaji's mind. There, we saw an instrument intended to give somewhat of an idea of the Unstruck Pranava Sound. Yoganandaji was mesmerized by the sound of the instrument. Later, he himself built an instrument like that. With a few words written on a circular [mission statement], he tried to have everyone maintain this kind of tranquil atmosphere even in our ashram in the city. The enthusiasm, inspiration and joy of that time brings encouragement to the heart even today. In the Christian year of 1916, upon having passed the M.A., Basu Kumar became the head of all of our works. Eventually, a house of books named "Shankar Library" was founded. The good reputation of the ashram began to spread as workers, devotees and admirers came from many places. With the blessed inspiration of Guru Maharaj [Swami Sriyukteshvarji], the seed of Yoganandaji's organizational and propagational work was sowed in this way in a private corner of the city.

CHAPTER 10

In the year 1916 (during the rainy season, as far as I can remember),* one day Yoganandaji suddenly came to us and told us, "I must tell you something, don't say this to anyone yet—I am going abroad [to a foreign country]. My friend Amar Mitra is greatly encouraging this and has also brought about the opportunity for this. At the instigation of Roy Bahadur Yogendra Chandra Ghosh Mahasaya—the son of the eminent high-court judge, Chandra Madhav Ghosh—an association has been formed to send youths of Bengal to foreign countries to be educated in science and art. Amar and I have been offered the chance. I have been selected to go to Japan to learn about farmers. I have to arrange everything in just a few days. Much of the expenses of travel and education will be provided by the association, but some of the expenses will have to be managed by oneself." The association stated that upon having completed the education and returning back to one's country, after one is established in some work, one should gradually pay back the money to the association. In this way, the association would be able to provide opportunities for even more youths.

[*Translator's note: The parentheses and the text within them are in the original.]

At this time, Yoganandaji took me along to see his elder brother Ananta Lal in Gorakhpur. Upon arriving there, we found that his elder brother was ill, and the illness eventually worsened into typhoid fever. We became engaged in serving him as much as we could. Hearing such news, their father Bhagabati Charan Ghosh Mahasaya came to Gorakhpur from Calcutta. We could not stay for very many days because Yoganandaji had to go abroad. Of course, we did not comprehend the severity of the illness at that time. Still, after returning to Calcutta, Yoganandaji sent Nirmal Chandra, a student at the ashram, to take care of his elder brother.

During our stay in Gorakhpur, we went to the Gorakhnath Temple—somewhat away from the city—to have darshan of Mahatma Gambhirnath Babaji Maharaj. We had received Gambhirnath Babaji Maharaj's darshan a few years ago in Calcutta itself, when we were in the company of Rebati Mohan Sen Mahasaya, the kirtan-singer devotee of Mahatma Bijoy Krishna Goswami Mahasaya. In the purity of dawn, in the peaceful and sanctified atmosphere of the temple, we were privileged to sit near Babaji Maharaj's profoundly tranquil, meditative form and receive his silent blessings. At another time, Yoganandaji had come to Babaji and was very happy to have been able to talk about matters of sadhana with him. When I said, "But Babaji is 'mouna' [silent or mute by choice]." At that, Yoganandaji laughingly said, "Even he spoke at the stirring of Divine Love."*

[*Translator's note: The "Babaji Maharaj" referred to in this paragraph is NOT Mahamuni Babaji Maharaj, the Great Guru of Yogiraj Shri Shri Shyamacharan Lahiri Mahasaya. Many great saints in India are called "Babaji Maharaj," which is a term of fatherly respect.]

We returned to Calcutta. Arranged by Amar Mitra, Yoganandaji's clothes and outfits were made; his hair was cut and styled nicely. Yogananda once again became Mukunda Lal. Guru Maharaj had wished that Yoganandaji should at least travel wearing a turban instead of a hat. But that did not happen in the end. Even though he was dressed as Mr. Mukunda Lal Ghosh on the outside, he remained steadfastly as Yogananda on the inside. The stay on the ship would be for one month; the books he took for reading during this time were mostly philosophical. When another young co-habitant of the ship's cabin saw the gathering of those books, he caustically said, "Hey, all of this philosophical stuff won't work in the middle of the ocean." After multiple changes of the date of departure on the ship, I seem to remember that the date was settled on a day around the end of September 1916. Together with Basu Kumar and other friends, some members of the Satsanga Sabha, Roy Bahadur Yogendra Chandra Ghosh and other highly respected persons, we arrived at the ship's departure jetty at the Kidderpore [Khidirpur] Docks. We received permission from the ship's managers so that some of us could gather in the ship's cabin.

We decorated our dear one with garlands of flowers. I had written and taken along a text of felicitation for the journey along with a song. That felicitation was read, and the song was sung, by Charubabu (disciple of Guru Maharaj, a singer of yoga-sangeet in practically every satsang gathering, and dear to Yoganandaji—Charu Chandra Guha Mahasaya of Kidderpore).* Even though the lyric and melody were composed by me, I was basically speechless at that time. For that particular moment, everyone seemed to be tearfully moved upon hearing the music and words. The farewell was [ultimately] addressed in silence. Even though Yoganandaji had kept that writing for a long time, that is nowhere to be found any more. The words are not remembered either. A few of the words from the lyric of the song come to mind:

Brother Yogananda, you had put us in rapture with joy

With honey-soaked melodies, put the world now in that same rapturous joy

[*Translator's note: The parentheses and the text within them are in the original.]

Evening had crossed into night. One by one, everyone came down from the ship. Dear friend Basu Kumar also left the cabin at night with a heavy heart. Yoganandaji kept me for a little while longer. Even before it got dark, tears had come to his eyes. Finding me alone, he embraced me and broke down and wept. Then the tears stopped. Somewhat managing the emotion in his heart, he told me again and again, "As soon as your B.A. matriculation is finished, you should be prepared to meet me abroad." He continued to say, "I don't know why, but my heart was growing restless in [India]; I wanted to go somewhere different. I received the opportunity. I am going abroad with the hope and belief that I will be able to make even more effort in spiritual practice." Basu Kumar also told me specifically, "Keep an eye on the improvement of the ashram. Attract the minds and hearts of good people. Take care to make the upcoming celebration (9th Ashwin, 25th September)* a good one…" etc.

[*Translator's note: The parentheses and the text within them are in the original.]

In the darkness of the night, I slowly came back down to the dock. There I saw that several friends and brother-disciples were solemnly sitting here and there in the shadows, all with heavy hearts. Eventually, in due time, we all went back to our homes. At the end of the night, I saw in my imagination: with anchors lifted, the ship was slowly moving along on the bosom of the Bhagirathi, in the direction of the ocean.

From the next day on, the activities of the ashram continued in an orderly manner under the leadership of Basu Kumar. Before, because of his Divinely Intoxicated state, Yoganandaji did not always keep complete attention on the rules. If some irregularities in our normal agenda of work would draw his [Yoganandaji's] attention, he would sometimes just laugh and say, "Rules are made for us and not we for rules [repeated in Bengali]."* In later years, it was also not entirely untrue that the transgression of rules related to our school administrative tasks did not upset us from time to time. When we would express our displeasure, he did not seem to mind very much.

[*Translator's note: The quotation marks and the text in English within them are in the original. The bracketed statement within the quotation marks notes that Yoganandaji also immediately translated the English into Bengali. Both English and Bengali versions of that statement are in the original quotation.]

During the journey, we received a letter from him from Singapore. He described the travel, wrote about different countries, and about finding Indian friends in different places—gathering them along with others and holding "satsang."* He had begun the letter with an outpouring of love: "I am thoroughly overcome with the love from all of you. That garland of flowers covered with such inner affection still hangs in my cabin. Reading the farewell felicitation writings over and over again, I experience the life-touch of all of you."**

[* and **Translator's note: The quotation marks and the text within them are in the original.]

The auspicious time of the Autumnal Equinox on 9th Ashwin was celebrated as usual. Chanting, devotional singing, a great gathering with the President of Sadhu Sabha, Swamiji Maharaj [Swami Sriyukteshvarji] at the Ram Mohan Library, distribution of sacramental foods and other such events were all held as before. Basu Kumar played the role of the primary presenter, and read a description of the events at the sabha as well. The holidays of the puja festivals were upon us. The study and teaching at the ashram stopped for a few days. Taking permission from Basu Kumar to see my mother, I also left for the village of my mother's family's house.

We went on writing to Yoganandaji to the address in Japan. Suddenly—and the puja holidays were hardly over—right at the beginning of November, Yoganandaji was back in Calcutta. The excessively externally oriented concept of daily life in Japan, promiscuity among men and women, and the endlessly restless activity made him very unnerved. It seems that he began to have frightful visions from that atmosphere and from falling ill at that time. Spending only about a week in Japan, he boarded a return ship. Still, to help India's growth [in valuing work ethics], he used to greatly praise the artistic nature and other matters of artisanship and work of the Japanese. He said that although the Japanese make cheap and pretty things for our market, it was also seen that they made very durable, high-quality and precisely made things for their own country. He had brought some very useful, well-made things with him, exemplifying [those qualities].

Because of the lack of money, he somehow managed the journey as a deck passenger on the returning ship. Within a couple of days, he met Dr. Satyendra Nath Mishra, the ship's physician. Gradually, that introductory meeting changed to a closer friendship. Much time was spent with him discussing spiritual matters. The doctor was drawn to Yoganandaji. He made comfortable arrangements for Yoganandaji around his own living area, [and] with reverent heart, received some instructive wisdom on spiritual sadhana as well. Later, at Yoganandaji's advice, he came to Calcutta and received initiation from Guru Maharaj. He even founded a Satsanga Sabha in his own house in Shikdar Bagan Para. Understanding the effect of Yoganandaji's personality, [Dr. Mishra] began to encourage him to go to the West, particularly England. Later, "doctor-babu" had visited America himself. He also became very close friends with us. He departed for the other side a few years ago. Even today, we remember him keeping everyone always in a happy state of mind and his encouragement and support in many ways.

On the ship, Yoganandaji had had a great deal of discussion on spiritual matters with an American couple. After talking about several religious groups, Yoganandaji offered that the greatest ideal of religion is "Ananda-Brahman" [God-Bliss] to which human beings are naturally attracted, and relating to that subject, he expounded upon the science of Kriya Yoga. The gentleman was mesmerized by the mantra of Yoganandaji's words and encouraged him to go to America. He also requested Yoganandaji to write down the matters of his spiritual talk. Because of that request, he quickly wrote down a draft-sketch of that talk in a notebook. This draft-sketch was what became the foundation for Yoganandaji's famous book, "Science of Religion" (Dharmavijnana).*

[*Translator's note: The parentheses and the text within them are in the original.]

During this time, because of elder brother Ananta Lal's illness growing worse, father Ghosh Mahasaya brought him to Calcutta. His treatments continued in Calcutta. But he made all treatments fail and left for the other world. Yogananda was abroad at that time. Finding upon his arrival that his elder brother was no longer there, Yoganandaji was heartbroken. His father had kept himself under control at the departure of his eldest son, but he was full of grief within, and it is needless to say that he received some comfort by having Mukunda at his side at this time.

Having touched the ground of his homeland, Mukunda Lal again became Yogananda in nature and dress. The enthusiasm in our ashram became quite stirred up, within rules or not. The Calcutta Satsanga Sabha created and founded by Guru Maharaj Swami Sriyukteshvar Giriji in Simla Para continued to be held in the gulley of Pitambar Bhattacharya in Garpar on every Saturday. The Kriyavan sadhak Charubabu would come from Kidderpore every Saturday and sing and play music at the sabha. Every Thursday, with arrangements made by Tulsi-da, the puja of Mahavir, Ramanama Sankirtan and such continued on. His main assistant was Prakash Chandra. They regularly gave out sacramental offerings of fruits and sweets after puja and devotional singing and such. According to Yoganandaji's direction, after the sabha on Saturday, we used to partake in the khichuri [mix of rice, legumes and vegetables], rice pudding and other sacramental food cooked by one of the young boys at the ashram, Suyodhan, and pass the night in the ashram itself.

Nirmal and Suyodhan lived in the ashram and studied in the Athenium school in nearby Garpar. One day, Yoganandaji noticed that the righteous teaching that the boys received in the ashram was some-what corrupted by the comrades in school. He became worried about this matter and after consulting with us, stopped the boys from going to school and made arrangements for such studies in the ashram itself. Gradually, the idea for a residential school, or an ashram school, began to dwell in him.

One day, a few days before, at Upen-da's invitation, we went to their house in Triveni on the occasion of the Sri Jagaddhatri puja. After eating the sacramental food there, we visited Triveni's Kapilashram, the Hansashvarira Mandir of Bangshabati, and the tomb of the Sanskrit scholar Daraf Khan, and thereafter went on to Khardaha. On the banks of the Ganges in Khardaha at that time, there was a Vaishnav gathering going on for almost a month, put on by the Maharaja of Kashim Bazar, Manindra Chandra Nandi, who was known for his heroic generosity and of having the character of a rajarshi [sage-king]. Thousands and thousands of people were receiving the sacramental food from the pujas. We also went and arrived at the huge food pavilion to have some of the sacramental rice and such. Upon arriving there, we saw the Maharaja himself standing there with bare feet and practically bare upper body, cordially inviting all guests and carefully seating every-one himself, and jokingly saying, "We can't really take the responsibility of keeping an eye on your shoes though." Although joking words like these were spoken, the simple behavior of this Maharaja of high character made a mark in Yoganandaji's mind. Much later, during the time of thinking about the plans for the building of the ashram school, he heard from people that the Maharaja of Kashim Bazar had freely donated money for the benefit of the country and people, for many types of causes and institutions.

Mentioning the need of ashram education for children's character building, Yoganandaji wrote a letter of petition in English proposing that a residential school be established, synthesizing the education in contemporary universities current with the time. From the time of the sweet coolness of the November dusk into the very late night in the adobe room of the ashram, he and Basu Kumar talked through the matter and the petition was completed. I was the third person in that room—at that time somewhat asleep. In the deep night, they both pushed me awake and said, "Take a pen and paper. Write down precisely what is going to be said." I sat up and took down dictation; some mistakes were also made in the daze of sleep.

In the morning, taking benediction on his head, Basu Kumar left with the petition paper in hand and arrived at the royal palace in Kashim Bazar, about a half-mile distance from Garpar. The Maharaja was taking his morning walk in the garden. There was never any special procedures set up to approach the generous-natured, friend-of-the-people Maharaja. Greeting the Maharaja in a simple manner, Basu Kumar said right away, "There is a petition [for a grant]; I have brought it." The Maharaja greeted him back in return and said, "Read it; I'm listening." After it was read, the Maharaja stood up, looked at the profoundly peaceful youth Basu Kumar, and said, "You are Godsent* [repeated in Bengali]. For a few days, I was also thinking about a permanent educational institution for such self-building. Give me your scheme**—your system of work." Basu Kumar answered, "There is a leader among our friends. After discussing with him, I will bring the papers this very afternoon."

[*Translator's note: "You are Godsent" is written in English in the original. The bracketed statement following notes that it was immediately translated in Bengali by the Maharaja.]

[**Translator's note: The word "scheme" is written as that, but transliterated in Bengali in the original.]

With elation in his heart, Basu Kumar returned to the ashram and spoke about all that happened. Immediately, Yoganandaji sent out for a stack of writing paper to be bought, and with the help of Basu Kumar, and consulting with us as well, created a draft of the goals and procedures and activities of the imagined school. When the time came, Yoganandaji and Basu Kumar went to the Maharaja, became acquainted with each other, and discussed the matter. The Maharaja himself became delighted and enthusiastic upon coming to know about the righteous resolve of the endeavoring and renunciate youths. It was told to him that we had begun a small version of [this] work, based on those very ideals, in Calcutta itself. He was invited to see the ashram. The day of his coming was also set.

For our part, we cleaned and whitewashed the adobe room, cleaned the narrow path, and made [the ashram] as beautiful [hospitable] as we could. Prakash Chandra's efforts in this task very much comes to mind. The room was set up and decorated; neighbors and some other special, sympathetic dignitaries were invited as well. With the two students who were residents of the ashram and the other young school-students who used to come to study at the ashram, we made preparations to present seven students. In the group of these students was Bishnu Charan Ghosh (Yogananda's brother and eminent physical culturist—still with a thin body in those days),* my brother Kshirod Mohan (a little chubby in those days—Yogananda used to affectionately call him "Shiva"),** and a few others. It was settled that we ourselves would perform the recitation of sacred verses, devotional singing and music. The child Prakash Chandra's beautiful voice, Yoganandaji's training, as well as my small abilities on the esraj [bowed string-instrument] took a special place in the occasion. The Maharaja arrived in due time, with joy in his countenance. After the customary cordialities, the occasion went on quite as we had planned. The Maharaja was satisfied and took his leave, and told us to come to him, without delay, to discuss the matter of founding the school. I used to also take part in these discussions.

[*Translator's note: The parentheses and the text within them are in the original. Sri Bishnu Charan Ghosh later became the founding father of modern physical culture in Bengal, using both western bodybuilding methods and hatha yoga in conjunction with each other. The reference to the "thin body" is made in irony, because Bengalis know him as one who had the body of a champion bodybuilder.]

[**Translator's note: The parentheses and the text within them are in the original.]

After talking and discussing over the matter, it was settled that the work of the school would begin in one of the Maharaja's bungalow houses by the Damodar river, adjoined with the Damodar rail station of the Asansol branch of the B.N.R. railway. The Maharaja would take the responsibility for all expenses, but seven rupees would be charged to the students for the expenses of their food and such. At the commencement of the school, he would take on the complete expenses of six students as well. Some counsel was taken from Acharya Shastri Mahasaya [Hansaswami Kebalananda] on the matter of the activities of the school. Later, on Guru Maharaj Swami Sriyukteshvar Giriji's directive, the founding day for the school was set for 9th Chaitra, 22nd March, 1917, during the time of the auspicious Great [Spring] Equinox.

It is worth mentioning here that the astrological time of the Chaitra Equinox is usually called the Great Equinoctial Transition in the almanacs. But Swamiji Maharaj proved with his calculations that even though it is spoken about this way in the serial almanacs, the transition periods had changed because of the changes that had taken place in the positions of the planets and the stars thousands and thousands of years ago. Therefore, if those who work in the area of astrology do not use corrected almanacs, their work will definitely be faulty. After independence, at the instigation of Dr. Meghnad Saha and such other eminent scientists with political power, the almanacs were investigated and adjusted, and it was found that Swamiji Maharaj's conclusions were correct. Our government set the time of transition and the beginning of the [Bengali] new year according to this new time [concluded upon after correcting the almanacs].

The occasion of this auspicious day of the Great Equinoctial Transition has been celebrated yearly in Puri's Karar Ashram of the Sadhu Sabha, founded by Guru Maharaj. Yoganandaji was prepared to join in this celebration from before. He told Basu Kumar to take over the work of founding the school on that auspicious day. He requested his friend, Tulsi Narayan, to take Prakash Chandra and go with Basu Kumar and take care of all that was necessary. Yoganandaji took me and headed for Puri.

Taking six children and friends with him, Basu Kumar crossed Asansol to the Damodar station and arrived at the Maharaja's bungalow house in the village of Dihika, on the banks of the Damodar river. The eminent historian Nikhil Nath Roy, the principal collector for the Athora courthouse near the Maharaja's house, had arranged everything. An attorney who was highly established in Asansol and who was a supporter of righteous endeavors was made the master of ceremonies, and on the auspicious astrological time of 9th Chaitra, 22nd March 1917 of the Christian calendar, in a tranquil and sanctified atmosphere, the ashram school was founded with a sacred ceremony. Eventually, a wire came from Puri carrying Yoganandaji's highest regards, and everyone was enkindled with inspiration anew.

In due time, Yoganandaji arrived in Dihika with a new teacher and assistant. Manomohan (Satyananda)* took the responsibility for the ashram in Calcutta as well as other works. From time to time, he went to the new ashram and joined in on the different duties of the school. After a while, in order to keep an eye on the observation of rules and such, he took his friend Shivananda Swamiji with him as well. Charubabu used to go there every week and teach music.

[*Translator's note: The parentheses and the text within them are in the original.]

This bungalow house sat on top a high, mound-like spot. In front, the Damodar river flowed on in its serpentine way. A little farther ahead was the railroad bridge, set like a picture. The mountain range could be seen far in the distance. A large tropical forest was nearby. Small waterfalls, a scattering of huts belonging to villagers, and the vast expanse of red earth reaching out to the horizon-sky made the place seem as if it was from a dream-world. It felt like this was the true pilgrimage place for the experience of "Shantam Shivam." From time to time, a B.N.R. train would break the silence, arriving at the little station below, out of one's sight. In an atmosphere of meditation combined with dutiful work—in the vision of a new era—the ideals of an abode of spirituality became intensely awakened even in the workers of the newly founded Brahmavidyalay (Maharaja Bahadur's favorite name was "School of Divinity").*

[*Translator's note: The parentheses and the text within them are in the original. The name "School of Divinity" is written in English in the original.]

The God-surrendered Yoganandaji carried on the inspiration from the teachings of Jnanaguru Maharaj:

anashritah karmaphalam karyam karma karoti yah

sa sannyasi cha yogi cha na niragni na chakriyah

*[Yogiraj's** commentary: Doing all dutiful work without the desire for the fruits of action—that is the one who is a sannyasi—that is the one who is a yogi; by saying "I do not touch fire and do not do any work"—one is neither a sannyasi nor a yogi.]

[*Translator's note: In this case, the bracketed statement is in the original, contained within brackets and not parentheses. In this translation, the bracketed statements have usually been the translator's, used for clarification purposes.]

[**Translator's note: "Yogiraj"—Sri Sri Shyamacharan Lahiri Mahasaya.]

The karma yogi Yogananda continued to give his right hand Basu Kumar (Dhirananda)* and left hand Mahomohan (Satyananda)**— designations which he affectionately gave us himself [right hand and left hand]—these two—new inspiration for work.

[*and **Translator's note: The parentheses and the text within them are in the original.]

CHAPTER 11

The work of the school moved forward in the ashram in Dihika. Children from the different districts of Bengal—and even the children of Bengalis living in other provinces such as Bihar and Assam—began to enroll in the school. From Brahmamuhurta [dawn]—after the morning cleansing and such—devotional singing, chanting and recitation of sacred verses would begin. After that, there would be breakfast, studying, eating vegetarian food [lunch], some ordinary work of the school, house-cleaning, a light repast, sports, practice of yogasanas, gardening work from time to time, meditation and spiritual talk, all of which would take up the day and evening, and after the evening meal, bedtime would be around 10 at night. Instead of chairs and tables, it was arranged such that [the students] would sit on an asana [floor seat] with a [low] desk. A spiritual gathering was held every Saturday after dusk. Some of the workers from the train station and a few villagers from that sparsely inhabited area would attend this gathering. Next to the ashram, a separate primary school was begun for the santal [aboriginal tribe] boys and other local children in a thatched-roof-hut. Swami Yoganandaji himself took up the responsibility of that boisterous and joyful place of learning. At the leadership of the school director Yoganandaji, sometimes the teachers and students would band together and go out to the mountains, forest, river, waterfalls, fields and such lovely places of natural beauty. With swimming and taking dips, eating in the woods and singing devotional songs [and such], the happy and fun times would go on and on. Yet he would also reprimand if there was neglect in work, excessive sleeping and such erroneous behavior. Expert at cooking, Swamiji himself would create new vegetarian dishes from time to time. If the meal was delayed because of this, he would laughingly give the reason for it to the teachers and say, "It's a little bit delayed because of creating a new dish. But this is also something to be learned." Sometimes he would lightly express high-mindedness by jokingly saying, "Rules are made for us and not we for the rules [repeated in Bengali]."* At the time of bathing, from time to time, devotional songs and chanting would go on while bathing by the river and delay the holding of classes. And sometimes, he would become so absorbed in teaching a class, that the hour would pass and he would forget that another teacher was supposed to come to the class at that time. The boys called Swamiji and the teachers "dada" [elder-brother]. In this way, a familial atmosphere was growing.

[*Translator's note: The statement within the quotation marks is written in English in the original. The bracketed statement notes that Yoganandaji immediately repeated the statement in Bengali.]

Yoganandaji's spiritual nature and the ideals of the institution continued to give inspiration for work. He was also particularly keen on treating guests and visitors graciously and lovingly. Basu Kumar managed the helm of the school, keeping watch and seeing that teaching, studying and the associated activities would be carried out properly. If there was any disorderliness in the flow of work, he would make us aware of it and take control of the helm. Sometimes there would be even be childish arguments, somewhat because of not knowing about something, agitation from irregularities, and trying to keep an eye on orderliness. Still, everyone would accept and bow to the school director Yoganandaji's orders and work accordingly.

In order to give the school the form of guru-griha [house of masters] or acharya-ashram [abode of the knowledgeable]—as instructed by the sages, Yoganandaji invited acharya-guru Shastri Mahasaya (Hansaswami Kebalananda Maharaj)* and gave him the position as the primary teacher of dharmacharya [spiritual culture]. Although our elder, Kavibhushan Mahasaya, employed by the prestigious Calcutta Mahakali Pathshala, came to the ashram, mixed with us as equals, and conducted the matters of reciting new verses, hymnals and mantras in a manner quite right for the situation. Disciplined in righteousness—or in present terms, an orthodox brahmin—Kavibhushan Mahasaya became taken by our—particularly Yoganandaji's—simple behavior and spiritual connection. He used to lightheartedly say, "Brothers, the lightning touch of your inner beings is casting away all of my conflicts." At the wishes of the patron Maharaja Bahadur, a hatha yogi named Alokananda Brahmachari came to the school and made preparations for teaching many different kinds of yogasanas. Although quiet and reserved at first, at Yoganandaji's touchstone effect, he too became cheery and upbeat.

[*Translator's note: The parentheses and the text within them are in the original.]

With the growth of studentship, more teachers were necessary. Yoganandaji remembered an ideal-bound M.A. student and devotee of the Sri Ramakrishna Mission, Shashi Bhushan Ghosh. After having had spiritual discussions with him and upon seeing his powerful perspectives and leanings, [Yoganandaji] thought of him as a fitting teacher and called on him for this time of growth. The co-headmaster of the Maju School, the resident of Bankura (first residence in the Burdwan district)*—this youth became drawn by the ideals of our ashram, became "Shashi-da" [elder brother Shashi] to us and joined the work of the school. Former students of the Calcutta ashram—Nirmal—became the head of the students [and] Sushodhan—became the director of the kitchen—and they continued their studies and went on serving [in the ashram]. Yogananda's brother Bishnu Charan (the eminent physical-culturist)** was also a student at this ashram at that time. This is where he began his studies of yogasana and muscle-strengthening.

[*and** Translator's note: The parentheses and the text within them are in the original.]

Wanting to see the new feats accomplished by his sannyasi son, the supremely respected Bhagavati Charan Ghosh Mahasaya came to the school, and upon observing everything, gave us his enthusiastic support as well as advice on things. His son had now become the "householder"* and guardian of an immense domicile. Swami Sriyukteshvar Giri Maharaj paid an auspicious visit in order to see his dear disciple's acharya-ashram. He also gave us new insight on the methods of teaching and left us with his blessings. He used to regularly say that in order to have national progress, cultural awareness and true independence, an educational system founded on the scheme of learning and teaching as practiced in ancient ashrams—but modified to suit the present times—was necessary. A self-sustaining and very orderly educational system was needed to instill discipline and build character; it was only then that there could be philosophical vision. Teachers would also develop in the environment of such ashrams.

[*Translator's note: The word "householder" is in quotations in the original.]

Under Acharya Shastri Mahasaya's direction, the study of Sanskrit was getting a good deal of attention. Many times, friends would come to the ashram and would enliven and fill us with enthusiasm. The great friend, Dr. Nagendra Nath Das (in later life, a university professor of biology; now departed)* came to the school and installed a simple telephone line in the tin-roofed room—where Yoganandaji used to spend a great deal of time with the young students. It was from this Dr. Das that Yoganandaji learned photography. During his travels to the West, Dr. Das had also gone to the ashram established by Yoganandaji at America's famous city of Los Angeles, and had been very inspired at being there. Then one day, the righteous patron, heroically generous, simple, humble and idealist Lord of Kashimbazar, Maharaja Manindra Chandra Nandi Bahadur arrived at the school. His coming brought about renewed zeal and new ideas and plans on carrying out the work.

[*Translator's note: The parentheses and the text within them are in the original.]

Upon beginning this work again with new fervor, an old conversation with Guru Maharaj came to mind. When Yoganandaji, pulled by the passion for renunciation in his younger days, said that he wanted to go to the Himalayas and spend his days there in meditation and devotion—at that time, His Holiness Sriyukteshvar Swamiji said, "Do not go against the rules of nature. You and your companions learn and study well. Then, when you are fit for it, become engaged in the service of humanity. It is nature's order that one should do the dutiful work of the world after the time of formal education. Whether you marry or not, you will definitely have to engage yourself in the service of humanity. Then, in due time, the character of renunciation and sannyas will blossom properly in the mind and heart. If love is not born while in the midst of human beings, do you think that love will be awakened by mountains and jungles?"

Established sixteen years ago, the master poet [title: Kaviguru] Rabindranath Tagore's Shantiniketan Brahmacharya Ashram had now become quite a success. Certain gentlemen associated with that ashram came to see our school out of curiosity. They had thought that this ashram—financially supported by the righteous-blooded patron Maharaja Manidra Chandra Nandi Bahadur, and created and directed by a Hindu sannyasi—was conservative in nature—meaning—was very deliberately following stubborn orthodoxy, and could be some-what in opposition to the liberal philosophy of Shantiniketan. But upon seeing this new ashram in the phenomenally beautiful natural setting, they were captivated, and upon conversing and discussing things with Swamiji [Yoganandaji] and other workers, [the gentlemen] came to know of [the faculty's] open outlook and were quite pleased. They returned to Calcutta and immediately wrote to Brahmacharya Ashram guru Rabindranath right from there, and gave him a detailed description of our school. Rabindranath let them know that he was happy to know of the school. He believed that even though [that school] had taken up a somewhat different methodology, the same fundamental thing was at work, and that endeavoring in a different way would actually bring beneficial results. Expressing a desire to meet Yoganandaji, he wrote, "We must keep in contact with each other."

In the Christian year 1916—I think in August—Yoganandaji took me and visited Shantiniketan. Upon receiving word of this, Rabindranath sent a dignitary to welcome us right at the Marfat Bolpur station and took us [to Shantiniketan], where [Rabindranath] took great care of us, attending to us as distinguished guests of the ashram. He expressed enthusiasm in the establishment of the new brahmacharya ashram [Yoganandaji's school]. A teacher for the ages in the area of education for human development, and loved by his students, the joyfully coun-tenanced poet Rabindranath said in his naturally smiling way, but with a little seriousness, "I do not have anything to say about whatever methodology of teaching is taken up, but I would like to request one thing: please give the kids a little bit of freedom. Our youth have been dying with authority chasing them since childhood. Pressured by the authority of mother, father and teacher when young. [After growing up,] pressured by the authority of the boss in the office and so on—how much of this pressure can they withstand? Let some joy come to their faces." We were very inspired by Rabindranath's words. He was also pleased. From that day on, somehow I was also blessed by the master-poet's special attention and affection. Later, I had other opportunities to come to this great man. This has been and remains one of the most special treasures in my life.

Seeing Shantiniketan Ashram at that time—with its unostentatious, pure and simple atmosphere, a serene feeling as shown in the sagacious Dvijendranath Tagore's meditative eyes, the simple lifestyle and dedication to teaching by the members of the faculty—such as Pandit Bidhushekhar Shastri, professor Kshitimohan Sen, science professor Jagadananda Roy—the freedom of the youth to move about as they wished, cultivation of music, holding classes under trees, and ashram-guru Rabindranath freely and easily mixing with everyone—all of this filled us with new inspiration. It was here that we found out that Acharya Bhupendra Nath Sanyal Mahasaya had become a dear and trusted friend of Rabindranath from basically the very beginning of the founding of the Shantiniketan Brahmacharya Ashram, and that he had done a great deal of guardianship work [for the school's principles]. It was he who brought Pandit Bidhushekhar Shastri Mahasaya to this ashram. It was from conversing with this Shastri Mahasaya that we found out that our Shastri Mahasaya [Kebalanandaji] was the recipient of many titles, and that [Kebalanandaji] was basically thought of as a beacon-like teacher of the prominent pundits of Bengal. Yogananda was stupefied, amazed and proud at hearing about this unassuming but extraordinary teacher, and upon returning to the ashram [Yoganandaji's school], expressed his wish to reveal [Kebalanandaji's] true story to everyday people.

In the past, Shastri Mahasaya had received the name of "Kebalananda" from a sannyasi acharya in Benares. Making a special request to [Kebalanandaji], Yoganandaji convinced this elderly brahmin acharya Pandit Mahasaya [Kebalanandaji] to don an ochre garment. Garpar's Habu-da also came and joined us as the ochre-robed "Premananda." Remembering that vow of sannyas taken in the Christian year of 1911, leader Yoganandaji dressed his dear friend, the renunciate, dutiful, service-oriented and highly knowledgeable Basu Kumar as a sannyasi, and newly initiated him with the name of "Dhirananda," [a name] which appropriately reflected [Basu Kumar's] nature. The students also wore yellow-colored garments. Symbolizing renunciation and tapasya, the ochre- and yellow-clothed teachers' and students' disciplined ways awakened in the ashram the holy memories of the eras of the ancient sages.

In this wonderful atmosphere, all of a sudden Yoganandaji had a dream where he seemed to see that the boys of the school were gradually leaving the ashram and were disappearing to who knows where. This hallucination of the mind disturbed him a bit also. Maharaja Bahadur was notified again and again about the shortage of space that had been brought about by the increased number of students. Suddenly one day, the Maharaja sent a letter: "Instead of building a new space in Dihika now, please bring the school to Kashimbazar." Everyone was dumbfounded at this order. Yoganandaji saw the maleficent manifestation of his dream. Although the Maharaja was pleaded in many ways to not change the location, he did not let go of his plans. A fanciful wish had risen in him to take this school—gradually being known more and more in its good reputation—and establish it near his own capital town of Kashimbazar to give it a form that his heart desired. For this, he spent a great deal of money to fix up and prepare an old mansion, which he gave to everyone with affection and tender care. Built many years ago—almost from the time of Hastings—and overgrown with foliage from the woods, the hugely constructed rooms were damp and in an unhealthy condition. Thus, almost everyone fell ill. The Maharaja became alarmed and brought everyone to a building right next to the king's palace. There was no lack in medical treatment and care, but everyone had become disheartened, and thinking that malaria could be contracted in the local environment, everyone became afraid. The immensely positive and generous Maharaja assured us: "Let us not be afraid. Everyone can go for a change of air to Ranchi. I have a house there."

Hearing about Ranchi, everyone breathed a sigh of relief. Without delaying, Yoganandaji ran to his father, his helper in all endeavors and ever his encouraging supporter. [Yoganandaji] received some financial help from him and took his fellow teachers and students and headed for Ranchi. In the month of August of the Christian year of 1918, everyone arrived in Ranchi at the beautiful 70 bigha estate [approx. 23 acres] of the Maharaja with its spread-out mansion, and upon having a change of atmosphere, everyone regained their health and began the work of the brahmacharya school. Innumerable mango, plum, lychee, guava, pear and other such trees in that garden brought great energy and enthusiasm to everyone. After consulting with the physician, it was arranged for the time being for everyone to stay in Ranchi for at least six months.

On the other hand, the happy memories of Dihika remained awake in everyone's mind. Yoganandaji set it up and [let us know] that we must keep that ashram in our beautiful "place of pilgrimage."* For this, several workers were kept at that same bungalow of the Maharaja [the Dihika ashram], and eventually, a parcel of land was purchased nearby.

[*Translator's note: The quotation marks and the text within them are in the original.]

In the meantime, Yoganandaji had come to know Narendra Lal Khan Bahadur, the king of Narajol, and thereby had petitioned the king to found a brahmacharya ashram by the banks of the Damodar river in Dihika. Introducing me to the Raja Bahadur, Yoganandaji told him that I would be the proposed head of that ashram. Upon seeing me as a young brahmachari, [the king] was pleased. Yoganandaji sent Swami Shivananda and two students with me to Midnapore [Medinipur] to start the arrangements. The Raja Bahadur took great care of us and had us stay at his temple-house in Abasgar, on edge of the town of Midnapore. Because of sudden illness there, we returned only after staying one month. The Raja Bahadur promised that he would be able to give us some help after the ashram was founded. But because of the work in Ranchi, our having plans for other organizational work, and not being able to raise all of the funds for the [new] ashram, I did not end up going to set up that new ashram after all. Acharya Shastri Mahasaya, along with disciple Swami Shivananda, kept the flame alive in Dihika. A new [small] house was built on the newly purchased piece of land as well. We went there with Yoganandaji and spent a joyous time. The itinerary to begin the work of the ashram was also presented, but because of the ever increasing work in Ranchi, not much attention could be given in that direction [Dihika]. For the time being, those plans were shut down. Shastri Mahasaya and Shivanandaji came to Ranchi and it is actually from there that they attended to the progress of the school. Recalling our previous goals and vows, in the month of March of the Christian year 1919, Yogananda Swamiji named me Satyananda Giri, dressed me as a sannyasi, and brought new energy and drive to my life. It was at his orders that I joined Dhiranandaji there as a co-worker and became engaged in the service of the school. Swami Shivananda was in charge of the huge fruit garden and farmland in Ranchi. Because of his strict vigilance, neither the students nor anyone from outside had the courage to cause any mischief with the garden. A lover of gardens and farmers, Yoganandaji attended to the garden with his friend Shivananda from time to time.

Later on, the Maharaja had actually agreed to have the school in Dihika. But seeing that the environment in Ranchi was especially good, Yoganandaji permanently established the school in Ranchi. Practically all of Ranchi's different sects and their members received the ashram-school with respect and affection. Biharis, Bengalis, aboriginal peoples, and even Christians and Muslims felt our openness and became sympathetic to the ashram's work. They would even join us in chanting in the city during festivals and in many kinds of organizational work as well. Other than in Western countries, there is no other land [in the subcontinent] that has as many followers of Christianity as in Ranchi. Our ashram was itself in the Christian neighborhood; but we never felt any discomfort because of that. Instead, we received their affection and empathic feelings. The Muslim neighborhood was nearby. They also used to come and open-heartedly and mingle with us happily.

CHAPTER 12

For the local students in Ranchi—particularly the Oraon, Munda, and students from other such aboriginal tribes, Yoganandaji began a primary school at one end of the ashram with the financial help of the Maharaja [Nandi] Bahadur himself. Even though we did not have the beautiful and orderly setup of the schools conducted by the Christian missionaries, there was no shortage in the studentship in our primary school. Yoganandaji instructed that as soon as the children arrived at the school, they should wash their faces, hands and feet, and in the recess after midday, they must be given a repast with chick-peas and date-sugar and such. Eventually, the education here—up to the sixth grade—was set up to be taught in the medium of Hindi. The fear that the propagation of Christian missionaries could be hindered because of this primary school had risen in a few people's minds, and because of that, the European lords of the government had tried to use technicalities to somewhat create obstacles [for the school] as well. Whatever the case may be, because of the magnanimous behavior of the Christian contingent [in the area], no feelings of indignation could even come up in our hearts.

The number of students in the ashram-school continued to increase incrementally. Some Bihari students also enrolled. Although the main language medium in the ashram classes was Bengali, a special effort was made to make arrangements for teaching in Hindi. More teacher-workers were needed. Shashi-da was there. A few days before, my school-mate, the grandson of Yogiraj [Sri Sri Shyamacharan Lahiri Mahasaya]—Ananda Mohan Lahiri had also joined us. These two were the ones who were there, one with us, in every situation. The righteously principled brahmin scholar Ramendra Nath Bhattacharya, the highly educated Bijoy Krishna Dutta, Banbihari Bhattacharya (now a professor of Kanthi College)* and a while later, the respected researcher of Buddhist scriptures—Nagendra Nath Biswas—these mahasayas joined in, and with their sincere service, took to the ashram as if it was their own. Because of the coming of these young and passionate educators, the flow of learning and culture of the ashram became bright and effulgent; the school also grew in prestige. Today Shashi-da, Nagen-da (later, Swami Nirvanananda)** and Ananda-da are in the after-world, but the memory of their deeds remains undimmed to this day.

[* and **Translator's note: The parentheses and the text within them are in the original.]

At this time, the eminent attorney Kumar Krishna Dutta Mahasaya, who was associated with cultural education, was endeavoring to construct an exemplary educational institution in the Rikhia region of Deoghar. Upon meeting with Yoganandaji, he became even more enthusiastic. Yoganandaji was enthralled when he saw the expansive, peaceful, comely and healthful place surrounded by mountains, forests, bodies of water and farmland. Later, [Yoganandaji] took the leader of all auspicious occasions—the Maharaja of Kashimbazar— and me to see the huge place of Kumar-babu's future plans. Swami Sriyukteshvar Giri Maharaj after seeing everything, had also said that that was a fitting place for an acharya ashram. Later, because of many reasons, it was not possible to found that school at that time.

The fundamental idea for the high-level educational methods that we have today—meaning: the environment of an ashram, a foundation of service to the community, being fit for self-reliance, being able to work in the area of agricultural arts, thoroughly learning one's mother-tongue by the age of 14 as well as being taught in that language, and after having somewhat of a comprehensive education, beginning to learn English—this type of system had been conceived by Kumar-babu almost fifty years ago. The Sanskrit language was also appropriately included in the curricula. His son Asimkrishna (now an attorney),* along with his brother, indubitably proved the success of this system that was thought up by Kumar-babu.

[*Translator's note: The parentheses and the text within them are in the original.]

A few days before this time, an unmarried disciple of the venerable Shastri Mahasaya—and Yoganandaji's classmate from the Hindu

School—Ramendranath Singha, M.A. B.L.—suddenly left his position in their Hitlar Company in Bahubazar, and joined in the work at Ranchi; and in a short while, received initiation into sannyas from Yoganandaji himself and became known as Swami Ramananda Giri. But in just a year, he left for elsewhere. More local residents joined in the work of the ashram school, as well as the primary school adjacent to the ashram that was dedicated for the education of the indigenous peoples and the general public.

In the expansive and lovely wooded place in Ranchi, Swami Yogananda had created quite a happy environment with the students and teachers. The scenes of Shantiniketan came to mind. We also began to hold classes under trees. Some days, Swamiji would be completely immersed in teaching class and go past the allotted time. He had to be alerted that the time for teaching another subject was being lessened.

Here, he found the opportunity to employ a particular discipline of physical culture that he created to help improve the physical conditioning of the students. This system was what was later known prestigiously as the "Yogoda" physical exercises. Kriya yogis benefited from practicing this system of exercise.

About a year before the founding of the school, a book written by a German physical culturist named Miller came into Yoganandaji's hands. He was enthused and excited upon reading in the book about muscle-building through mental power. Seeing me, he said, "I have found exactly what I was looking for." This book had greatly helped in systematizing the "Yogoda" method. Swamiji had experienced that power could be gathered via the inexhaustible internal will of human beings, by which, different muscles could be controlled and strengthened; without using tools and machines, the body could be made strong and powerful by natural techniques [body and mind] alone. Several students learned this and received great benefits from it. From time to time, he would practice this with his fellow teachers as well. The bodybuilding education of Yoganandaji's youngest brother—now the eminent physical culturist Sri Bishnu Charan Ghosh—actually began here. Of course, later on, [Sri Bishnu Charan Ghosh] received inspiration from the famous physical culturists Chittun and other great athletes. [Yoganandaji] also arranged to have students learn asana, concentration, meditation and other such aspects of yoga. The initiation of Kriya Yoga was generally given to very few that were fit for it, and was reserved basically for older students.

At this time, my school-mate, poet and social servant Bholanath Bhanja (now departed)* received initiation from Swamiji, became known as Shraddhananda Brahmachari, joined in the work of the ashram and created an environment of literary studies. He even formed a discussion group comprised of teachers. Ill health forced him to take leave. Yoganandaji used to take him, sometimes with students, and walk around the groves of the garden, sit awhile under a tree, and Shraddhananda would be by him and write down Swamiji's statements. It is sad to say that we have not been able to find that priceless collection. We had received other members of the staff through Shraddhananda as well.

[*Translator's note: The parentheses and the text within them are in the original.]

Seeing that the land in Ranchi was quite fertile, a desire was born in Swamiji's heart to grow vegetables and herbs. He would work in the field, sometimes with students. The simplicity and discipline of the aboriginal gardeners fascinated all of us. Two gardeners, Budhu Munda* and Sakharam Oraon,** particularly attracted Swamiji—and us as well. Now almost 90 years of age, the elderly devotee Budhu, who took the ashramic name of Budhubaba, still thinks of Swamiji with a grateful heart. Sakharam is in the after-world. In 1914, Sakharam had gone to Europe as a coolie to aid in World War I. Swamiji used to sit with him and listen to many things about that continent.

[* and **Translator's note: "Munda" and "Oraon" are names of different aboriginal tribes, and not the surnames of "Budhu"ji and "Sakharam"ji.]

Students and teachers going together to the mountains, forests, waterfalls, rivers and such places, and eating outdoors, spending the night outdoors, singing and chanting in nature—these activities filled the school with new life. Almost 50 miles from Ranchi, the challenging mountain-climb in Lohardaga, making a journey by foot through the very rocky and tremendous jungle-road—with indomitable enthusiasm—in order to see the famous Hudru waterfalls, spending the night in caves in the mountains—the memories of such scenes stir up wonderful feelings in the heart even to this day. The unstoppable zeal in an event on a certain day still vividly comes to mind. It was decided that the students and teachers together—about 60 people—would spend the night in a solitary mountain near the Jagannath temple, about 7 miles away from the ashram, and that we would also cook outdoors and eat there. A little before evening, we arrived at the mountain with our things. Just a little while later, a huge storm of rain and wind started up. Who will go where, where will we keep the things, where or even when will be able to cook—we were besides ourselves with these concerns. The rain would not stop. We decided that we should just eat whatever snack-food we had and somehow gather in two or three caves and somehow spend the night. Yoganandaji said, "That will not do. We cannot admit defeat. Come on everyone, get up, and let's go to that village in the distance and get some dry wood. We will cook right in this cave. We have to get water too. Look, see that pond in the distance." It was raining intensely at the time. A few students got up, took off their garments and dressed in their langotis [typical underwear for males], ran towards the village. I also got excited and ran, getting soaked in the rain. The head of the village knew us. He was dumfounded upon seeing us like that in the night and asked everyone to stay in their house. But after hearing our plans, he hurriedly gave us dry wood and some other things. Taking all of those things on our heads, we ran in the darkness, and identifying shadows from a distance, we arrived at our gathering place. The rain subsided a little. Water was brought from the pond. The cooking was done in a small cave. The taste of that warm khichuri [mix of rice, lentils and vegetables]—that we ate on leaves spread out in a long cave—still feels like nectar [even in memory]. Yogananda used to say, "No showing sour faces; thinking that there is danger will not do." We too would become energized by his words of gusto. I am not ashamed to say that I would feel grumpy some days. In any case, the happy memories of those exciting and enlivening times still bring up the zestful fervor of youth.

From time to time Swamiji would cook new types of vegetarian dishes. Using some creative tricks and certain spices, he would take ordinary vegetables, cottage cheese [paneer], poppy seeds and such and give them some of the look and feeling of eating fish, eggs, meat and such things. He used to have fun serving them in the dim light at night. He loved to feed people. He could eat as well. His favorite foods were regular chachchari [dry dish of spiced vegetables cooked in oil], fried large potols [an okra-zucchini type of gourd], alur dom [special Bengali potato curry], biuli karai dal [pigeon-peas cooked in an Indian wok], mushrooms, singhara [samosa], halua [semolina with raisins, butter and sugar], khichuri [see prev. para.], payes [Bengali rice pudding] and all such things. Guru Maharaj used to say, "Fooling the nose, mouth and eyes and then nicely presenting that food is what is called 'good eating', right?" Yoganandaji used to laughingly remind us of this statement. It seemed that he would become engaged in research and experiment when it came to this subject. One day, he sat to prepare an adhesive from leftover flour-wash to fix his harmonium [keyboard musical instrument with bellows], but he continued to stay in his room even as evening had come. As night fell, he sent word that dinner will be a little late. He just would not leave his room. A stove was lit in his chambers; cooking utensils and spices were brought there. As we sat to eat at night, he served a new vegetarian dish. Chewing it, I saw that it was not that easy to tear. Some kind of a meat-skin-like thing was cooked with onions. But there were no onions. My mind became somewhat uneasy. Yoganandaji was laughing about his accomplishment. What happened was this: when he went to make the adhesive after washing the flour, he saw that that slab had become like a piece of skin. Seeing that, the whim arose in him to create this decorative dish. He used to take some simple vegetable (particularly potatoes)* wrap the flour-skin around it, use many types of spices (particularly the proper proportions of hing [asafetida] and ginger),** fry it in oil, and making it more colorful, create a kalia [rich curry] out of it. If cooking is not done in a timely way, with all of the right spices and other ingredients, it does not come out tasting or looking right in everyone's hands. I remember one day that he invited a significant gentleman who was vegetarian and served him this beautiful delicacy of his. Upon seeing and smelling it, the gentleman was shocked and quickly jerked his hand away. Triumphant in this victorious culinary journey, Yoganandaji was completely filled with coddling delight. At festival time, he would take the students, pick big amlakis [emblica] and papayas from the garden and make preserves with them, and the time of doing this would feel like the preliminary ceremony welcoming the festival. Once he had had bel fruits picked from the garden, made a tub full of bel-sherbet [cool fruit-drink] out of them, and had all of the guests that had gathered drink to their hearts content.

It was as he was duty-bound to take care of visitors. Separate eating arrangements were made for them and he used to give that charge to a responsible staff-member and a student. In this way, the reputation of the treatment of guests at the Ranchi school was known all over. If at any time, even in the dead of night, any visitor would come, if it was needed, even arrangements for cooking would be made for that person at that time. Although the students would sometimes cower and be fearful of the teacher-acharya Yogananda Swamiji's strict discipline, they enjoyed his lightheartedness and humor from time to time as well. Once, he was with some students and teachers and spent time chatting with them late into the night. In the deep night, before going to bed, a student was sent to check on all of the sleeping facilities. He went around to check and then returned, saying that a calf had entered a room at the empty guest-house. Swamiji got up, pretended to put on a face of great concern, and said, "Go bring our guest. We must take care of our visitor." The calf was brought in and attention and care was given to it. Then he said, "Call the guest-attendant. We must make halua [sweet semolina] right now. The guest must have a repast." The guest-attendant in charge—Sushodhan—got up from sleep and not seeing anything at all, quickly cooked the usual halua and came. In the midst of everyone's raucous laughter and in front of the astonished and now awake eyes of the guest-attendant, Yoganandaji affectionately went on feeding halua to the calf. In the uproarious hilarity, the sleeping quarters of the school were now completely awake.

Yoganandaji had a penchant for keeping peacocks, deer and such other animals on the ashram grounds. He received a baby deer as a gift and began to give him great care and affection. It seemed as if he had just received a son. One day, in his absence, there was some neglect in the feeding arrangements of the baby deer. Because of this, the baby suddenly became sick. Yoganandaji returned and became quite aggrieved upon seeing the meek creature's condition, and began to treat and take care of the deer himself. But all failed; the infant deer died during that very night. We were all deeply hurt along with Swamiji at losing that beautiful, energetic and playful little creature. It pulled so much at his heart that he even saw that little helpless deer in a dream. At the death of the dear, Yoganandaji felt that the deer would be liberated from animal births and be born in a higher birth. Feeling this, Swamiji was at peace.

In October of the year 1919, Paramhansa Swami Pranabananda Giri Maharaj came to Ranchi and stayed in the home of one of his disciples. He was making arrangements at that time to leave Benares and live in Hrishikesh. With him was the disciple Brahmachari Sananda. Along with brother Ananda, several of us students and teachers were fortunate to have the Holy Swamiji's blessings and prasad. He expressed hope for the progress of every aspect of the school and emphatically advised that the students should abide by the righteous path and become self-reliant in life, and instead of giving into behaving aberrantly and crazily with the excuse of being impassioned with spirituality, they should adopt the attitude of servitude and be engaged in the service of family and society with love and care. It is needless to say that he openly expressed his best wishes and happiness towards the institution founded upon Guru Yogiraj Lahiri Mahasaya's philosophy [the Ranchi school]. A few days later, Yoganandaji was enthralled at having the company of this great being—a direct disciple of the Yogiraj who was close to Him and lived in the same city with the Master. There was already a deep friendship between Yoganandaji's father—the highly respected disciple of the Yogiraj—Bhagabati Charan Ghosh Mahasaya and his gurubhai Swami Pranabananda Giri Maharaj. A nectarous atmosphere was formed when they both met in Calcutta, when Swamiji was on the way to Hrishikesh. Swamiji Maharaj [Pranabanandaji] said right in front of Ghosh Mahasaya that a fitting father had had a fitting son, and expressed his happiness at that as he gave them his sagacious blessings.

At the time of departure for Hrishikesh, Swamiji [Pranabanandaji] left by saying that this is the last time that he will come. These words became unmercifully true a few days later, when he attained Mahasamadhi in Hrishikesh. When Brahmachari Sananda returned to Ranchi, Yoganandaji and we Kriya Yoga acharyas listened intently— with reverence and awe—to the description of this great being's departure from the body while in yogasana via the use of a special technique of Kriya Yoga. The great sadhak Swami Yoganandaji experienced the use of this sadhana technique in secret, and tried as much as possible to explain it [to us] in words.

On 22nd March, in the auspicious day of the Spring Equinox, Swamiji began the celebration of the foundation-day of the school in Ranchi. Because that day was set as the yearly festival-day of the Sri Guru Maharaj-founded Sadhu Sabha in the city of Puri, at his request, the ceremonial activities began on Sri Panchami and was a week-long event. It is in these festival gatherings that he began to form his public speeches. Many were drawn to him; some actually began to see him as the true yogi that he was. At this time, for the sake of expanding the work and raising funds to keep the school going, he started an association called "Brahmacharya Sanghashram." He specifically asked Swami Dhirananda to attend to the work of the association, and asked me to attend to the work of the school. But the work of the school went on growing in such a way that Swami Dhirananda had no possibility of attending to anything else. Especially because Swami Yoganandaji himself had to often travel elsewhere, he [Swami Dhirananda] had to take the heavy load as head of the teachers. Besides that, he was the one—with the welcomed growth of the school—who truly kept things in order, and was a key figure in the school's success.

CHAPTER 13

As the studentship continued to expand in the Ranchi school, in order to properly take care of the resident students, an arrangement was made upon having discussions with the [head] teacher Yoganandaji where students would be educated in three divisions according to age and aptitude. For the few quiet and good-natured students in the "brahmachari" division, sometimes he himself would be there to supervise the studies—and he paid special attention so that they would be drawn to and be engaged in spiritual sadhana. With the thought that the second tier of students would eventually blossom into the "brahmachari" character through satsang, he named that division "satsang." For the children, the "shishu" division was set up. Each division had one teacher in charge. One specially picked, responsible student was assigned as leader or student-director of each division. Although sometimes Yoganandaji would be spiritually absorbed or indifferent to worldly interests, he would always take great care to keep a close eye on all work and would especially keep watch on the behavior of the students. While maintaining the attitude of an attentive and affectionate father and trying to be kind when wrong was done, it seemed that sometimes he would become extremely harsh as well. He also knew that my soft nature sometimes could not be supportive of that harshness. When it was necessary to give rambunctious students tender and loving care, he would often ask me to do that. I have seen that sometimes he would become upset and unmercifully deride someone, and immediately afterwards would break down with his gentle heart, become outwardly pained, and try to heal that person's hurt. This "strict-gentle" nature of Swamiji was seen throughout his life in every kind of work, organizational activities and personal interactions. Sometimes being a little excessively authoritarian, having financial difficulties because of indifference to money management, lacking in attending to ordinary rules and regulations because of living in his own way—because of these and other such things, his fellow-workers and teachers became distraught from time to time, yet when they came in personal contact with him, they got along quite happily and they carried on the work of the school [with that happy attitude]. Swamiji used to try to naturally arouse the enthusiastic zest in them by being engaged with them in exercise, drills, running and jumping, holding discussions, and eating and relaxing. Although we would have some negative feelings here and there because of the usual weaknesses in any person, we actually lived pretty much a happy life with the educator Swami Yogananda. The fellow-workers and teachers that were in the ashram at this time were of exemplary character, demonstrated by their discipline in work, passion for learning, energetic work efforts and attitude of service. It seems that nowadays this kind principled behavior cannot be found at all. The strongly founded good name of the Ranchi Brahmacharya Vidyalaya was established because of these dedicated servant-workers. After having worked almost twenty years in [that] one place, I can freely proclaim this.

Adjacent to the students' living quarters were several small rooms for the teachers. Yoganandaji, Dhiranandaji and I had our three rooms next to each other. Often at night, Yoganandaji would have me join him in his room. After chit-chatting for a while, I used to just go to sleep right in that room. I remember once when we were speaking about some spiritual matters and went on right into the dawn. Students and teachers used to gather at dawn in the big room of the students' quarters—right next to his room—and he used to lead them in the recitation of verses related to morning invocations. Every Saturday, a spiritual gathering was held in that same room. The recitation of verses, music, lectures and chanting would take place in these gatherings. When he was present, that event would go on late into the night. Spiritually thirsty seekers from outside would also join the gathering at times. Swamiji used to sing in the style of the popular types of songs. Still, when drums and cymbals were added, his heart-intoxicating devotional songs used to fill everyone with spiritual ecstasy. He used to pay special attention to making sure that all guests properly received prasad at the end of the gathering.

He liked to listen to Tagore songs, Indian Classical Music and other such music. He used to even hire accomplished singers and invite them to the ashram. Upon hearing that a certain bright young musician—later known as the eminent musical scholar Jnanendra Goswami—had come to Ranchi to establish his singing career, he was invited to the ashram-school. It's as if the melodies he sang into the deep night with his sweet voice still play on in our ears. My ears have probably never heard the beauty of Tagore songs like I heard him sing them. "Make this house of mine Yours and light the lamp of this home..." This song became permanently embedded as one with Swamiji's heart for the rest of his life. It was at that time that I learned from him that the master poet Rabindranath Tagore composed the melodies of many of his songs with help of the late Doyen of Music— Radhika Goswami Mahasaya.

I had said before that he had a special attraction for Shyama Sangeet [songs to the Goddess Kali] during his childhood days. Now, in these gatherings, music and devotional songs related to sadhana were prevalent, such as: 1) "The boat of satsang has docked at the bank of this Earth, whoever wants to catch it come quickly! Oh look there, the path of the Great Ones is in sight—it's getting late my friend..." 2) "How can you stay like this in this worldly place, forgetting your true nature. The One whose Love's Intoxication for which you run around, call Him, why don't you, with your whole being..." 3) "What is the way, O Yadupati. In which way will I not be swallowed by the waters of Time and Death..." Singing the songs and devotional chants preferred by Sri Guru Maharaj, he would instantly become immersed in meditation and would become ecstatic with the flame of love in those songs. In later days, he would become thoroughly absorbed in the feelings of love from the songs of sadhana and would be completely taken over in samadhi. At this time, the students were very interested in theater. One day, while Yoganandaji was having fun with the students, he suddenly said, "Come, let us put on a play right now. The theme of the play shall be wisdom of actions and shall be devotional, and each person will get up on stage and improvise his dialogue." He was in the scene of wisdom, and with the use of tiger-skin and such, took on the part of a yogi. Dhirananda was probably not there that day. I believe that I had to take on a devotional part. Because of the circumstance, I even danced for the sake of spiritual learning and also took on the part of a hunter for that reason. The students were also with us and joined us in acting in the drama. We [the teachers] were "Swamijis." We— especially myself—carried ourselves with a certain seriousness of work. But everyone was surprised to see me openly mixing with everyone, my dance and humor, because of which—being pulled by their affection—I again had to take part in dramatic roles. [Yoganandaji] saw several plays in the usual theater [professional]. Among those performances, he sort of liked the play "Ramanuj," but "Shankaracharya" by Girish Ghosh [eminent disciple of Sri Ramakrishna] impressed itself in his heart most of all.

So much spiritual discussion went on with Yoganandaji in his room as he sat on his bed. Basically, having come into the flow of the working world because of Guru Maharaj's directives, he was drawn from time to time to the matters of the expansion of the work and the propagation of spirituality. One day, on this subject, we spent the entire night talking about Swami Vivekananda's life and his prolific work. [Yoganandaji] emphatically paid homage to the fact that [Vivekanandaji] had showed the sannyasis of today a beautiful, powerful and loving path for the work that they had to do. And another day, he became filled with the feelings of the cherished discipline of Lord Buddha, and continuously repeating [Lord Buddha's] promise of Liberation-sadhana, wrote that [verse] down on the wall of his room, so that it would always be remembered.

A few days later, he began to live in a somewhat more alone and solitary way. Sometimes he would suddenly call us to gather in his room for some spiritual talk, right when we were busy with work. If it was brought up that there would be problems in the work, he used to say, "How about a little feeling of trust, no? Will it be right if we are completely drowning in work?" To relieve himself from the complex bindings of the ever-increasing school, from time to time, he used to take us and some high-minded students, sit peacefully and calmly on a field under streetlights, and have spiritual discussions there. He used to say in the conversation at that time that he was creating an environment in the midst of that workflow where he could especially take care to prepare for spiritual work. There was a time when, in the guise of chit-chatting after dinner, a few teachers and some of the older students used to sit and have spiritual discussions. Yoganandaji himself set the rule that we should sit only for a short while, but as we continued talking, that rule was broken. On some nights, if someone would fall asleep after sitting a long while, he would create a great drama with that person for fun and have us rolling with laughter. And some nights, the jocularity would reach such a level that he would say, "Oh!

We are staying awake and everyone else is sleeping so nicely! That will not do. We have to wake everybody up." Saying this, he himself went to room after room, waking up the students and having a raucous and hilarious time with everyone. If we sometimes had resentment in our minds because of strict reprimand related to neglect in work, these lighthearted times helped to rid us of those resentments.

On the subject of samadhi and God-revelation, one day he said with great joy, "Gurudev has taught me how to die—meaning, how—by being established in sadhana—one can leave the body under one's own control—I have learned that sadhana." Although he practiced Kriya Yoga with unwavering discipline, he said that his first taste of samadhi and God-revelation happened in Serampore by the holy touch of Sri Guru Maharaj. He described this beautifully in his English autobiography. Here is a small extract from the Bengali translation by Sri Indranath Seth Mahasaya (Yogi Kathamrita)* : "I experienced that the Center of the Supreme Heavenly Abode was actually a place deep within myself and that the place of experience within was spawned by the Same. It was as if the entire creation was emanating from my Being and the radiance of an incredibly beautiful Light was spreading through the Sahasrar. 'It is His river of nectar flowing through the world'.** A flow of liquid nectar was rushing through body and mind—waves upon waves. I heard the Omkar Sound, the Sound of Brahman—the thunderous Pranava Resonance—the First Pulse of the creation of the Universe. Suddenly, breath came back into the lungs. Oh, if I could only express how my heart was filled with disappointment, I cannot tell you. That Great Being of mine was completely gone. Again I came back and was imprisoned by this insignificant and miniscule physical cage—this thing that cannot contain that Colossal Person of the Atman. Like the prodigal son described in the Bible, I left my Immense Abode of the Cosmos, and again entered this tiny 'pot' of the body."

[*Translator's note: The parentheses and the text within them are in the original.]
[**Translator's note: The quotation within the main quotation is in the original.]

About this experience, he had also explained, "When the disciple has strengthened the mind-heart via meditation in such a way that no experience, however large, can overcome him, it is then that Guru bestows upon him the experience of Brahman-Bliss...* When there is great progress and strength gathered by the unceasing sadhana of yogic practice, and pure devotion—it is only then that the mind-heart can withstand the incredible impact of the gigantic experience of Omnipresence...** The tremendous longing to attain God draws that person towards God with an unstoppable force, and the All-Seeing, All-Knowing, All-Love that is the Lord also is pulled to the devotee by the devotee's love and is bound to him."

[* and **Translator's note: The ellipses [...] are in the original.]

Even though there was japa, meditation, chanting and other such things, as for the matter of God-experience, Yoganandaji felt that the sadhana practice of Kriya Yoga as taught by the Yogiraj [Sri Sri Shyamacharan Lahiri Mahasaya], was the most excellent path and one that was easy to practice. He would always say that this was the air-plane method.* Sitting in a steady and comfortable asana, practicing pranayam-kriya, the mind-body stationary, the mind drawn into the stage of pratyahar, where in the pure and tranquil state the God-spoken Unstruck Sound—the beautiful Pranava Resonance—is taken up, Union with Satchitananda—the Divine Effulgent Lord—that it could be experienced through an easy method—he used to speak about this fundamental message of Kriya Yoga practice from his personal experience and Divine Knowledge. That the seed of sadhana planted in the fertile spiritual field within this God-surrendered being blossomed into True flowers and fruits of Spirit—this goes without saying.

[*Translator's note: The words "airplane method" are in English in the original.]

Sometimes, while performing the duties of head teacher, there would be differences with other teachers in opinion and mentality, but Yoganandaji and those same teachers would become enamored with each other after having satsang on spiritual sadhana (regardless of the particular teacher's religious affiliation).* On some days, after the prayers at dusk, he used to sit with the students and—expressing great contentment and joy—would say, "Oh, I can see the potential of beauty and purity awakening. Along with receiving their academic education, the students here are also receiving the sacred touch of the Lord."

[*Translator's note: The parentheses and the text within them are in the original.]

In the beginning, the students at the school addressed us swamijis and other teachers as "dada" [elder brother]. Later, under the advice of certain venerable and respected ones, the sannyasis were addressed as "swamiji." Yoganandaji was "bara [top or elder] swamiji," Dhiranandaji was "meja [middle] swamiji," and I (Satyananda)* was "chota [younger] swamiji." After some time, it was decided that Yoganandaji should be addressed as "guruji" and that the venerable Shastri Mahasaya should be addressed as "guru maharaj ji." However, Yoganandaji did not give initiation to the students at this time.

[*Translator's note: The parentheses and the text within are in the original.]

Even though he did not give formal initiation, the spiritually oriented students were focused on Yoganandaji as if they were disciples. In this group, a very intelligent child of 12/13 years of age in the seventh grade named Kashinath Bandopadhyay especially drew Yoganandaji's attentive affection. It is needless to say that this talented child was dear to everyone. Among all his brothers at home, he was known to be a dutiful, studious and erudite boy and he was truly cherished by his elders.

During the holidays from school in the year of 1919, Kashinath went home as did the other students. I heard later that Yoganandaji did not want to let him go at that time. He said afterwards that a warning of danger connected to Kashinath and his home had come to his mind. Kashinath died during the holidays after a suffering for a few days with a terrible bout of typhoid. At that time, Yoganandaji was in Calcutta, and upon hearing the news of the sudden death of Kashinath, sat down like a madman right in the middle of the road. Deeply hurt, Swamiji became restless to find out about the disciple's subtle form or the soul. Through the science of hypnosis and several other such methods, he found that disembodied soul nearby, and he firmly believed that he would meet Kashi after his reincarnation. One day, in my very presence, he used the science of hypnosis to put a student into the hypnotic state and asked him, "Who are you that has come here?" and he received the answer from the child's very mouth, "I am Kashi." Swamiji became excited and asked him many other questions in the private room. He looked up at me once and said, "I guess you don't believe in all of this?" I answered him, "I don't have the nerve to say that I don't believe, because how much knowledge do I have? But I don't have much desire or interest in these matters, and I find that my own explanations [understandings] come to me about the appearance of these spirits." Whatever the case may be, Yoganandaji said many times that he received wisdom and help through the use of supernatural methods in this way.

The peaceful and pure environment of the first location of the Brahmacharya Vidyalaya—on the banks of the Damodar in the village of Dihika—remained firmly imprinted in our hearts. There was a strong feeling that we must keep an ashram center there. With this attitude in mind, at the wish of the venerable Shastri Mahasaya—the head teacher of spiritual studies, who also wanted to keep the flame alive in Dihika—arrangements were made for the venerable Shastri Mahasaya and his companion-attendant Swami Shivanandaji to reside there. We went there with Yoganandaji a couple of times. A cottage was also built on the 12 bigha [approx. 4 acres] of land that Yoganandaji had acquired there. But there is nothing there now. After Shastri Mahasaya left Ranchi, Yoganandaji moved from his room next to the students' quarters and took up residence in the relatively larger room located in the southwest corner of the main building of the school. He used to invite us to his room and we used to pass the time addressing many subjects and issues. From time to time, he also called the students and checked their studies. On the veranda adjacent to the room, he sometimes cooked food separately for his own health. We used to come independently of each other, one person at one time, on certain days to eat with him. It seemed that a feeling of absent-mindedness could be sensed in him at this time.

The freely donated and large amounts of funds from the heroically generous and bountiful Karna-like patron—the Maharaja of

Kashimbazar—sometimes took a long time to arrive. Swamiji became a bit concerned about the future of the Vidyalaya. He began to think about many different ways of possibly raising funds. He even thought about permanently establishing the school on another piece of expansive land on the outskirts of the city of Ranchi. Even with financial difficulties, the work of the school, keeping the spiritual environment intact, the work of the garden, and service to guests and visitors—carried out as Swamiji specifically directed—went on unabated.

CHAPTER 14

Though the Brahmacharya Vidyalaya was founded in 1917 of the Christian year, the work of the Satsanga Sabha in Calcutta (known today as Yogoda Satsanga Sabha)* went on as usual. The yearly celebration of the auspicious day of the Autumnal Equinox as calculated by Swami Sriyukteshvar Giri Maharaj on 8/9 Ashwin [Bengali calendar] continued to be held as before. At this time, the students and teachers would come to Calcutta just before the puja-holidays break at the school. Upon securing a new residence in Calcutta, the students were given the chance to go about and see many places and events. Two days of public gatherings, headed by special dignitaries for each day, were held at the Ram Mohan Library. On one day, there were recitations by students, devotional songs, lectures by members of the public and such other activities, which comprised the day of yearly gathering by the school, and on the other day, spiritual talks, chanting and other such activities comprised the day of the yearly celebratory gathering held by the Satsanga Sabha. Arrangements were made for the general public and devotees to partake in prasad together. The yellow-clothed contingent from the school at the Calcutta sabha held a particular attraction for the inhabitants of Calcutta. Once, I even saw an article in the respected Amrita Bazar newspaper—"Rishi Boys in Calcutta." One of the specialties in Calcutta was that there were city-wide devotional chants and celebrations throughout its roadways covering 4/5 miles. The heroically generous, righteous-blooded Maharaja of Kashimbazar—Manindra Chandra Nandi—also attended the festival from time to time. Through these events conceived by Swami Yoganandaji, the name of the school continued to spread.

[*Translator's note: The parentheses and the text within them are in the original.]

One morning in the summer of the year 1920, Yoganandaji went to check on the work going on in the storehouse, and after looking over things for a while, he went over to a secluded corner, leaned onto a small cot and fell into a light sleep. Immediately after that, he rushed towards the schoolhouse and said to us, "Look, I just had a dream that I am traveling about in America." I have always seen that if something made a significant enough impression on him, he would totally become firmly resolved to see it come to fruition. Although that statement he made might seem to be a passing joke to ordinary people, Dhirananda and I could not completely blow it off. The same state of being was seen in work as well. He went on talking about his distant journey in such a way—it seemed that everything was already set; all that was necessary was to start the voyage. Yet there was nothing at all that was arranged or set. At any time, he would take his harmonium and go on singing about dream-awakening like a fountain...*

I will go throughout the world like a flood—singing
Longing, and like a madman
With hair flowing, picking up flowers
Spreading wings painted with rainbows
I will scatter and spread laughter in the rays of the sun and pour out my life

From peak to peak I will run
In mountains and hills I will smother myself
Laughing and giggling, singing merrily, clapping with joyful rhythm

Swamiji then went to Calcutta for money, to acquire a passport, and to make arrangements to have appropriate clothing made as well. As far as money, he received much help from his father, and he also got his father's assurance that he would help Yoganandaji even after he went to America. It should be mentioned that Sri Prabhas Chandra Ghosh also gave him regular financial help for a while.

At this time, we all of a sudden came to know that there was going to be a great international convention with many religious representatives in the American city of Boston, for the sake of promoting [religious] openness. Heramba Chandra Maitra Mahasaya, an acharya of India's Brahmo Samaj and a professor at City College, was a member of the working committee of that convention. When Yoganandaji went to gather information about America, Maitra Mahasaya told him about this, and knowing that Swamiji's religious perspectives were also open-minded, encouraged him to be the one to go and represent India. With Dhiranandaji's assistance, Yoganandaji's book, "Science of Religion" (Dharmavijnan),* was properly published. Sri Tulsi Narayan Basu and I also were able to help somewhat in the publication of the book. In this book, he tried to make the readers understand that religion is universal and one; that all human beings longed for Bliss; that God is Bliss Itself; and that His Presence can be experienced within our very selves. Through the study of scriptures, japa and worship, dharana-dhyan and such methods, Truth can be experienced. Through the easy practice of Kriya Yoga sadhana, the sadhak attains Union with the Divine Truth in a systematic and rapid way, and realizes the Supreme.

[*Translator's note: The parentheses and the text within them are in the original.]

The ship was originally scheduled to leave in the month of July, but the date was pushed back, and we returned to Ranchi to continue with the work of the school. In Calcutta, Swamiji went on meeting with friends, relatives and those with experience about America in order to prepare [for the journey]. In later years, he told us that at this time in the Garpar house in Calcutta, when he was in deep and contemplative meditation about traveling this new road, he was fortunate to have Babaji Maharaj's darshan, and was highly inspired upon receiving His good wishes and blessings.

In Ranchi, we prepared to say a formal farewell to Yoganandaji. Shraddhanandaji composed music, and the teachers presented him with an English prose composition honoring his farewell. Swamiji also replied to this in English. This was his first English speech. Hearing this speech that day, no could even imagine the eminent brilliance that would signify the speeches of his future. He went to Calcutta after this occasion. Several of us also accompanied him.

Upon reaching Calcutta, we found out that the date of departure for the ship had been further delayed. After the war, cargo-loaded ships with passengers would travel in this way to America and arrive there after the long journey of almost one month. It became easier to gather up the necessary things because of the ship's delayed departure. Importantly, there was time now to complete the printing and binding of his book. During this time, Yoganandaji was called with a heartfelt invitation to the house of his childhood friend—now departed—Kamal Chandra—who was a magistrate at the time.

On the day of departure, with tear-filled eyes, he took his goodbyes from the Garpar house that afternoon and arrived at the Kidderpore dock. We friends and dear ones all gathered there. At the scheduled time, staying with the regulations, Swamiji departed from us and boarded the ship. We continued to talk to each other from the stairs and then from the deck. Right at this time, Swami Sriyukteshvar Giri Maharaj arrived. It was not allowed for anyone else to board the ship to meet anyone at that time. Nevertheless, through the help of Swamiji Maharaj's disciple, Atul Chandra Roy Mahasaya, a high-level stevedore at the Kidderpore docks, Swamiji Maharaj went to Yoganandaji's private cabin on the ship, and gave him many different kinds of advice and instruction on the subjects of the propagation of Kriya Yoga in America as well as organizational endeavors, and blessed his dear disciple to be triumphant in the world. The departure bell for the ship rang. Swamiji Maharaj came down from the ship. Yoganandaji quietly stood on the side of the deck. Slowly, with the sun going down, the ship left the jetty and continued onward towards the ocean. With heavy hearts, we all headed back for our own homes.

A few days later, we received a letter from Yoganandaji directly from the ship, describing many things about the journey. He was asked to give a lecture in the meeting room of the ship at the request of the fellow passengers. When he went to speak, he struggled a little at first. But as he remembered Sriguru, he quickly untangled the problematic knots, and gave a heart-rendering speech which was praised by the listeners.

After traveling for most of the month on the ocean, the ship arrived at the docks of the American city of Boston around the end of September. Finishing up with the usual rites of introduction and welcoming, he settled into the quarters assigned for him. In the congress, or convention, there were even representatives from countries such as Japan contributing in the program. He was the only representative from India.

His lecture at the convention took place on the 6th of October. The subject of his talk was already in printed form in his book. The publisher of the journal of the American Unitarian Association—the organizer of the congress—wrote about the lecture in his description of the events of the congress, mentioning Yoganandaji's positively radiant language, the visionary perspective on the matter of the universality of religion and other such things as these. Yoganandaji gradually began to draw the attention of the public after this lecture. He was invited to many events concerning various subject matters, and this work of lecturing and such continued on.

There was no real suitable place of residence for him in the beginning. Although he received financial help from his father, managing the expenses there was actually a bit difficult; because of which, he had to be thrifty with the expenses related to living quarters and food. Eventually, upon assimilating into the general people of that country, he came to understand that if the wisdom of sadhana and the attained knowledge of India were properly and intelligently preached, the residents of America were ready to gladly receive it and would not be hesitant to donate money for that. America is the land of the immensely wealthy. With the Americans' empathy and help, the spiritual work of India would be significantly benefited. He wrote to us extensively about all of this and let us know that people were needed to help in the work of organization-building over there. If we could make it work over there properly, then it would greatly help the work of the Ranchi school as well. Once, he wrote clearly, "Look. You all know that I can do the work of propagation, and people do come together, but running it in an orderly way is something I cannot write about. So, either Dhirananda or Satyananda, one of the two of you will have to come here to join in this work with huge potential. Both of you, be ready. Whomever I call will have to come without delay."

A few days later in Boston, an older lady named Mrs. Hayes became Yoganandaji's disciple and made arrangements for Swamiji to stay in her home. Appreciating her spirit of service, care and spiritual tendencies, Swamiji initiated her and gave her the name of Sister Yogamata. After establishing himself a little bit, he sent Guru Maharaj, father, relatives and us several beautiful presents. We also became excited from hearing about his steadily progressing success. Dhiranandaji regularly sent him the complete news from here, and Yoganandaji also sent back ideas and advice with his replies from time to time. With the help of several endeavoring persons who had become devotees in America, he founded a small ashram in a lovely environment by the banks of a lake in the suburbs of Boston, and sent us pictures of that place. He also wrote that some places/land had to be acquired in Calcutta, and that— no matter what—a house/building had to constructed; and he also asked us to look for a piece of land measuring about 5–6 katha [approx. 3600—4320 sq. ft.]. Because a truly permanent place had still not been determined for the Ranchi school—even though Maharaja Bahadur had purchased a 40-bigha [approx. 13.2 acres] of land on the outskirts of Ranchi as that possible future site of the school—under the advice of Guru Maharaj, arrangements were made for a residential school— which actually was previously conceived—to be set up in the in [Sriyukteshvarji's] Puri ashram. A trust deed was prepared with these five: Sadhu Sabha president Swamiji Maharaj, Swami Yoganandaji, Swami Dhiranandaji, Sadhu Sabha secretary Atul Chandra Chaudhury, and Maharaja Manindra Chandra Nandi Bahadur. The fundraising association that Yoganandaji had previously founded as the "Brahmacharya Sanghashram" was written into the trust deed as a branch association. Because Swami Yoganandaji was not present, I was assigned to be his deputy trustee. Besides that, immediately after the trust deed was legal, Swamiji Maharaj bestowed upon me the position and title of "ashram-swami" of the Puri Karar Ashram (now called Yogoda Ashram).* A working association to direct the affairs of the ashram was also created. At Yoganandaji's direction in 1921, leaving everyone in the Ranchi ashram in tears, and in tears myself, I took on the responsibility of the Puri ashram and began work there. Atul Chaudhury Mahasaya used to send monthly financial help. We were also supposed to receive some help from America, and besides that, we discussed that some money could be gathered through the efforts of Dhiranandaji. The heroically-generous Maharaja Bahadur was also petitioned for help. The work began with a few students. It was with Atul Babu's regular funding that we were able to begin the work. The fees from the students and fundraising at times also helped to pay the expenses. Being in close proximity with Guru Maharaj at this time remains a priceless treasure in my life.

In the meantime, as Yoganandaji's work continued to expand in America, he felt the need for a partner. Dhiranandaji and I were told to be ready. At that time, I had expressed in my reply that I did not wish to go. Justifiably, he was a little saddened by that. In any case, he wrote in 1922, "Dhirananda must come right away. Satyananda, take up the fortitude to direct the Ranchi school." Again I had to see the tears in everyone's eyes—[this time] in Puri—and had to return to Ranchi. At Yoganandaji's direction, one of Yoganandaji's young-adult disciples named Haridas Bandopadhyay was initiated by Dhiranandaji, named Swami Hirananda Giri and, after discussing the matter with Guru Maharaj, was sent as to be the head teacher at the Puri ashram. The fellow-workers and students from before happily and enthusiastically welcomed me back. We also gave Dhiranandaji a fond farewell and put him on the ship in Calcutta. Because of a particular obstacle, Guru Maharaj ji was not able to come to the docks. Later, he said somewhat quietly and somberly that he felt that the beginning of an inauspicious future was connected with this journey that Dhirananda was taking.

Dhiranandaji reached Boston after one month. The satsang association had become quite known by that time, and Yoganandaji let us know that because of that, Dhiranandaji's welcoming was held with a good deal of celebration. Now, both of them began to work together. Books were printed. Many types of educational pamphlets and circulars under the name of "Yogoda Shiksha Pranali" were also published.

At this time, Yoganandaji was enthused by several devoted youths. And a devotee in his middle years named Dr. Lewis helped greatly in the expansion of the work. Dr. Lewis' automobile was also used for Swamiji's service. Up to 1924, the work went on with Boston as the center. At a certain time, a youth named Mohammed Rashid arrived at Swamiji's place, after having finished his studies at an American University. I have heard from Rashid that he was actually a fellow passenger from Calcutta with Swamiji [during his journey to America]. He was drawn to Swamiji from that very time, but not much interaction happened. He went on to continue his studies. After the completion of his studies, he searched out Swamiji, came to Boston, became his disciple, and instigated Swamiji to leave the boundaries of Boston, travel the huge American land, and spread the message throughout. An automobile was found. Two other youths came along as companions and attendants. Mohammed Rashid himself became Swamiji's secretary. The other youths became drivers of the automobile. During this auspicious journey, he went around giving lectures in different cities. In the western state of California, on Mount Washington on the outskirts of the city of Los Angeles, he saw a beautiful house and was very drawn to it. Swamiji said that when he was traveling in Kashmir, he saw a house like that atop a mountain in a dream. The money that was raised from the lectures went to buy that house, and some money was owed to lenders. In later years, that loan was paid off, and the house, completely renovated, became one of the sights to see in America. At present, the land there measures almost 25 acres.

Swamiji returned with everyone to Boston after his travels and immediately began to make preparations to set up the main center in Los Angeles. By that time, Dhiranandaji had established himself quite well in Boston in the area of teaching and mathematics, but at leader Yoganandaji's wishes, he shut everything down, went to Mount Washington in Los Angeles, and took on the responsibility of that center. Yoganandaji—as was in his nature—went on traveling and propagating the message. In 1925, a magazine named "East-West" began to be published from this main center. It is this magazine that is now widely known as the "Self-Realization Fellowship Magazine." Eventually, it would be set up so that the Yogoda Shiksha Pranali could be sent out weekly throughout the world to seekers and member-students. Swamiji also wrote several spiritually oriented books at this time.

CHAPTER 15

Many kinds of propagational work also went on in America along with the publishing of literature. People came out in different cities to listen to Swamiji's lectures which were held in educational institutions, churches and such places. Following the procedure of publicity in the American nation, promotional leaflets and posters with his picture on them were circulated in the city in which he was about to come to give his talk. It was in his nature to keep his attention immersed in country-wide travel and in experiencing the beauty of nature. And so, besides his lecturing and work of propagation, he would also go to snow-covered lands, deep forests, waterfalls and other such places, and would become absorbed in meditation there.

At this time, he added the word "Yogoda" to the original title of "Satsanga Sabha." He named the American foundation "Self-Realization Fellowship." As propagation bore fruit, branches of this foundation were established in many places in America.

[Also] at this time, he created a serial set of teachings following a syllabus that were set up to be delivered by mail to registered members every week. Dissertations on health and eating, talks on the development of the mind and heart, and visionary teachings on spiritual sadhana and other such things of the syllabus were printed in cyclostyle print on booklets.

Like taking a correspondence course*—meaning, lessons sent through mail—as in many educational institutions, innumerable numbers of students were becoming members of this main center. Regular discussions and studies of the methods of sadhana were also held in the branch centers with the help of these booklets.

[*Translator's note: The words "correspondence course" are in English in the original.]

Gradually, Swamiji began to mingle with many significant persons in America and engaged in exchanging his viewpoints with them. He met the American president as a special and successful Indian citizen living in America who was also representing a British colony. As far as it is known, no Indian sannyasi has since been in the presence of the American president in a publicly formal way.

Swamiji was very glad and inspired to have the company of the botanical scientist Luther Burbank. Through his scientific work, as if cutting through mysterious webs and picking out thorns from a prickly pear, he was able to quicken the growth of some trees from ten down to three years, and amazed everyone by increasing the fruit production of an ordinary fruit-tree. It was as if he related to the trees and plants in his garden as loving friends. Swamiji was taken by this passion to work and generosity of heart demonstrated by Mr. Burbank, and bestowed him the honor of saint—meaning sadhu. Mr. Burbank also said that he was benefited by taking up the practice of Swamiji's Kriya Yoga method. When the elderly Mr. Burbank departed from his body just a short time later, Swamiji was deeply aggrieved. Yoganandaji conducted a eulogy according to Indian customs in memory of this sadhu Burbank, with flowers and fruits, and with the recitation of Vedic mantras in the sanctified environment of his ashram.

Several places in the southern part of America [United States] are known for their separatist and racist attitudes. Swamiji used to also go to those places for the work of propagation. And one time, a segment of the separatist groups insidiously expressed their antagonism towards him. Unperturbed and calm, he was able to be indifferent to their hatred. The regrettable fact is that at this time—and within a short time—certain jealous and small-minded Indian persons, who were envious of Yoganandaji's well-founded reputation and widespread fame, tried to make sure that he was discredited in the eyes of the general public, instead of showing their support for him. The efforts that they made failed because of Swamiji's firmness of strength. Even sadder than this is that Swami Dhiranandaji became ill at this time and shortly afterwards, left the ashram and ended his association with Yoganandaji. It is needless to say that Swamiji was deeply hurt by this sudden act.

At this time, a Bengali student named Brahmachari Nirad and another Bengali youth named Khagendranath—who came a short while later—continued the work of the institution as Swamiji's disciples and assistants. Sometime afterwards, they also left for their individual endeavors.

Because he had not yet been able to be free of the debt held on the large house in Los Angeles, Swamiji was naturally anxious. But he had always maintained his faith in God while facing many adverse situations. He went on doing his duty maintaining that same faith in this unsure situation. From far away, we came to know about his state of mind and the insecure situation of his institution through his letters. Right at that time—it seemed as if it was through the blessing and compassion of the Lord—an immensely wealthy man with a spiritually thirsty heart came to the ashram. Mr. J. J. Lynn, a veritable god of wealth from Kansas City, came to [Swamiji's ashram] with the humblest of hearts, hoping to find peace and seeking spiritual shelter. Through Divine Grace, they met within a short time. Swamiji was gladdened by the inspiring spiritual feeling within [Mr. Lynn.] Mr. Lynn began to come regularly to the ashram for satsang. He freed the ashram of its debts through his wealth and went on to help financially for the future growth of the ashram. We have heard, and people who went there have also said that they were very surprised at seeing this tremendously wealthy and generous man's soft nature, trusting spirit which was appropriate for discipleship, and extremely normal and unostentatious behavior. Swamiji bestowed upon him the title of Saint—or sadhu—Lynn. Mr. Lynn now had peace in his new life, and felt as if he was immaculately purified. Very frequently, he came to the ashram and sit absorbed in meditation.

Freed of debt, the workers at the ashram took up their tasks with new zeal. There were obstacles along with progress. Overcoming all of that, everything started to fall into place. The books that were published at this time were: "Science and Religion" (it was the subject matter of this book that was the theme of Swamiji's first lecture in America at the religious convention),* "Songs of the Soul" (collection of poetry),** "Metaphysical Meditations" (the essence of spiritual meditation),*** and "Scientific Healing Affirmations" (healing illness and disease through internal divine power).**** Of course, several more books were published afterwards.

[* through **** Translator's note: The parentheses and the text within them are in the original.]

In the meantime, as the work continued to expand, Yoganandaji began to be concerned about workers who would be fit to do the job. He wrote to me saying that a group of young workers should be sent. Instead of abruptly sending inexperienced youths, I brought up the prospect of sending our former student Sriman Jotindra Nath Bandopadhyay. Swamiji had also mentioned his name. Mr. Rashid, Swamiji's working-secretary, came to India to manage the departure of workers from here. He was invited to both Calcutta and Ranchi. After he examined everything, he left completely convinced that Jotindra Nath was the most appropriate as well. Within a few days, we named him Brahmachari Jotin and in August of 1928 of the Christian year, we wished him a good journey and sent him off. After learning from Swamiji while being in his company for a while, Brahmachari Jotin founded a branch center in the city of Washington, the capital of the United States. Swamiji used to praise Jotindra's endeavors and methods of propagation. He also let me know, "You've sent quite an able young man. This brahmachari has become so established in the city of Washington, that even I have to admit defeat." Yoganandaji used to feel the pride of his defeat and the victory of his spiritual son and disciple in this way. A few years afterwards, Jotindra Nath received the initiation of sannyas and took the name of Swami Premananda Giri. In later times, it was with Swami Premananda's inspiration and financial help that the Sevayatan institution came about.

Through the exchange of letters, we used to request Swamiji [Yoganandaji] to come to his home country. Fifteen years had passed, and there was no sign of him coming home. In the meantime, the patron of the Ranchi school, the Maharaja of Kashimbazar— Manindra Chandra Nandi Bahadur, left for the afterworld. Anxiety set in on the work and operations of the Ranchi Brahmacharya Vidyalaya because of financial lack. Although he knew all of this, Swamiji was not able to help that much. He was informed of the tireless work and love that my fellow-workers were giving to keep the school alive. Because of their incomparable service, the work of the ashram-school went on unabated.

Because of working on so many things, my body became ill. Afflicted with sickness, I was forced to recuperate away [from the ashram]. I returned to Ranchi after having recovered a bit when I received an unexpected letter from Swamiji in the month of July in the year of 1935 from London. In that, he wrote, "Though it may be unbelievable, it is true. I am in London and will be seeing the land of India very soon." This news was spread all over. Preparations were made to welcome him properly. I was still in ill health. I asked the former students of the school to make special efforts to receive him with the highest respect [when he arrived] in Calcutta. They partnered with Swamiji's brothers—Sri Sananda Lal and Sri Bishnu Charan Ghosh—and began to attend to everything. With the significant work of the eminent physical culture scientist Bishnu Charan Ghosh, a welcoming association comprising of noteworthy citizens was formed.

We received news saying that Swamiji was highly appreciated in London after lecturing in a very large gathering filled with many people. The English audience in the gathering were amazed at finding out about spiritual practice—particularly Kriya Yoga—and demonstrations of the Divine through yoga. Some even received initiation in Kriya Yoga.

While he was traveling in Europe, he witnessed an incredible spiritual miracle happen to a saint named Therese Neumann in Bavaria. The lady was completely devoted to Lord Jesus Christ from childhood. Immersed in meditation, this saint felt the crucified Lord Jesus' pain at the time of His death so intimately that on every Friday—from her head and chest, particular parts of her hands and feet (the places where Lord Jesus Christ had to wear a crown of thorns, and where iron nails were spiked into him—as [Biblical] descriptions have said)*—those places would become wounded by themselves and blood would come out from those very wounds. In this state, in pain yet in absorbed in Divinity, she would lose normal consciousness. The lady was also indifferent to the ordinary needs of food and sleep. It was as if she carried on her life with nothing but the Light of God.

[*Translator's note: The parentheses—()—and the text within them are in the original. The bracketed—[ ]—word within the parenthetical is the translator's, and is used for the purposes of clarification.]

After seeing many places and things in Europe and then Egypt, Swamiji arrived by sea on 22nd August of the year 1935 at the port of Bombay. With him was his working-secretary and disciple Mr. Richard Wright and a woman-disciple in her middle years, Miss A.T. Bletch.

I had already let him know on his journey that Mahatma Gandhi was in Wardha, which was on the way from Bombay to Calcutta. [Gandhiji] had been very pleased upon seeing the Ranchi school; so if he met with that school's founder, he would be quite happy. Following this thinking, Swamiji arrived at Mahatmaji's ashram. That was an especially memorable day as they met and talked. After listening to a scientific and logical explanation of Kriya Yoga, he also received the method of that yogakriya. Mahadev Desai, who was Mahatmaji's dear friend, headed a gathering on the courtyard of the Wardha ashram where he arranged for Swamiji to give a talk. Eventually, Swamiji said his good-byes to Mahatmaji and the venerable residents of the ashram and headed for Calcutta.

With everyone's help, a welcoming ceremony worthy of Swamiji's stature was arranged. Amidst the ever-repeating chants of praise, Swamiji, the inspired youth Mr. Wright—his disciple and at once his secretary, and the service-dedicated disciple, the respected Miss Bletch arrived in due time at the Howrah station, on the Nagpur line of the Bombay Mail [name of train]. Sri Shachandra Nandi, the young Maharaja of Kashimbazar (now departed),* headed the innumerable friends and devotees who garlanded Swamiji and his companions, ecstatically shouting glorifying and holy proclamations. And representatives of newspapers also did their duty by taking photographs.

[*Translator's note: The parentheses and the text within them are in the original.]

With everyone at his side, Swamiji arrived at his father's house at 4/2 Ram Mohan Roy Road in Garpar. An expectant crowd gave him a grand welcome there as well, with an elevated stage and shehnai music. The meeting of father—then aged—and son was truly heart-rending. The relatives who were present also had their eyes fill up with rapturous tears. After fifteen long years, Yogananda had come home; the accumulated memories seemed to come alive and Swamiji was overcome. Guru Maharaj sent his welcome-blessing through a representative. I was bound to Ranchi because of ill health. I also sent him my deeply reverent salutations.

CHAPTER 16

Returning to his homeland after so long, waves of joy overflowed as [Yoganandaji] saw and met everyone. He also went to Serampore to meet with and offer his reverence as disciple to Sri Guru Maharaj. Initially, Yoganandaji decided that there should be a central monastery in Calcutta, even though the Ranchi school was already there. He looked at several houses in Calcutta for this purpose. However, his father asked him again and again to first pay attention to Ranchi. In just a few days, he headed for Ranchi by automobile. There were some problems on the road with the automobile as well. With him was Bishnu Charan, nephew Ajit-da, Bijoy Mullick, Ananda Lahiri, Sailen Dasgupta and another one or two people. Because of my illness, I had written to Swamiji that Sailendra should work as his attendant in my place. Swamiji had also received Sailen with truly great affection. In Ranchi, many people had gathered to welcome [Yoganandaji], but because of being delayed by car trouble, they arrived in the deep night, and many of those that had gathered went away disappointed. Still, the residents of the ashram welcomed him in the night itself. He embraced me in such a way that I was not able to hold back my tears. On the next day, residents of Ranchi gave him their welcoming. He also gave talks in different places in Bengali and English.

Even after being in America for such a long time, his behavior was like the normal ways of this country [India]. People began to come to him to be healed of many kinds of health problems. [Yoganandaji] helped a great deal of ailing people through natural treatments and mental science. We had heard that he had given comfort in this way to many people with health problems in America as well.

After blessing everyone with joy for a few days in Ranchi, [Yoganandaji] returned to Calcutta. There, the residents of Calcutta gave him an immense welcoming in Albert Hall. People flocked to see him. Among them, some were sick, some sought initiation, and some only wanted to have his darshan. For Kriya Yoga initiations, Swamiji arranged one day for men and one day for women. After giving initiation to the men, he told them, "Study and understand it properly from Satyananda." Even an eminent person like Professor Prabhudatta Shastri received initiation personally from Swamiji.

Just a few days afterwards, on the 9th of Ashwin [or] the 25th of September, the time for the yearly celebration by the Calcutta Yogoda Satsanga center arrived. Although I was ill, he asked particularly those of us in Ranchi to participate in that celebration. So, I also presented myself there at the appropriate time. At that time, our former students, Sailesh Mohan Majumdar (now Swami Shuddhananda)* and Sailendra Bejoy Dasgupta, were working as directors of operations for a students' residence, established on Bechu Chatterji Street. Swamiji [Yogananda] would come there from time to time and join in on the weekly sabha held on Saturdays, and would fill everyone with joy with spiritual discussions and devotional singing and such things. When I arrived, I went to stay at that same students' residence. The festival in Calcutta went on as expected. It is needless to say that a great number of people gathered there because of Swamiji's coming.

[*Translator's note: The parentheses and the text within them are in the original.]

During Swamiji's stay in America, Swamiji had met the prince of Mysore [region of South India]. Swamiji had already seen many places in South India. Now, he went there with the official invitation of the prince. A large gathering was held in Bangalore. Many people received initiation there. Swamiji was also given a welcoming ceremony in the Mysore palace.

After traveling and returning from the southern part of India, Swamiji stayed mostly in Calcutta. From time to time, he used to go to Ranchi. Gradually, his pull towards Ranchi grew stronger. He spoke with the Maharaja of Kashimbazar and purchased that land, house and garden measuring almost 23 acres for thirty thousand rupees. Then, meaning in the year of 1935, the value of an estate house like that was more than eighty thousand rupees. But the Maharaja wanted the school to be set up, and thus let go of that house for that low price. 25 years before this time, the late Maharaja Manindra Chandra Nandi Bahadur had purchased that house also for thirty thousand rupees. Even at that time, with property values as they were then, the price of that estate was considered low.

Discussions went on about changing and improving the property of [the] Ranchi [school]. Because there was not much money at hand at that time, not much was done right away. Swamiji was very drawn to the students' residence in Calcutta. He told us to attend to it and make sure that it was stable. During the last days, he himself took residence in that small house. He used to also go from time to time and stay in the house of his great friend Sri Tulsi Narayan Basu's on Raja Dinendra Street next to Garpar. While he was staying there, he became aware of the enterprising abilities of Prakash Chandra Das and later, [Yoganandaji] relinquished the responsibilities of very important endeavors to him. Afterwards, [Das Mahasaya] was the one who supervised the work as well.

Prabhas Chandra Ghosh was extremely dear to Swamiji. From time to time, he would even go to Prabhas Chandra's house in Kharagpur and spend a couple of days there. And whenever Prabhas Chandra had time, he would come to Calcutta and be blessed by Swamiji's company. He was appointed to the position of vice president of the newly established Yogoda Satsanga Society. Sananda Lal Ghosh, Bishnu Charan Ghosh and Dr. Prakash Chandra Ghosh—who was Prabhas Chandra's brother—all became engaged in the membership association of the society. Of course, Ananda Mohan Lahiri, Panchkori Dey (Shantananda Brahmachari)* and I also were registered board members. A short while later, I was the one who had to take up the responsibility of general director. Shantananda was the assistant director. Before leaving India, Prakash Chandra Das (the now departed Atmananda Swami)** and Sri Ramkishore Roy Mahasaya—the Kriyavan attorney from Ranchi who had helped in the organizational work in many ways—were appointed by Yoganandaji to be registered board members. Ramkishore-babu was a devotee of yogacharya Sudhakar Kumar Nath Mukhopadhyay Mahasaya. It was his efforts that enabled Swamiji to collect some priceless books of shastra with the spiritual commentary by the Yogiraj [Sri Sri Shyamacharan Lahiri Mahasaya]. These books were with [Ramkishore Roy Mahasaya's] uncle, Debendra Nath Roy Mahasaya, a disciple of the Yogiraj.

Debendra-babu's son Sriram Bishnu Roy and other fellow devotees took discipleship under Swamiji.

[* and **Translator's note: The parentheses and the text within them are in the original.]

The joyous meeting with Sudhakar Kumar Nath and Swamiji in Burdwan is an event worth mentioning. Kumar Nath said, "[Teaching] the method of Kriya Yoga sadhana, and propagating it—Swami Yoganandaji has truly given us a priceless gift, as the nectarous Bliss springs forth from this sadhana."

While he was in India, [Yoganandaji] met with many sages and saints. He went to the Belur Math and offered his reverence. He met with Anandamoyi Ma and also brought her to the Ranchi ashram once.

When Swamiji was in America and was not able pay much attention to the Ranchi school—after letting him know—a foundation set up for the well-being of the school named "Brahmacharya Sangha" was registered. He had previously created a foundation while he was living in India called "Brahmacharya Sanghashram," but that was never registered.

In any case, Swamiji now desired that all of the work should be done under one organization, with the name of Yogoda Satsanga Society, and that this organization should be connected with the Self-Realization Fellowship in America. Everything worked together while Swamiji was in India. When he went to America, he kept writing that no organization can develop if there are differing ideas; thus, those who could not be a part of Yogoda with their whole beings should separate.

Naturally, many were saddened in their hearts by this motion. Nevertheless, many of the former staff members began an institution in Ranchi called "Brahmacharya Sangha" and a regular school was started there as well. The residential school Brahmacharya Vidyalaya stayed with the Yogoda Ashram. For a long time, a separate primary school was adjoined to the ashram-school. The work of that primary school was started particularly for the indigenous aboriginal students such as Oraon, Munda etc. The activities there went on regularly and as usual. Swamiji himself had formed that place. This institution was very dear to him.

Every week, Self-Realization Lessons were published from the American center and it continues to this day. The lessons contain instruction on spiritual practice, general life skills, food, and ways to maintain health and well-being as well. Those who become members are the ones who receive those lessons in regular intervals. Because Swamiji decided to publish lessons like those also from the center in India, those booklets were named "Yogoda Lesson" and began to be published twice a month for the members [in India]. Sriman Panchkori Dey (Brahmachari Shantananda)* took complete responsibility for that task and began the work. Just like in America, these lessons were also cyclostyle printed. In India, people of many different religions received these teachings, particularly in the area of Bombay. I had the responsibility of answering questions related to these.

[*Translator's note: The parentheses and the text within them are in the original.]

CHAPTER 17

Following Swamiji's directions, Bishnu Charan sent one of [Sri Bishnu's] prodigious students—Sri Krishnakali Bandopadhyay—to be a teacher of physical education at the Ranchi ashram. Because of Krishnakali's beautiful and simple nature, as well as his method of teaching, youths from the ashram and also many others from outside enrolled in the gymnasium in the school. Krishnakali taught known exercises as well as the Yogoda method of exercises designed by Swamiji. The work of the school also went on regularly.

In the year of 1936, Swamiji went to travel the northwest of India. He took part in the Prayag Kumbha Mela in the month of Magh (Bengali calendar). He lectured there also. Over here in the ashram in Puri, Guru Maharaj fell ill. He was restless to see his dear disciple Yoganandaji. Yoganandaji returned from the Kumbha Mela. Right at that time the Holi festival [festival of colors] had arrived. Everyone became engrossed with him in the Holi celebrations. Hearing about Guru Maharaj's condition, he set out for Puri the next day. But when he arrived there, he was completely heartbroken because Guru Maharaj had left his body on the day after the Holi festival—the second day of the lunar fortnight. As per the rules that apply to sannyasis, Swamiji held a burial of Guruji's body in the courtyard of the ashram, and later, he made arrangements for a bhandara as well.

After this, Swamiji traveled and worked some more and then set out for Bombay to eventually head for America. Everyone's eyes were filled with tears and Swamiji shed tears himself. Suddenly, after a few days, a letter came from Bombay saying that the ship that he was supposed to take could not be taken, and that he is coming back.

When he returned, he told us that he witnessed Sri Guru Maharaj appear in his physical body in Swamiji's hotel room in Bombay, and that they had had spiritual discussions as well. He likened this event to the resurrection of Lord Jesus Christ. Many of the devotees in America also accepted this event on that premise.

Then in the month of August, with everyone again in tears, [Yoganandaji] left for America. When he arrived there, he saw that his dear disciple—Sadhu Lynn—had a gift waiting for him—a new ashram-house on an expansive ocean-side property in Encinitas. Swamiji began to have different kinds of construction done to that ashram by the beach. He had a temple built there, and the tops of the temple were gilded. He named the temple "Golden Lotus Temple." It was built right on the side of the ocean, and because of problems with erosion, the temple had to be taken down. Now there is a beautiful ashram there, with places for retreats and such. More ashrams have been set up in different American cities and the work continues there. Swamiji's talks are being known and heard, and many places in the world are spreading his message through setting up ashrams and such.

In India, particularly in Bengal, the previously founded Satsanga Sabha continues the work, now being called by the name of "Yogoda Satsanga Sabha." I still have to look after most of its work.

Upon arriving in America, Swamiji again asked for workers to be sent there. I wrote to him that there was no young man as capable as Jotin (Swami Premananda),* but I could also send [Yoganandaji's] disciple Sri Sachindra Nath Chakraborty. Initiating Sachindra Nath with the name of "Brahmachari Premeshvarananda," we sent him off to America. In the meantime, Sri Sadananda Mukhopadhyay and Sri Anil Kumar Basu were both initiated into the path of brahmacharya with the names "Brahmachari Sadananda" and "Brahmachari Animananda" [respectively], and joined the work in Ranchi.

[*Translator's note: The parentheses and the text within are in the original.]

From time to time, Swamiji used to direct us in organizational matters. But because of giving different people different instructions at times, we used to face some problems with work.

The main place of work for the Sadhu Sabha that Guru Maharaj had set up in Serampore [Srirampur] was in his paternal home [the ashram in Serampore]. After he left his body, we could not keep that house for the ashram, despite numerous efforts. A trustee had been assigned for the Puri ashram; so, there was no difficulty in keeping the ashram established there. Already in 1921 of the Christian year, Sri Guru Maharaj had let Yoganandaji know that he [Sriyukteshvarji] had appointed me as "ashram-swami" of that ashram. But when Swami Dhiranandaji went to America, I again had to take on the responsibility of the Ranchi [school] in the year of 1922.

In the Christian year of 1941, to carry out the work exactly as he wanted, Yoganandaji gave the name of "Swami Vinayananda Giri" to Brahmachari Premeshvarananda and sent him to India as his deputy and partner and head of the organization in India. It is needless to say that many were unhappy with this arrangement. Nevertheless, everyone bowed their heads and accepted guru Swamiji's orders. Prakash Chandra became Swami Vinayananda's primary assistant. Even though I was the head teacher at the Ranchi school, Swami Vinayananda gradually started to take up all of its responsibility. At that time, I was feeling like taking a leave. I went about here and there, but I continued to take part in the festivities of the Yogoda Satsanga Sabha in many different places.

In particular, the Yogoda students' residence so dear to Yoganandaji— directed and run by Sri Sailesh Mohan Majumdar (now Swami Shuddhananda)* and Sri Sailendra Bejoy Dasgupta, both of whom were former students of the Ranchi school as well as Kriyavans—eventually closed down as well. During the time that Yoganandaji was in India [after returning from America], Sailendra Bejoy was with him practically all day every day and attended to him in many different ways. Swamiji had a great wish that he would take Sailendra Bejoy to America. Even after [Yoganandaji] went back to America, he wrote to me about this many times. But at that time, Sailendra Bejoy did not particularly have much interest in that direction.** Many felt that stopping the work of this center [the students' residence] in Calcutta because of the new situation was significantly detrimental to Yogoda Satsanga. At that time, Swamiji did not quite understand [what happened] on this side. Swamiji's disciple and physical culturist Sri

Krishnakali gradually drew himself away from Ranchi. Later, another physical culturist, as well as the director of the free medical dispensary at the ashram—Sri Shashi Bhushan Basu—also ended his association with the Ranchi school.

[*Translator's note: The parentheses and the text within them are in the original.]

[** Explanatory note: Sailendra Bejoy Dasgupta was a beloved Kriya disciple of Swami Sriyukteshvar Giri.]

The work of the Ranchi school went on with the partnership of Swami Vinayananda and Swami Satchitananda (Brahmachari Animanada).* It is worth mentioning here that after Swamiji left his body, Prakash Chandra and Prabhas Chandra had gone to America. At that time, Rajarshi Janakananda (the name given by Swamiji to Mr. Lynn)** was the head of America's Self-Realization Fellowship. Before he had left his body, Swamiji had set aside the sannyas names of "Atmananda" for Prakash Chandra, and "Satchitananda" for Animananda [Prabhas Chandra]. From Rajarshi Janakananda, Prakash Chandra took the name of "Swami Atmananda Giri," and after returning from America, Atmananda Swami gave Animanda the name of "Satchitananda." In any case, after working for a while [at the school], Swami Vinayananda left Ranchi and became engaged in the work of the Yogoda Ashram in Dakshineshvar. Later, Sri Girindra Nath Dey (Swami Vidyananda)***of the Lakshmanpur ashram took over the responsibilities of the Ranchi ashram. Swami Satchitananda assisted in the work of the ashram, and particularly with the help Ramkishore Roy Mahasaya, began to do some propagation. The work of the Ranchi ashram has gone on through many changes, even before [Swamiji's] departure from the body. Now, Swami Vinayananda, Swami Satchitananda, Swami Vidyananda and several staff-members from the past are there.

[*,** and ***Translator's note: The parentheses and the text within them are in the original.]

CHAPTER 18

In 1943, Swami Premananda sent letters and telegrams from America to Sailesh Mohan (Swami Shuddhananda)* saying that the news of the famine back home was also known throughout America. To aid in the situation, [he also said that] some money was being sent from America. That money helped a bit. Then, Swami Premananda sent a proposal saying that an institution dedicated to service ought to be set up in some village, and that a group should be created with Swami Satyanandaji as the head, and that the work [of that institution] should be started. I had a trust deed drawn up, but I had my name left out. The institution was named "Sevayatan." Even though I left my name out of it, I became wrapped up in it. Instead of setting up different societies, a single institution was set up that could work together in the future with the Yogoda Satsanga Society. We let Yoganandaji know about our plans. We sent him an invitation to come here. He wrote that he would come and began to prepare for that as well. A few days before that, he had written to me asking me to come to America to work there and said that I could stay in any of the centers for however long I wished. I replied to him that it was he who was needed in this country [India]. Everything could be arranged after he arrived here.

[*Translator's note: The parentheses and the text within them are in the original.]

Later, Swamiji asked me to again take over the responsibilities of the Ranchi ashram with the previous workers from Yogoda. And he also wrote saying that he would like Sevayatan to join Yogoda. I asked him to please come here first. He was ready to come in the year of 1952.

Unfortunately, on the 7th of March of that same year, he attained Mahasamadhi in America itself. Sri Binoy Ranjan Sen, the Indian ambassador, had gone to Swamiji's ashram a few days before that and very much enjoyed Swamiji's company. Swamiji took great care to prepare many kinds of food with his own hands and treated this respected guest with heartfelt hospitality. Sen Mahasaya had said later, "I have met many sadhus and sannyasis, but such a big-hearted person is rarely seen."

A welcoming gathering for Sen Mahasaya was held on the 7th of March in 1952 in the Baltimore Hotel in the city of Los Angeles. Swamiji also took part in that welcoming gathering which was put on by the residents of America. Although Swamiji was feeling a little ill that day, he arrived at the gathering and went up to give his lecture at the appointed time. As he finished the talk, immediately after he offered his self-penned English poem to India, he fell to the floor and expelled his last breath. The proceedings were halted. Everyone was in shock and grief. Devotees took his body to the ashram. The yogi's body remained in 21 days in a condition without any decay. We received this most astonishing news as well.

After he left his body, his extremely dear disciple from America—Mr. Lynn, whose guru-given name was Rajarshi Janakananda—took the seat as head of the organization in service to his guru, representing Yoganandaji as his deputy. Swamiji's especially faithful disciple Miss Fay Wright (Sister Daya)*—now Daya Mata—became a significant partner and carried on with the work.

[*Translator's note: The parentheses and the text within them are in the original.]

Although the mahapurush and yogi Paramhansa Yoganandaji had left his body, he remained firmly present as guru in the hearts and minds of the devotees.

It is natural that the memory of the person whose presence I had had since childhood as companion, friend, and the charioteer of life's chariot should remain alive—by itself—in the mind and heart. I have known him as a human being. I have experienced the spiritual light radiating from this human being—always—and ever-undimmed. Perhaps some conflicts also came to mind as far as the working world. But his inner spiritual beauty forever holds his image within as an extraordinary master.

Kriya Quotes from Swami Satyananda Giri

excerpts from *Acharya Sanglap* (Conversations with Swami Satyananda Giri) recorded by Sri A.K. Sarkar

English Translation by Yoga Niketan

This translated book maintains that an almost literal translation of the Bengali words of the original author best serves both seekers and Kriyavans. No attempt has been made for the translations to be poetic or interpretive for the above-mentioned reason. If the reader notices irregular English grammar (including non-traditional sentence structure, punctuation, etc.), please understand that it is intentional. The translator has tried as best as he could to keep the work as close to the Bengali phrasing in the original without it being unreadable or incomprehensible.

Pranam, The Translator: Yoga Niketan

Swami Satyananda Giri Maharaj

SWAMI SATYANANDA GIRI MAHARAJ ON KRIYA

"Before the start of Kriya, or Prankriya, the practice of Mahamudra helps to bring about in the body and the nervous pathways/currents the condition of strength and steadiness, [and] clarity and health appropriate for sadhana. As one continues the practice to attain this condition, the practice of the technique of the Second Kriya is made possible with the method of piercing the tongue-knot by the technique of Khechari Mudra. In the Second Kriya, taking the recourse of specific syllables of mantra along with the practice of abiding in the different chakras, the instruction of special Kumbhak is given. The proper practice of the Second Kriya, breaking the heart-knot, results in bringing about the experience of the Unstruck Sound [Anahata Nada] Pranava. Included in the Second Kriya is the instruction for a type of Kriya-technique for applying a particular kind of pressure or strike [Thokar] on the Anahata Chakra. The Third Kriya's practice is taught for establishing oneself firmly in the wave/path of Pranava Nada, and the technique to attain Nada in the Fourth Kriya, experiencing the different chakras, leads to breaking the Muladhar-knot."......Swami Satyananda Giri, Acharya Sanglap, book 2 page 67

Question: Familiarize us with the mudras necessary in Kriya Yoga.

Answer: Lahiri Mahasaya spoke of three particular mudras necessary for Kriya Yoga. Mahamudra, Yoni mudra and khechari mudra. These are stated in the scriptures. But understanding Lahiri Mahasaya's special ways of using the methods [is important]. Of course, the transmission of the techniques is received only from Guru.

In Mahamudra, he has made special use of the in-breath and the out-breath. Even as we want to walk on the path of the Pranayam of Kriya and Dhyan, we hear of nadi-shuddhi and bhuta-shuddhi. Mahamudra does the work of that nadi-shuddhi in a particular way. By this, one can be freed from the attacks of physical afflictions. Performing Mahamudra takes away the experience of denseness in the body, and the body naturally becomes fit for sadhana such as pranayam. The innate feeling of delight in body and mind comes about. Among physical exercises/techniques, Mahamudra is somewhat similar to "Pashchimottasana" [from hatha yoga].

Lahiri Mahasaya held Yoni Mudra in a highly important position. This mudra is practiced as the mind becomes tranquil after the practice of pranayam and such. One has to shut off the exterior senses when practicing this mudra. By the use of the breath, one has to pull on the Kundalini Shakti at the Muladhar, and in the point between the eyebrows, the place that can be truly called the abode of the Lord—the abode of Guru—the abode of Kutasthachaitanya—stilling the mind there, one experiences the revelation of Light. This type of technique greatly helps the mind to progress on the high spiritual path. That Light is what can be truly called "Yoni" or "Brahmayoni." This can be basically said as the substantive essence: The Mula [Fundamental] Prakriti creates the World-Samsara via that Brahmayoni. Therefore, through that Yoni, meaning pathway, we have created the World-Samsara and have become bound by it. Via meditation upon that Yoni, one can become established in the Fundamental Consciousness-Truth beyond the external world and [experience] overflowing Bliss springing forth. It is in this cave of Light within the sadhaka that the Spiritual Substance is hidden, and it is this that is the path of the Great Ones—

"dharmasya tattvam nihitam guhayam" "mahajano yena gatah sah panthah" ["The Substance of Dharma is hidden in the cave."] ["The path that is/has been traveled by the Great Ones."]

The other one is Khechari Mudra. Entering the tongue in the nasal passage in pathway of the upper palate is called "the practice of Khechari Mudra." Although this is a physical technique of hatha yoga, it [brings about] a steady and still condition and is necessary to draw the mind inward. When this condition [the achievement of Khechari] happens, the sadhaka experiences somewhat more steadiness and stillness and becomes ready to advance to the second level of Kriya."...........Acharya Sanglap book 1 pages 8–9

"one has to concentrate on the movement in the path of the Yogasutra-mentioned sushumna nadi to bring about that experience in the spinal column itself. Through this, that path continually gains magnetic power by the technique of Kriya, which results in turning the outgoing currents of the [other] nadis inward by the attractive power of that magnetic force, and [thus] the mind is also magnetically drawn within in that way. This results in the ending of the restlessness of inhalation and exhalation, after which, the state of pranayam where there is disconnection from the movement of in-breath and out-breath is eventually attained. This results in the stillness of mind, and with the disciplined practice of pratyahar and dharana—dhyan and samadhi are eventually attained in the paravastha of Kriya. Through this practice itself one can attain realization on the path of samadhi, with the luminous experience of the various chakras—the abodes where power is transmitted—and the Unstruck Resonance of Pranava. It is because of this foundational and essential fact that Yogiraj has said that all states of sadhana can be attained with the reverently disciplined practice of the First Kriya.

But according to the physical and psychological states and makeup [constitution] of individuals, He gave instructions for practice of the performance of different stages of Kriyayoga sadhana—First, Second, Third etc.—and their methods and techniques. For example, in the First Kriya—discovering the path of sushumna along with practice of Khechari Mudra—when that practice is firm and strong, in the Second stage, one experiences the various chakras and eventually experiences Sound [Nada]. The Third Kriya is there for one to take up that Nada in a specific way and become completely established in that Nada. It is in this way that there are directives that have given for progress on the path of Kriya, stage by stage"......Acharya Sanglap 2 page 51

After this comes the matter of Second Kriya. For this, Khechari Mudra is necessary. With this, by the help of this inturning physical technique, one is also aided in turning the mind inward as well. Then, the abidance of the different chakras on the path of sushumna and the practice of kumbhak in pranayam are the elements upon which one focuses. This results in being able to hear the Unstruck Sound [Anahata Nada] and the experience of dhyan is heightened. This Nada or Pranava Shabda is what Maharajji [Swami Sriyukteshvar Giri Maharaj] pointed towards in his Kaivalya Darshan [English title: The Holy Science] scripture as the way for a sadhaka to walk on the path of samadhi in the perfected state ("pranavashabda eva panthah"). In his work, he showed and taught us that that Universe-pervading Nada resides in Its Totality within the body of the sadhaka. The Resonance is what magnetically draws the sadhaka to experience Brahman in practically every state of being or situation. Gradually, with greater and greater Light springing forth, the door of sushumna is effervescently manifested (dhvanerantargatam jyotih). Continuing to experience the incredibly beatific visions, the yogi is able to become established in the paravastha of Kriya. It is this method that he [Swami Sriyuktshvarji] graciously tried to have us realize in a simple and usable way. The disciples of Yogiraj—our respected elders—have shown us the path in this manner.

page 26, vol. 2 of Acharya Sanglap.

---

2) Question: Give us an analytical explanation of Lahiri Mahasaya's Kriya Yoga.

Answer: In the matters of Kriya Yoga, Lahiri Mahasaya particularly emphasized Kriyayoga Sadhana and Kriya Paravastha. "Kriya" sadhana may be thought of as the sadhana of "the practice of being in Atman." "Kriya Yoga" brings about the awareness of the Self/Atman. In "Kriya Paravastha," surrender in Atman is experienced. As the body of Kriyayoga Sadhana, Lahiri Mahasaya has given directives for three acts; this has already been stated before. The first is **Mahamudra**—by the performance of which the feeling of denseness/stiffness of body is cast off. The nadis within the body become prepared for Kriya, meaning that the process of nadi shuddhi is activated. The body becomes conducive for sadhana. The second is to do **Pranayam** in asana.

3) Question: What is special about Kriya Yoga Pranayam as compared to ordinary pranayam?

Answer: From scriptures, we know that pranayam has three parts— purak [filling the lungs], rechak [purging the lungs] and kumbhak [sealing the breath]. In the beginning of the sadhana of this Kriya Yoga's internally moving Pranayam, the kumbhak is not visibly apparent. By the use of a special easy and simple method of the purak-rechak act, from the steadiness of the sadhak's sadhana, kumbhak comes effortlessly and naturally. This somewhat falls into [the area of] what is spoken of as "Kevali Kumbhak" in the scriptures. However, in more advanced stages of sadhana, the use of special techniques of kumbhak are facilitated. These techniques of sadhana are transmitted via Guru.

4) Question: What happens with gradual advancement in Kriya?

Answer: Advancement on the path of Kriya [consists of] breaking the tongue-knot by the aid of Khechari Mudra; breaking the heart-knot by the aid of Pranava, or Nada, and breaking the Muladhar-knot by the bursting spring of Light, where the awakening of the Kundalini Shakti is experienced.

5) Question: Speak of the third act.

Answer: The third act is **Yoni Mudra**. Pranayam Kriya results in the mind ascending upward. At that time in the Brahmayoni in the Ajna Chakra, one has to do a special kriya of Light-witnessing using this act. First the subtle light in the body is experienced. Gradually through being in dhyan, one can progress to Paravastha. With the experience of Nada and Pranava-Resonance, the revelation of Light becomes more and more brilliant, and the eye of Prajna blossoms open.

—Acharya Sanglap, book 1 pages 14–16.

(editor's note—-the words in bold print are that way in the original Bengali. We have presented them here in that same way)

What is understood to be the "tongue-knot"?

Answer: Just as asana and such are needed in the field of sadhana, in the same way, there is a special necessity for breaking through the tongue-knot, or [the performance of] Khechari Mudra. With the help of some physical and a certain amount of mental effort, the tongue can be inserted into the hole in the upper palate. This act in many ways helps the disciplined life. In this manner, the tongue arrives at the junction point of the nasal passage inside the hole in the palate. Along with the practice of Kriya Yoga and the advancement of mental absorption, the tongue continues to go up even further. It is said in the scriptures that when the tongue arrives at the end of its full journey, the state of "jada-samadhi" comes about. This Khechari Mudra is what can be called as "breaking through the tongue-knot." Gradually, there is advancement of this condition. Samyama is also acquired gradually. In a particular state experienced during the practice of this technique, a certain type of fluid comes upon the tongue that improves the health of body and mind. It is this fluid that is described in the scriptures as "Sahasrarchyut Sudha" [Nectar falling off the thousand-petaled]—that nectar which yogis drink as they move forward on the path of Immortality. It is by this that an earthly knot, meaning a significant knotting of the ties of material bondage—is undone and released. Through this, progress on the path for the sadhaka is made consider-ably easier and clearer..............from Acharya SanglapVol 1 page 26

Question [to Satyanandaji]—Speak about breaking through the heart-knot.

Answer: We understand the abode of the heart to be in the area of the bosom [chest-center]. Experiences of happiness, sorrow, peace etc. are felt emanating at particular parts of the chest-center area. If one is able to untie the knot here, [more of the] bindings of material/psychic bondage are cut away and the path of yoga is further cleared up. In the special procedure of Kriya Yoga, a directive is given to apply a physical and mental technique over and over in the heart area. This results in the springing forth of the Unstruck Resonance [Anahata Dhvani] in the heart area. We call that Resonance the "jhankar of Pranava" [profound ringing of OM]. Listening to that Nada [Sound] again and again, the mind becomes more and more free from earthly bondage. Deep immersion into the Pranava Shabda [Word] is itself "samadhi" [to make one]—the most excellent path to attain Kaivalya. It is this that can be called "samadhi into Pranava in the paravastha of Kriya. In this way, the knot or node that contains things such as meanness of heart, bindings of guilt and defilement etc. is released open, and the sadhaka moves ahead on the path of liberation.

This state can also come upon the mind through ordinary meditation and such. But in Kriya Yoga, there is a directive for an easy technique by which this state can be attained permanently.

—Acharya Sanglap, Vol. 1, pages 26–27

Question [to Satyanandaji]: Speak about breaking through the Muladhar-knot.

Answer: Speaking about it in the ordinary way, Muladhar is the abode of the earth element, meaning generally—the place of the awareness of physical things. Ordinarily, our minds move in that direction, meaning that the mind is drawn in the downward direction. With the aid of spiritual sadhana, the mind moves upward (the ascending movement occurs).* Yogis, in the particular language of their Kriyayoga sadhana say, "One has to do the sadhana of putting the mind in the sushumna and take it from place to place on the road of the six chakras up to the Ajna Chakra." It is by this that the Muladhar-knot is broken. The dormant Kundalini-Shakti in the sadhaka awakens and rises toward Kutasthachaitanya.

[*The parentheses and the translated text within are in the original.]

About the breaking of the heart-knot, it has been said: By a particular Kriya, Anahata Nada [Unstruck Sound] springs forth in the heart area, which results in the awakening of the feeling of Boundless Profound Peace, and along with that the Tranquil and True Light of Kutasthachaitanya is revealed—"dhvanerantargam jyotih" [the Light within the Resonance]. In the stillness of witnessing that Light, the door of sushumna is opened. That is the true Illuminated Path. "maha-jano yena gatah sa panthah" [the path that has been/is traveled by the Great Ones]. With the experience of Light, the Anahata Nada emanates clearly throughout—down through the Muladhar, and right along with that, the ascension of Shakti is experienced. This is the mystery of breaking through the Muladhar-knot. Needless to say, breaking all the knots does not mean that the knots have been completely broken. The deepening of the progress of this is also experienced slowly, one after another, on the path of the sadhaka's gradual advancement.

This is from pages 27–28 in Vol. 1 of Acharya Sanglap

The time of the in-breath and the out-breath is called "mantra." The seed of this mantra can be said to be the "Hamsa Mantra" [or, "Hangsa Mantra"]. The time of taking the breath in—"Ham" [or "Hang"], and the time of releasing the breath—"Sah." This current goes up to the Ajna Chakra and becomes established as the "Soham" [or, "Sohang"] seed. In the tranquil and still state, engaging oneself in the meditation of that "Soham," one can attain the ambrosia of the paravastha of Kriya. Hearing the term "Soham" makes us think of some huge philo-sophical thing. But here, the meaning of "Soham" for the sadhaka— "That I Am,"—that realization where I no longer have a separate existence and I am merged in That—this knowing comes about natu-rally by which the spiritual meditation of this paravastha is enriched, and by listening to the Nada via the sadhana of higher Kriyas, one experiences the revelation of Light in the area of that Bindu...page 54 vol. 2 of Acharya Sanglap

On this matter, I want to say another thing once again—that just the act of in-breath and out-breath is not pranayam. This [Kriya proper] may be called "Pranayam's Kriya." The calm and still condition that comes about after taking up the Hamsa seed upon the performance of this Kriya can be said to be the first steps in Kriya's paravastha, and immersion in that is the imperative duty of the Kriya Yogi. Being focused on the natural movement of the breath (watching the breath)* can be a way of concentrating the mind. The aforementioned Hamsa Mantra seed is practiced along with this and there is attainment. The mystery of the japa of the Name, breath by breath, is also experienced in this technique via the instructions of masters of particular sampradayas. [*The parentheses and the text within are in English in the original.] page 55, Vol. 2 of Acharya Sanglap

---

It is the pranayam of the First Kriya which he [Swami Sriyukteshvar Giriji Maharaj] used to speak about taking up and practicing in extensive amounts. In the easy practice of this pranayam, there is no facilitation for the performance of strenuous kumbhak. Simply and easily, by attaining the state of natural kumbhak in the spaces between purak[in-breath] and rechak [out-breath], the sadhaka can gradually attain the state of Tranquility—this he [Sriyukteshvarji Maharaj] taught us clearly. Using the aid of the mantra of in-breath and out-breath is instructed for the performance of ordinary pranayam. But beyond the practice of in-breath and out-breath, he also showed and taught the inner way of performing the seed mantra of the in-breath and out-breath—the "ham-sa" mantra—in a simple way and establish it as "so-ham"* in the Ajna Chakra. Vol 2. page24,

[Translator's note: In scriptures, "so-ham" is the mystically mirrored "ham-sa." Spiritual lexicons state that "so-ham" means "That I Am," or "I Am That."]

FIRST KRIYA

The Three Acts of kriya:

Question (to Satyanandaji): Give us an analytical explanation of Lahiri Mahasaya's Kriya Yoga.

Answer: In the matters of Kriya Yoga, Lahiri Mahasaya particularly emphasized Kriyayoga Sadhana and Kriya Paravastha. "Kriya" sadhana may be thought of as the sadhana of "the practice of being in Atman." "Kriya Yoga" brings about the awareness of the Self/Atman. In "Kriya Paravastha," surrender in Atman is experienced. As the body of Kriyayoga Sadhana, Lahiri Mahasaya has given directives for three acts; this has already been stated before. The first is Mahamudra—by the performance of which the feeling of denseness/stiffness of body is cast off. The nadis within the body become prepared for Kriya, meaning that the process of nadi shuddhi is activated. The body becomes conducive for sadhana. The second is to do Pranayam in asana.

Question: Speak of the third act.

Answer: The third act is Yoni Mudra. Pranayam Kriya results in the mind ascending upward. At that time in the Brahmayoni in the Ajna Chakra, one has to do a special kriya of Light-witnessing using this act. First the subtle light in the body is experienced. Gradually through being in dhyan, one can progress to Paravastha. With the experience of Nada and Pranava-Resonance, the revelation of Light becomes more and more brilliant, and the eye of Prajna blossoms open.

............Acharya Sanglap, book 1 pages 14–16.

1) <u>MAHAMUDRA</u>:

"Before the start of Kriya, or Prankriya, the practice of Mahamudra helps to bring about in the body and the nervous pathways/currents the condition of strength and steadiness, [and] clarity and health appropriate for sadhana.................Acharya Sanglap, book 2 page 67

In Mahamudra, he has made special use of the in-breath and the out-breath. Even as we want to walk on the path of the Pranayam of Kriya and Dhyan, we hear of nadi-shuddhi and bhuta-shuddhi. Mahamudra does the work of that nadi-shuddhi in a particular way. By this, one can be freed from the attacks of physical afflictions. Performing Mahamudra takes away the experience of denseness in the body, and the body naturally becomes fit for sadhana such as pranayam. The innate feeling of delight in body and mind comes about. Among physical exercises/techniques, Mahamudra is somewhat similar to "Pashchimottasana" [from hatha yoga]...............Acharya Sanglap book 1 pages 8–9

As the body of Kriyayoga Sadhana, Lahiri Mahasaya has given directives for three acts; this has already been stated before. The first is Mahamudra—by the performance of which the feeling of denseness/stiffness of body is cast off. The nadis within the body become prepared for Kriya, meaning that the process of nadi shuddhi is activated. The body becomes conducive for sadhana. The second is to do Pranayam in asana.-

...Acharya Sanglap, book 1 pages 14–16.

Question: Familiarize us with the mudras necessary in Kriya Yoga.

Answer: Lahiri Mahasaya spoke of three particular mudras necessary for Kriya Yoga. Mahamudra, Yoni mudra and khechari mudra. These are stated in the scriptures. But understanding Lahiri Mahasaya's special ways of using the methods [is important]. Of course, the transmission of the techniques is received only from Guru.

In Mahamudra, he has made special use of the in-breath and the out-breath. Even as we want to walk on the path of the Pranayam of Kriya and Dhyan, we hear of nadi-shuddhi and bhuta-shuddhi. Mahamudra does the work of that nadi-shuddhi in a particular way. By this, one can be freed from the attacks of physical afflictions. Performing Mahamudra takes away the experience of denseness in the body, and the body naturally becomes fit for sadhana such as pranayam. The innate feeling of delight in body and mind comes about. Among physical exercises/techniques, Mahamudra is somewhat similar to "Pashchimottasana" [from hatha yoga].—Acharya Sanglap, book 1 pages 14–16.

2) PRANAYAM (Kriya Proper)

"one has to concentrate on the movement in the path of the Yogasutra-mentioned sushumna nadi to bring about that experience in the spinal column itself. Through this, that path continually gains magnetic power by the technique of Kriya, which results in turning the outgoing currents of the [other] nadis inward by the attractive power of that magnetic force, and [thus] the mind is also magnetically drawn within in that way. This results in the ending of the restlessness of inhalation and exhalation, after which, the state of pranayam where there is disconnection from the movement of in-breath and out-breath is eventually attained. This results in the stillness of mind, and with the disciplined practice of pratyahar and dharana—dhyan and samadhi are eventually attained in the paravastha of Kriya. Through this practice itself one can attain realization on the path of samadhi, with the luminous experience of the various chakras—the abodes where power is transmitted—and the Unstruck Resonance of Pranava. It is because of this foundational and essential fact that Yogiraj has said that all states of sadhana can be attained with the reverently disciplined practice of the First Kriya......Acharya Sanglap 2 page 51

From scriptures, we know that pranayam has three parts—purak [filling the lungs], rechak [purging the lungs] and kumbhak [sealing the breath]. In the beginning of the sadhana of this Kriya Yoga's internally moving Pranayam, the kumbhak is not visibly apparent. By the use of a special easy and simple method of the purak-rechak act, from the steadiness of the sadhak's sadhana, kumbhak comes effortlessly and naturally. This somewhat falls into [the area of] what is spoken of as "Kevali Kumbhak" in the scriptures. However, in more advanced stages of sadhana, the use of special techniques of kumbhak are facilitated. These techniques of sadhana are transmitted via Guru.— Acharya Sanglap, book 1 pages 14–16.

The time of the in-breath and the out-breath is called "mantra." The seed of this mantra can be said to be the "Hamsa Mantra" [or, "Hangsa Mantra"]. The time of taking the breath in—"Ham" [or "Hang"], and the time of releasing the breath—"Sah." This current goes up to the Ajna Chakra and becomes established as the "Soham" [or, "Sohang"] seed. In the tranquil and still state, engaging oneself in the meditation of that "Soham," one can attain the ambrosia of the paravastha of Kriya. Hearing the term "Soham" makes us think of some huge philosophical thing. But here, the meaning of "Soham" for the sadhaka—"That I Am,"—that realization where I no longer have a separate existence and I am merged in That—this knowing comes about naturally by which the spiritual meditation of this paravastha is enriched, and by listening to! the Nada via the sadhana of higher Kriyas, one experiences the revelation of Light in the area of that Bindu...page 54 vol. 2

On this matter, I want to say another thing once again—that just the act of in-breath and out-breath is not pranayam. This [Kriya proper] may be called "Pranayam's Kriya." The calm and still condition that comes about after taking up the Hamsa seed upon the performance of this Kriya can be said to be the first steps in Kriya's paravastha, and immersion in that is the imperative duty of the Kriya Yogi. Being focused on the natural movement of the breath (watching the breath)* can be a way of concentrating the mind. The aforementioned Hamsa Mantra seed is practiced along with this and there is attainment. The mystery of the japa of the Name, breath by breath, is also experienced in this technique via the instructions of masters of particular sampradayas.

[*The parentheses and the text within are in English in the original.]

Acharya sanglap page 55, Vol. 2

3) YONI MUDRA

The third act is Yoni Mudra. Pranayam Kriya results in the mind ascending upward. At that time in the Brahmayoni in the Ajna Chakra, one has to do a special kriya of Light-witnessing using this act. First the subtle light in the body is experienced. Gradually through being in dhyan, one can progress to Paravastha. With the experience of Nada and Pranava-Resonance, the revelation of Light becomes more and more brilliant, and the eye of Prajna blossoms open.

—Acharya Sanglap, book 1 pages 14–16.

Lahiri Mahasaya held Yoni Mudra in a highly important position. This mudra is practiced as the mind becomes tranquil after the practice of pranayam and such. One has to shut off the exterior senses when practicing this mudra. By the use of the breath, one has to pull on the Kundalini Shakti at the Muladhar, and in the point between the eyebrows, the place that can be truly called the abode of the Lord—the abode of Guru—the abode of Kutasthachaitanya—stilling the mind there, one experiences the revelation of Light. This type of technique greatly helps the mind to progress on the high spiritual path. That Light is what can be truly called "Yoni" or "Brahmayoni." This can be basically said as the substantive essence: The Mula [Fundamental] Prakriti creates the World-Samsara via that Brahmayoni. Therefore, through that Yoni, meaning pathway, we have created the World-Samsara and have become bound by it. Via meditation upon that Yoni, one can become established in the Fundamental Consciousness-Truth beyond the external world and [experience] overflowing Bliss springing forth. It is in this cave of Light within the sadhaka that the Spiritual Substance is hidden, and it is this that is the path of the Great Ones—

"dharmasya tattvam nihitam guhayam" "mahajano yena gatah sah panthah" ["The Substance of Dharma is hidden in the cave."] ["The path that is/has been traveled by the Great Ones."]

…………Acharya Sanglap book 1 pages 8–9

It is the pranayam of the First Kriya which he [Swami Sriyukteshvar Giriji Maharaj] used to speak about taking up and practicing in extensive amounts. In the easy practice of this pranayam, there is no facilitation for the performance of strenuous kumbhak. Simply and easily, by attaining the state of natural kumbhak in the spaces between purak[in-breath] and rechak [out-breath], the sadhaka can gradually attain the state of Tranquility—this he [Sriyukteshvarji Maharaj] taught us clearly. Using the aid of the mantra of in-breath and out-breath is instructed for the performance of ordinary pranayam. But beyond the practice of in-breath and out-breath, he also showed and taught the inner way of performing the seed mantra of the in-breath and out-breath—the "ham-sa" mantra—in a simple way and establish it as "so-ham"* in the Ajna Chakra. Vol 2. page24,

[Translator's note: In scriptures, "so-ham" is the mystically mirrored "ham-sa." Spiritual lexicons state that "so-ham" means "That I Am," or "I Am That."]

KHECHARI MUDRA

The practice of the technique of the Second Kriya is made possible with the method of piercing the tongue-knot by the technique of Khechari Mudra......Swami Satyananda Giri, Acharya Sanglap, book 2 page 67

Lahiri Mahasaya spoke of three particular mudras necessary for Kriya Yoga. Mahamudra, Yoni mudra and khechari mudra. These are stated in the scriptures. But understanding Lahiri Mahasaya's special ways of using the methods [is important]. Of course, the transmission of the techniques is received only from Guru...............Acharya Sanglap book 1 pages 8–9

Entering the tongue in the nasal passage in pathway of the upper palate is called "the practice of Khechari Mudra." Although this is a physical technique of hatha yoga, it [brings about] a steady and still condition and is necessary to draw the mind inward. When this condition [the achievement of Khechari] happens, the sadhaka experiences somewhat more steadiness and stillness and becomes ready to advance to the second level of Kriya."............Acharya Sanglap book 1 pages 8–9

After this comes the matter of Second Kriya. For this, Khechari Mudra is necessary......page 26, vol. 2 of Acharya Sanglap.

Advancement on the path of Kriya [consists of] breaking the tongue-knot by the aid of Khechari Mudra; breaking the heart-knot by the aid of Pranava, or Nada, and breaking the Muladhar-knot by the bursting spring of Light, where the awakening of the Kundalini Shakti is experienced.—Acharya Sanglap, book 1 pages 14–16.

What is understood to be the "tongue-knot"?

Answer: Just as asana and such are needed in the field of sadhana, in the same way, there is a special necessity for breaking through the tongue-knot, or [the performance of] Khechari Mudra. With the help of some physical and a certain amount of mental effort, the tongue can be inserted into the hole in the upper palate. This act in many ways helps the disciplined life. In this manner, the tongue arrives at the junction point of the nasal passage inside the hole in the palate. Along with the practice of Kriya Yoga and the advancement of mental absorption, the tongue continues to go up even further. It is said in the scriptures that when the tongue arrives at the end of its full journey, the state of "jada-samadhi" comes about. This Khechari Mudra is what can be called as "breaking through the tongue-knot." Gradually, there is advancement of this condition. Samyama is also acquired gradually. In a particular state experienced during the practice of this technique, a certain type of fluid comes upon the tongue that improves the health of body and mind. It is this fluid that is described in the scriptures as "Sahasrarchyut Sudha" [Nectar falling off the thousand-petaled]—that nectar which yogis drink as they move forward on the path of Immortality. It is by this that an earthly knot, meaning a significant knotting of the ties of material bondage—is undone and released. Through this, progress on the path for the sadhaka is made consider-ably easier and clearer...............from Acharya SanglapVol 1 page 26

The other one [mudra] is Khechari Mudra. Entering the tongue in the nasal passage in pathway of the upper palate is called "the practice of Khechari Mudra." Although this is a physical technique of hatha yoga, it [brings about] a steady and still condition and is necessary to draw the mind inward. When this condition [the achievement of Khechari] happens, the sadhaka experiences somewhat more steadiness and still-ness and becomes ready to advance to the second level of Kriya."...........Acharya Sanglap book 1 pages 8–9

HIGHER KRIYA:

But according to the physical and psychological states and makeup [constitution] of individuals, He gave instructions for practice of the performance of different stages of Kriyayoga sadhana—First, Second, Third etc.—and their methods and techniques. For example, in the First Kriya—discovering the path of sushumna along with practice of

Khechari Mudra—when that practice is firm and strong, in the Second stage, one experiences the various chakras and eventually experiences Sound [Nada]. The Third Kriya is there for one to take up that Nada in a specific way and become completely established in that Nada. It is in this way that there are directives that have given for progress on the path of Kriya, stage by stage"......Acharya Sanglap 2 page 51

HIGHER KRIYA

SECOND KRIYA:

Entering the tongue in the nasal passage in pathway of the upper palate is called "the practice of Khechari Mudra." Although this is a physical technique of hatha yoga, it [brings about] a steady and still condition and is necessary to draw the mind inward. When this condition [the achievement of Khechari] happens, the sadhaka experiences somewhat more steadiness and stillness and becomes ready to advance to the second level of Kriya.".............Acharya Sanglap book 1 pages 8–9

After this comes the matter of Second Kriya. For this, Khechari Mudra is necessary. With this, by the help of this inturning physical technique, one is also aided in turning the mind inward as well. Then, the abidance of the different chakras on the path of sushumna and the practice of kumbhak in pranayam are the elements upon which one focuses. This results in being able to hear the Unstruck Sound [Anahata Nada] and the experience of dhyan is heightened. This Nada or Pranava Shabda is what Maharajji [Swami Sriyukteshvar Giri Maharaj] pointed towards in his Kaivalya Darshan [English title: The Holy Science] scripture as the way for a sadhaka to walk on the path of samadhi in the perfected state ("pranavashabda eva panthah"). In his work, he showed and taught us that that Universe-pervading Nada resides in Its Totality within the body of the sadhaka. The Resonance is what magnetically draws the sadhaka to experience Brahman in practically every state of being or situation. Gradually, with greater and greater Light springing forth, the door of sushumna is effervescently manifested (dhvanerantargatam jyotih). Continuing to experience the incredibly beatific visions, the yogi is able to become established in the paravastha of Kriya. It is this method that he [Swami Sriyuktshvarji] graciously tried to have us realize in a simple and usable way. The disciples of Yogiraj—our respected elders—have shown us the path in this manner...........page 26, vol. 2 of Acharya Sanglap.

In the Second Kriya, taking the recourse of specific syllables of mantra along with the practice of abiding in the different chakras, the instruction of special Kumbhak is given. The proper practice of the Second Kriya, breaking the heart-knot, results in bringing about the experience of the Unstruck Sound [Anahata Nada] Pranava. Included in the Second Kriya is the instruction for a type of Kriya-technique for applying a particular kind of pressure or strike [Thokar] on the Anahata Chakra............Acharya Sanglap, book 2 page 67

THIRD KRIYA:

The Third Kriya's practice is taught for establishing oneself firmly in the wave/path of Pranava Nada...............Acharya Sanglap, book 2 page 67

The Third Kriya is there for one to take up that Nada in a specific way and become completely established in that Nada......Acharya Sanglap 2 page 51

FOURTH KRIYA:

The technique to attain Nada in the Fourth Kriya, experiencing the different chakras, leads to breaking the Muladhar-knot......Acharya Sanglap, book 2 page 67

"Dadu"

Acharya Sri Sailendra Bejoy Dasgupta
(1910–1984)

Exalted direct disciple of Swami Sriyukteshvar Giriji Maharaj

Dadu,
We are your children surrendered at your feet. Thank you for guiding
us with your light.
Please accept our quiet offering.

978-0-595-38675-8
0-595-38675-X

Printed in the United States
104277LV00004B/3/A